A MEMOIR A[BOUT RAISING]
BATTLING
AND LEA[RNING]
MOTHER

Don't Ask Why.

RYSTAL BELL

the Peppertree Press
www.peppertreepublishing.com

ISBN: 978-1-61493-863-7
Library of Congress: 2022921088
Printed: December 2022
Manufactured in the United States of America

TABLE OF CONTENTS

DEDICATION

For Mom.

Also, for Dad, Meagan, Katie and Rennie.

My husband: Sean, my two sons: Jaxon and Tanner and my nieces and nephew: Maddie, Chloe, Kinslee, Barrett and Hannah.

May you all find comfort in Mom and Memaw's story. Comfort in knowing where she is, how she got there, and where we can go too.

Here's to her memory, legacy and love, living on inside all of us forever. The struggle is real, but so are angels!

You are about to read very real and raw stories about the most difficult time in my life. I remember them. I lived them, and I suffer through them, still. Some names aren't mentioned, some names have been changed, and some specifics have been altered to maintain privacy.

Also, there will be some cussing. Sorry, Mom.

PREFACE

Life, a real definition behind the word, "hard." It's not easy, nor has it ever been promised to be easy. Some things in life will make you question your character, as well as your integrity, morals, and beliefs. God originally planned a perfect life for every human being He created, but that was abruptly taken away due to sin. Sin comes hand in hand with life. It's inevitable and it is supposed to be there. Every living and breathing body will experience life's hardest moments one way or the other. You can't outrun it and you can't hide from it. Unfortunately, we are not exempt from the things with which we disagree. Situations we don't want to be in will regretfully come up and it's how we decide to handle those situations that make up and form the meaning behind the word, "life." It's about your perseverance and your faith. It's all a big cycle and, in turn, it's the biggest lesson God intentionally teaches us. Everything in life is a lesson, big or small, but it's your dealing with it that shapes the outcome and it's all up to you.

God made promises that were sealed by the absolute highest authority, his Word. He promised happiness and blessings. He promised his unconditional love and acceptance. He promised to always be there for every beating heart and to guide and protect us through it all. In life, God may internally and emotionally be present if you choose to allow him but because he is physically not present, he gives a job to every person he creates. How are you going to play that out?

When life gets tough, the easy way out is to focus on ourselves, our difficulties and our unfair struggles. The promises God has made to us proves that you will never be alone. Life's lessons can be extremely difficult to conquer, and what better promise than that of God's to not have to conquer them utterly alone.

What if I told you that no matter what you go through, you're not the only one? What if I broke the news to you that there is, in fact, another person or another family somewhere out there that has or is going through the same thing or similar? Would you be surprised?

Since sin is very much real, unfortunately it brings a lot of unwanted baggage along with it. That baggage comes in many different forms, such as sickness, disease, racism, abuse, addiction and crime. Can you imagine what this world would be like without all the sin, sadness, grief, loss, and negativity? Just like you, I have an idea, too! Although this world can't control some of those, there is only one person who can control the outcome, and that's YOU.

I do not expect this book to help everyone. I cannot give you a step-by-step guide to follow in your days of grief and tremendous loss. I can't predict what will make your loss bearable and I can't promise to make it all better. I can only tell you what worked for me. But I do hope, that by sharing my very raw and real experiences as a human being, wife, daughter, mother, and sister trying to get through this hardship we call life, it'll be helpful to you and many others in some sort of way. I promise to not lie but to tell you there's truth in the pain you feel. If somebody tells you that grief and depression aren't such a big deal, they're lying to you! It's a huge deal and it's very much real. In this book, I will not sugarcoat the facts behind those feelings, but I'll share the very struggles that come along with them. I'm also going to tell you that overcoming all struggles is possible! That is not a lie—it's the truth and you, too, will see that. Happiness is purely an option. It's not mandatory, but it is highly recommended! We are given the choice to choose what we want out of life. So, choose wisely, Babe, the ball is in your court. We got this!!

INTRODUCTION

That day felt vastly different than most. Maybe it was the rapid pen tapping of the check-in clerk, or the twenty million copies of paper sliding through the printer behind the desk. It could have been the way the outside breeze whooshed through the doors that never seemed to fully close before opening again. The waiting room quickly filled up, yet the clock hands seemed to move entirely too slow. She sat there quiet, with raging nerves, fearing the unknown.

"Pam Heath?" Mom took one deep breath, stood up, and smiled, "Hi, how are you?"

As she draped herself with the Pepto Bismol-colored paper gown and hopped up on the crunchy crinkle of the OBGYN bed, she patiently waited for the doctor. During her wait, she must have read every "Did You Know?" pamphlet and semi-informative sign in the room, a few times over. The doctor knocked twice and invited herself in. "Pam! It's so nice to see you." she said to Mom.

The fifteen-minute visit, which felt like hours, led to a very unexpected conversation. She knew deep down something wasn't right. She knew her body and she knew it well. She had been through quite a lot in the past, but this was oddly different. This time, the strange feeling she felt deep down was accompanied with fear, anguish, nervousness, worry, a whirlwind of thoughts and emotions, and a deep dull pit in her stomach that had never been there before.

After the doctor walked in, no time was wasted. She pulled the stool up in front of Mom, sat down, and took her hand in her own. "How bad is it?" Mom asked, already bummed.

The doctor sadly replied, "Baby, it's bad. It's cancer and it looks like a car wreck in there!"

CHAPTER 1

MULTIPLE BLESSINGS!

"There's not just one healthy beating heart, Pam and Rennie. Look, there's actually two!" the doctor said, breaking the news to them. Their eyes opened wide. "Well ... that's amazing!" Mom said, surprised. Dad huffed, not even sure what to think about two new babies coming.

"Umm .... oh wait, wow! Nope, there's not just two—look! There are THREE babies, Pam!"

The room suddenly got quiet and Mom thought to herself, "OK, so this doctor just laid on us the news of twins! Scary, but exciting! And now he's got jokes? THREE? Nobody can just naturally get pregnant with three babies at one time!"

Well, news flash; she was wrong. One whole baby wrong! The doctor was shockingly serious.

It's TRIPLETS!

"Meagan," he said to my five-year-old sister, "you are going to have three little babies to help take care of!" The doctor said it cheerfully, most likely because he wasn't the one about to have to raise us. For a five-year-old, that was so exciting! She didn't quite feel the shock that Mom and Dad felt in that moment. Dad was questioning how in the world they just went from one child an hour ago to now an unrealistic flash into the future of four children. That really did not sound like a good idea.

Mom was lying there with her shirt half up, Doppler sliding across her belly, and suddenly she couldn't hear anything going on around her. All she could do was mentally begin to prepare herself about becoming a single mom with four kids, because there was no way in hell Dad was going to stay! She just knew for sure he was going to pack up and head out, like now!

Well, big decisions were made, and life went on. Right away, Mom knew the only way she was going to get through such a pregnancy, that back then wasn't that common, was to build her faith up in God. After many appointments, discussions, and choices, she was given a very unsettling "easy way out."

"A woman's body just isn't built to deliver multiples," she was told. That statement left her shocked, questioning how somebody besides God can determine if you really can do something like that.

Yeah, Mom wasn't the type of person to be dealt a deck of cards, just to give up before the game even starts. She was going to deal with the hand she was given, with or without help!

After a quick nine months, a belly that protruded out about three feet, and lots of anxious excitement, this quaint little family of three very quickly became a chaotic family of six! We were born—safely, all one minute apart!

Fame and glory came immediately after our birth and, for a new mother of multiples, it was overwhelming to say the least. Giving birth left her feeling excessively fatigued, but she thrived on helping others any way she could. Exhaustion didn't stop her from giving news interviews or providing advice from her experience in local newspaper articles. She wasn't thinking of herself, ever. She knew that by sharing this rare experience, it would show the next mother of multiples that this kind of thing really is possible, despite the statistics. She quickly gained fame following our delivery and she loved sharing what an adventure that had been. Not minding the interviews was one thing, but trying to tolerate the immediate demands from the media was another.

She was immediately given an offer to cast her newborns in the movie entitled, *Problem Child*. As much fun as that sounds, that's not who she was. She hadn't even had time to get to know us yet, so in no way was she going to let them swoop us away to live on some movie set in the first few months of our lives. She drew the line there, gave them our triplet stroller to use in the movie instead, and took her babies home.

From that moment on, life was challenging. I'm sure there were days when she thought there is no way she could possibly raise four young kids, three of which were the exact same age. Often when she told Dad, "I love you, have a good day!" as he rushed out the door to work, her sigh couldn't have possibly gotten any louder or any more obvious! The days were long, and the nights were even longer. She tried her best to juggle motherhood with one baby crying, the other throwing up, and the third crawling off to get into something that wasn't exactly baby proof.

The angelic little voice amongst all the chaos was what seemed like her only breath of fresh air. "Mommy, I'll help you!" Thank God for the independence of a five-year-old and the ever-so-loving presence of another human being in the home who could actually speak words! My sister, Meagan, was the oldest. She was so helpful, even when Mom hadn't asked for help. We were needy little humans and she brought Mom the comfort and joy that babies inevitably steal away.

At this time, Dad owned a business in construction and land development, so he was able to be home by dinnertime, most nights. He'd finally get to join in on all the fun that was going on at home during his peaceful workday. As we grew older, our house grew smaller. Thankfully, with his exceptional expertise in construction, he built us a four-bedroom home big enough to suit our family of six and even offer some breathing room at the same time.

Life was such a breeze by this point, *like what's the big deal raising multiples anyway?* Well, we were four years old and Meagan was nine when Dad decided to go back to college to get his business degree with a minor in Economics. Mom was pretty much Superwoman at this stage of life. She was able to handle anything else it began to throw her way. Dad worked his day job and attended night school two to four nights per week. This went on for eight *long* years. Some days went smoother than others. Some days flew by, but the majority of the days felt like the clock had run out of batteries by 8 a.m.

In our family, God always came first. If it wasn't for Him, not one of us would have been there. We wouldn't have had a roof over our heads and a pantry stocked full of snacks that always fed the neighborhood kids, too!

As kids back then, it was safe to hang out outside all day and night. The only meaning behind the sun going down was that it was finally time to play flashlight tag in the dark! You see, we had eighteen kids, just about the exact same age growing up on the same street at the same time. The minute we'd get off the bus from school, we'd throw our backpacks down in the corner by the front door, and run back out the door, so it felt like summer vacation all over again. In reality, it was just late afternoon, but our school worries always disappeared for the next several hours.

Mom had her mom-friends right down the street to whom she talked on the phone, because four houses down was too far away when you have a simmering pot of spaghetti sauce going on the stove! She'd twirl around the kitchen with the phone hugged to her ear as the spiraled cord wrapped around her body, multitasking conversations with dicing onions to throw into the pot before it started boiling over. Most of the time, she didn't have to set the phone down to pull the pot off the burner just to yell out the front door to come inside. By six o'clock, we were reminded that it was indeed "still a school night!" We'd just start getting all sweaty and mosquito bitten, sitting quietly in our hiding places, when Dad would come down the street and pull into the driveway. Just the sight of his truck meant you knew you only had a good five, maybe ten minutes, before you found yourself inside, scrubbing the dirt from under your nails, and folding paper napkins to place on the table before dinner was served.

We were always taught that being present in the moment meant more than the activities that filled our day. We sat down and had a family dinner every single night. Back then, there were no such things as cell phones, text messages, or iPads. In fact, if you weren't logged out of AOL Instant Messenger and it went off during dinner, you were grounded.

There wasn't a grab-and-go policy in our household. Mom always made a home-cooked meal, we'd set the table, and then sit down together to pray. Someone was always chosen by Dad to say the prayer while the rest of us bowed our heads and closed one eye while the other eye looked around to see who else was giggling and not following the directions either. We couldn't start stuffing our faces or even nibble at Mom's famous (burnt) garlic bread before the prayer was said. No matter what went on that day or how good the food looked steaming in front of you, coming together to give thanks first was a must.

"Katie, high-low?" Mom asked one night, totally at random. This was a new game Mom had come up with, and if I had to guess, it was probably a game she saw on Oprah, considering she was a regular viewer back then. We didn't have any other option but to participate. We laughed so hard every night because repeating that question six times around the table sounded so silly!

"What in the world does that even mean?" Katie asked. She was the inquisitive one out of the bunch. Meagan just sat there thinking how corny this game was, I'm sure. As for my brother, Rennie, and me, all we ever did was crack jokes about literally everything, while obnoxiously elbowing each other under the table.

"Well, you have to tell everybody what the highest part of your day was and then after that, you must end it with sharing the lowest part of your day," Mom replied.

Katie usually said something like, "The highest part of my day was passing twenty-six reading tests and getting an A+ in all my classes! The lowest? Well, it'd have to be when the zipper on my trapper-keeper broke on the bus." she concluded, smiling because she felt so accomplished. *Smarty pants!*

Meagan's most likely went this way: "Making the dance team today was definitely the highest, but my lowest part of the day was Rachel and I being moved to different desks in History class." She was bored with this game, but she was always made to answer anyway.

Rennie and I loved it because we never took it seriously.

Rennie said, "I'd say the highest part of my day was when I mooned all the girls in the lunchroom, and they laughed. The lowest? Hmm ... getting in trouble for pulling my pants down, because Mrs. Salt stopped serving cold square pizza and made me leave to go eat alone with my teacher!" Rennie said, so proud of his work. (I was proud, too! I mean, I saw those girls' faces as they giggled, blushing at his white pimply ass. That'd be the highest part of your day, too!).

"Myyyyyy dawg!" I chanted, right after Mom got onto him for indecent exposure in the second grade.

"OK, Crystal, that's enough. We don't need to cheer him on for behavior like that!" Mom said tilting her head at me like I should have known better.

"My bad," I said, trying to control my laughter.

"Now it's your turn, Crystal. High-Low?" she asked me.

Crap! Now it's my turn and I haven't even thought about it, because Rennie's is entirely too good to beat! "Umm, I think my high would be having the best-looking shoes in the class, 'cause everybody wanted them," I said.

"That's shocking," Meagan mumbled under her breath.

"And the low?" Mom reminded me that I still had to finish.

"Probably getting my favorite lip gloss taken away. Apparently sharing lip gloss isn't appropriate in the middle of science class. Ms. Star told me. That's the dumbest rule anyway. And she didn't even give it back. Mom, will you get it back for me, please?"

"Yes, Crystal, I will, but she's right. You should be focusing on bringing up your grades, not playing beauty parlor in the middle of class. There's a time and place for everything."

I guess she didn't like my answer.

"OK, everybody, great job! It sounds like you've all had an, umm, eventful day. Let's try again tomorrow."

Her sarcastic response meant we bombed the game that night, but hey there's always another day that Rennie will have a ton of highs to go around. I'm sure of it!

When you're a child growing up, you don't realize the significance behind those quirky conversations you share at the dinner table, and you can't comprehend the true meaning behind the words you actually pray for out loud. You don't realize the love that's put into the homemade spaghetti or even the easy-peasy thrown together mac-n-cheese with hot dogs you'd get only if you were lucky. The laughs and arguments seem so lame and unimportant to you as a kid. You're all too quick to throw to the wayside the lessons and meanings that came out of those every-day, overly detailed, and silly conversations.

After dinner, the only thing that truly mattered was who got to sit in "Dad's chair" to watch TV and who got to cuddle up next to Mom, sharing the same old and ugly-woven mismatched colored blanket with her to fall asleep. We wished our days away back then— *we couldn't wait to be old enough not to have a bedtime anymore!* We'd go to bed just hoping tomorrow came faster, because that meant we were one whole day closer to Christmas! In hindsight, those memories prove how necessary it is to have parents. Looking back now, I would give anything to be back on that awful-looking couch, in the same living room, and watching the same TV with my other family members.

My parents had a way of keeping us grounded, keeping us living in the moment together, and always keeping us close to God.

CHAPTER 2

ALWAYS MOM'S FAULT

Having an older sister came with advantages, but it also had its lessons. Meagan did a great job at paving the way for the three of us following behind her. There were arguments, boys, cuss words, makeup, loud music, clothes that seemed to always fit me regardless of my size, and ... an old excessively used gold Ford Taurus that conveniently came with a chauffeur.

When Meagan finally turned eighteen, Rennie acted like a jerk and blew the candles out for her, laughing and giving everyone high-fives. I chimed in behind him with, "Thank God you're eighteen now! You can order me stuff off those infomercials on TV, because Mom never does that!" They were useless things that I wanted, but I knew Meagan would do it.

"I know, it's always Mom's fault!"

That was the typical reply we got from Mom when we blamed something on her. Why do we have to come inside so early and do homework when the rest of our friends are still outside playing? Because Mom made us!

Everything seemed to be her fault back then. A "No" was thrown out way too many times when we thought she would go our way!

Then came the days when she trusted Meagan to watch the three of us while she ran errands. You know, the errands that were so incredibly uncool and unfair to have to sit through. Nobody likes going to the post office or sitting in the drive-through at the bank just to be bribed with those nasty, flat-circled, flavorless lollipops they always rewarded you with for sitting so nicely while they counted your moms' money. Much less the dreaded trip to the grocery store that always took what seemed like five painful hours. Back then, they didn't hand out stickers or free cookies at the bakery to the kids being punished and forced to attend those trips. We had finally graduated to the age of staying home alone, and it was a freedom we started to enjoy all too quickly.

As fun as it sounds to stay home alone, it was not fun when Mom got there! We always found something to accidentally break or shatter or something to spill or get into that didn't have our names on it. We'd give away all our snacks to our friends down the street or make phone calls on the house phone, expecting Mom not to find out. My brother, Rennie, would put more boogers on the wall (that eventually dried and never came off, by the way). My sister, Katie, was either eating butter straight from the container or trying to threaten me with a butter knife (no pun intended) because chances are, we were most likely fighting. That was our norm. I was often sneaking off stealing Meagan's clothes from her closet because she was out in the living room trying desperately to turn MTV off before Mom walked in the door.

Somehow, Mom always knew something was up. She never just assumed we were angels like we swore up and down we were. Dad would come walking in to find out right away about our eventful two-hour free time, because Mom was so ashamed that she felt overly compelled to share with Dad. We'd blame it on Meagan, and she'd blame it on Mom for not taking us with her in the first place. Wouldn't you know, echoing throughout the house: "I know, it's always Mom's fault."

She would take it, though occasionally with an eye roll or two, but she never had a problem with gaining the blame, yet again. She smiled most of the time—whether that was a sarcastic smile, or the type of smile that said my days are eventful, but I love them—regardless, she always had one. She figured that if she would stay the target of blame, it would take the pressure off the rest of the family and eventually it made her the strong one. She was stronger mentally and a lot stronger spiritually.

All eighteen of us kids on Jonathan Lane were hellions none the less, but we became best friends. Every family and house was very different than the next. Even the parents were different than the other parents, but somehow, we all fit together perfectly, like a two-hundred-piece puzzle.

Directly beside our house were the two boys we called "computer nerds." They knew how to work the old "floppy disk" desktop computer like the back of their hands. They didn't come outside to play very often, but when they did, it was all fun and games until we made fun of them and got in trouble for it, so their outdoor ventures never lasted very long.

Close to them was the cookie-cutter family with one boy and one girl. They always had such a nicely groomed home, but by the books rules. However, their son, well, he was a part of our crew.

Next door to him was a girl we loved to hang out with—although often not allowed to—but when we did, we soaked it all in. She'd share stories with us about when she got in trouble, and we always felt the need to loudly voice all the cuss words we were never allowed to say at home. Plus, she had ramen noodles and we never got those.

One house over from her, were our "soulmates" per se. The husband and wife became best friends to my parents. They had a son our age and a daughter a little younger. Let's just say Rennie finally met the brother he never had. For Katie and me, we finally had the little sister we knew we would never get. That was the fun house. Running in and out, slamming doors (mostly the fridge door), building blanket forts, and filming homemade movies just to ask mom if we could spend the night; that was how our days went the majority of the time. While the girls made brownies just to have an excuse to lick the bowl, the boys were in the bathroom with one sitting on the stool reading joke books to the other one taking a dump.

"Let's make a movie to ask Mom if we can spend the night." But that genius idea only worked every so often. If the homemade movie was a dud, because usually it was, we begged Suzi to call Mom to ask her if we could stay over. Most of the time, it was a "No," and we'd stomp our way back home repeating loudly, "Our mom is so mean!"

Across from their house was another family that had a daughter with whom we liked to hang out with, also. They, too, seemed "by the book." It was fun to hang out in their "front room" and play on the computer because we surfed websites that we were never allowed to view back home. She was sweet—even the boys thought so, too. So much, that Rennie decided it was a good idea to ask her to have sex with him at age eight. Granted he didn't even know what that meant at the time, but that didn't calm the pissed-off mothers and the raging phone calls from down the street! Mom marched his ass right back down to her house to apologize in person. Needless to say, her mom didn't like us much after that.

Next door to her was another family with two little boys and an older sister. She was our age. Katie and I were thrilled to have another girl in the neighborhood who was able to keep up with us. She got in trouble with us, was grounded at the same time we were grounded, and argued with us, because we always made her pick which one of us was her favorite Heath sister. (Of course, that pick seemed to change weekly.)

About two houses down from them, back towards our house on the cul-de-sac was a family from the Virgin Islands. They had two snippy dogs and two beautiful, milky skinned, dark-haired daughters. They both were Meagan's age and were a part of her "posse."

Finally, directly next to our house was the sweet nosey old couple, much like Martha and Mr. Wilson. However, in this case, there was way more than just one Dennis!

We always had the house with all the snacks loaded in the garage fridge. Probably because Mom had to buy stock in Publix Supermarket, having to feed the army that she was raising! We had the big pool out back, and the old (but new at the time) gray and purple Nintendo that came with a whopping two controllers, super accommodating! We had a big oak tree in the front yard that was perfect for climbing. There was a basketball hoop we'd often climb up and hang on from the rim. We also had a big green electrical box in the front yard that became "base" for every game we ever played.

The moms were remarkably like the rest of their families. The two that stood out the most though, were the "cool and fun" mom down the street and our "fun-but-sometimes-mean" mom.

As we all got older, drove our own cars and graduated high school, we quickly realized the roles our parents really did play. Although our mom was "mean," she always ended up being the "cool one" to all the others. Mom was overly generous and offered the most amazing hospitality to the entire neighborhood. From what I tasted, I mean heard, she made best the margaritas! She flooded the countertops with bean dip, chips and salsa, Capri Suns, and delicious homemade lasagna.

She was fun, hospitable, and determined to make every visitor comfortable enough to feel like they were in their own home. It was "Pam's way" or no way! We came to terms with the fact that her way was **the** way. She held firm to the rules she enforced and raised four kids like it was a cinch. Four kids that today are all grown, healthy, successful, and raising their own families. All of which enforce those same rules! It's funny how that works out.

Even now, truthfully, we become Mom in almost everything we say back to our kids who don't listen. Because even now when they're told, "No,"—you guessed it—we hear, "My mom is so mean!"

Now, I realize in fact, there were real reasons behind her answers. As parents, we all finally see that. *You did great, Mom!*

CHAPTER 3

TERMINAL TURMOIL

A s you can imagine, it's not an easy task for a woman's body to carry multiples. It was not an easy pregnancy. Her body had changed forever.

If you are a mother, you understand how once you have kids you still feel those super weird and random flutters like the baby is still inside your belly kicking. There are things that happen to you that you can't explain or control. It's really weird. Some of your body parts all of a sudden droop where they were never droopy before! Not only does your physical appearance change, but so does your inner appearance. Your mind thinks in a different way, and you take on more worry and guilt. You gain more emotions, you lose more sleep, and you grow even more love in your heart you didn't think was even possible from the start.

Some of us even gain more liking for coffee and wine, too. It's not so bad.

If you didn't know how much you knew your body then, now that you're a mother, you really know it.

However, in the spring of 2013, Mom started experiencing some very odd bodily symptoms that made it difficult to pinpoint the direct cause. She started feeling awkward and bloated almost constantly.

"I can't even eat, because I feel so full, but I haven't eaten anything all day," she said to me in the kitchen one day as I leaned over the counter flipping through her *HGTV* magazines.

"What do you mean, you can't eat, Mom? You have to eat something," I told her, just like she'd tell me when I was sick and too nauseous to even nibble on saltine crackers. She would also remind me to slowly sip lemon-lime Gatorade. Then she'd come back thirty-minutes later to make sure I downed it, all to stay hydrated and get better quicker.

"Crystal, I can't! You don't understand."

She was right. I didn't understand how she could feel like she had just left the Chinese buffet down the street, when nothing had even entered her mouth that day.

She started to bleed at times she wasn't supposed to bleed, and from places it wasn't normal for blood to flow. She knew something wasn't right and more painfully, so did I.

She was always so good at keeping up with her annual checkups and she had a very healthy lifestyle from which she never steered very far. However, Mom was no different than the rest of the world in the sense that losing the unwanted weight never came easy. No matter the hours she put into walking the treadmill, her abdomen continued to bulge. Now that she couldn't indulge in any type of food group whatsoever, she was unwillingly starving herself and even then, the weight kept piling on.

Katie was getting married in August that year, so Mom knew she would have to make an appointment to see the doctor very soon. It weighed heavily on her and it showed. The last thing she was going to do was ruin Katie's wedding with the news she highly suspected she'd receive, if her appointment came before the wedding.

When I stopped by to visit her, which was daily, I could tell something was bothering her. Our conversations weren't about the grandbabies anymore. They were about what was going on with her body and how confusing everything seemed. Something was really wrong, and trying to convince her to get to the doctor right away was a waste of our breath, because it wasn't happening any time before the wedding.

When something worried my mom, it worried me. I didn't know what was going on, just as much as she didn't, but seeing the unspoken worry written all over her face was enough to make me sick. Mom was like my security blanket—seeing it unravel right in front of me—I felt very scared.

"So … how's the wedding planning coming along?" I asked her, trying to ignore the elephant in the room, in hopes of avoiding looking weak in front of her, because the last thing she ever was, was weak. Let me tell you though, I was never able to hide anything from her. She saw my eyes just seconds away from welling up and the elephant in the room was now too big to hide or ignore.

"Crystal, I am fine. Everything is going to be OK, so stop worrying," she told me.

I tried not to worry because after all, she hadn't even been to the doctor yet and until then—well, let's just chalk it up to being menopause, can we?

Clearly, our lives were flooded with eventful happenings. It was never boring, but I will tell you, nothing was as exciting as our girls' trip to the Florida Keys for Katie's bachelorette weekend. It was one for the books and I'm very sorry you weren't there for it!

Mom reserved an exclusive docked houseboat for us, a few miles north of Key West. We partied hard! We spent our nights shooting Fireball, dancing on the bar top at Coyote Ugly Saloon, and parading around the drag queen pubs with a ridiculous amount of Mardi Gras beads suffocating our necks. That's the weekend Mom happened to adopt the nickname, "Kris Jenner," when she backed into a parked car at the marina and blew it off with a simple, "Oops, don't tell Dad!"

Nothing was wrong in our lives then. Well, popping open Michelob Ultra's at eight o'clock in the morning on the top deck of our houseboat was probably wrong, but we didn't care. The rest of the memories from that trip are not shareworthy and, truthfully, you wouldn't understand unless you were there anyway. Again, I truly apologize you didn't make the guest list for *that* trip.

"It's wedding time!" Katie cheered happily, but Mom grew anxious and overly stressed the closer it approached. She had this annoying thing about getting entirely too stressed out before any type of gathering, big or small. We dealt with the side effects of her stress, but the perfection that came out of that always made all the effort worth it. Seeing Mom walk down the aisle, nervously hooked to Rennie's arm, was a sight to behold.

After she walked to her seat successfully without tripping or choking on her own spit from the laughter Rennie caused in that short walk to the front row, Katie came glowing down the aisle. It was a perfect night.

The week following the wedding meant it was time that Mom faced her fears. The symptoms she'd been experiencing were only worsening at this point. That heavy weight she was carrying around with her not only affected her mind, but it was too heavy on her heart, so she scheduled an appointment to see her gynecologist.

We were all planning to leave the day after her appointment on a road trip to the mountains for another wedding. Life couldn't have been better, and her appointment wasn't going to be such a big deal, because after she had tests run and was prescribed medication, we'd be on our way to wine country.

"Bye! Have a great time! Enjoy your trip!"

Boy, did I love hearing those words from my coworkers on the days I exited the building to leave for a vacation. I skipped my way to the car and drove right down the road to the bank to withdraw some cash for the exciting trip we were starting in the morning. I pulled up to the ATM, put the car in park, and searched for my debit card in the pitless Prada purse that took me about five minutes to untangle from underneath the passenger seat.

My phone rang as soon I grabbed my cash from the ATM, so I answered it.

"Crystal, where are you? You need to come home right now!" Dad's voice on the other end of the phone was almost unrecognizable, with the amount of trembling fear I heard.

"Um, OK, I'm coming! Is everything all right?" I asked.

"You just need to get here right away!" he exclaimed.

"What's wrong?" I asked, but it was too late. He had already hung up.

My parents' house was only about five miles down the road, so it was close. So close, that it's where my thirty-minute lunch breaks were spent daily. That was always quicker than sitting in a drive-thru and Mom's Mexican tostadas were much better than any restaurants was anyway.

Unfortunately, that wasn't a phone call I was expecting. My life had just been transformed. It changed everything.

I happened to catch every red light that I could possibly catch. I got behind the slowest cars of every old person in town, and I'm pretty sure I prayed one long extensive prayer the entire way. I didn't say, "Amen," until I careened into the driveway on two wheels.

Oh no, this isn't good—I saw every "important" car parked in her driveway, you know, the ones you aren't supposed to ever see at that time of the day? Yeah ... those cars.

My heart sank and I felt sick to my stomach. I honestly don't even think I parked in a real parking spot. I'm pretty sure I ran my car up into the grass and hopped out before I even put it in park. Running inside, I had no idea what to expect or what I was going to walk into. I knew she had been to the doctor that morning, but nothing seemed to be of that much importance that *those* cars would be there and why Dad sounded like he was about to crumble on the phone a few minutes ago.

I barged in, slammed the door behind me, and bolted into the living room. My heart beat faster than I ran. I rounded the corner in the kitchen and immediately stopped cold in my tracks.

What I saw in that living room meant something was terribly wrong. I completely froze. Confused, I looked around to see both of my sisters sitting on the couch with their head in their hands. My brother on the other side of the room was staring at the wall like he was about to punch the world's biggest hole in it. My mom's best friend, Vicki, looked up at me with tears streaming down her face. Dad was next to her, draped over the back of the couch with his head hung low and shaking back and forth. I scanned the room in what felt like slow motion and fixed my gaze on Mom as she stood up to approach me. She knew I was scared and confused, and about to lose it!

"Mom?" I asked, scanning everybody's faces once again. "What's going on? What's wrong with everybody?" She grabbed my arms and embraced me as tears started forming in my terrified eyes. I felt pain in my body welling up on the verge of exploding. The words I heard after that were far worse than I could have ever expected.

"Your mom has cancer," Dad said, as she held me tight with a grip that nobody could have broken, because she couldn't possibly ever be the one to drop that kind of bomb on me.

My knees buckled and I fell straight to the floor. I was still tangled in her arms but shattering to pieces.

I lost it.

CHAPTER 4

THE WAITING GAME

Mom was the type of person who could turn any negative situation into a positive one, no matter how hard it seemed to the rest of us. She made you wonder how someone could be so faithful, so loving, and so caring at all times. She found a way to thank God for some sort of blessings every single day. She often taught even strangers lessons from her daily acts of kindness.

The grandkids called her Memaw and to them, she hung the moon! She was so much fun and so funny. Truly, she was their world. She was the wife who seemed so perfect and put together, and the mom who was so forgiving, completely genuine, and full of overflowing love, making you wonder if she was even real. Perhaps she was some sort of angel who was there just to teach you something and then poof away when you reached out to touch her.

You know as well as I do that everybody has a favorite person in life. We were best friends. She was my favorite—even verbally admitting it in times that hurt other people's feelings. I still did it though, because it was true–she was. She was everything that felt right, truly my home and my safe place, always.

"Your mom has cancer."

Talk about a knife that even Scarface wouldn't carry. That message went straight to my heart. The breath was knocked out of me as my body hit the floor. I screamed, "What? No!" as Mom cocooned me in her arms. She had my reaction already planned out, because she knew exactly how I'd take this devastating news. She was there to pick up the pieces and make me feel completely safe, even in all my sorrow.

She knew that breaking this kind of news to us was going to be the hardest thing she'd ever had to do, but she quickly went into survival mode and found a way to assure us that, in fact, everything was going to be okay. I looked around the room to see my siblings drowning in their tears and listened as Dad's foot pounded on the wood floor, as he tried to figure out what to do next.

I then threw my arms around my mom's neck and squeezed her tightly, as if nothing else in the world ever existed. All the while, she struggled to pull my crumpled body up from the floor.

Breaking through the instant devastation and screams, I asked her, "Why you, Mom, why you?"

I couldn't process what was just said out loud and thinking it might really be true, it was happening to her, and that will never be OK!

"Why not me? Why would I be immune to cancer? God has a plan, honey, but everything will be OK," she said so calmly.

That was not what we wanted to hear, but that's how she looked at it.

"His plan is the perfect plan, and we have to remember that," she explained.

I didn't understand how you could be given that diagnosis and still have the strength to even mumble the words, "Everything is going to be OK." If that was so, we'd all be home right now stuffing our suitcases with clothes we probably wouldn't have even worn in the mountains this week.

I sat down on the couch in an instant fog and joined the head-hanging crew. I didn't know what to think, believe, feel, or even what had just happened. The room became silent, as if everybody in there was searching for an answer to a question we had never had to ask before.

"The doctor has referred me to a gynecological oncologist to verify my findings and diagnosis and we will go from there. Don't get all worked up right now, you guys, because we really don't know much and there's no reason to make ourselves sick over something that isn't certain," she said.

"Your dad and I aren't going on this trip tomorrow, because I'm going to see the doctor first thing Tuesday morning. You can all certainly still go! In fact, I want you to go. We will enjoy our weekend and do what we have to do on Tuesday when I meet with my new oncologist. Again, don't worry. Keep praying and it will all be just fine."

First off, that was entirely too many words to process all at once. It didn't take but two seconds for us to quickly speak up. "Well ... we aren't going without you! We will be there with you on Tuesday!"

If your mom is the matriarch of your family like ours is, then you know just how it is to not want to do anything in her absence. Vacationing always meant Mom would be there. She was a safe haven. Trips were only worth it, if it included her.

Why would we go anywhere without her? WHY did God just give my MOM cancer?

"I can't believe this!" I said as I stood up from the couch.

I walked outside and stuck my feet in the freezing cold pool, called my husband, and had a meltdown at the sound of him saying, "Hello?"

"We aren't going to North Carolina. Something came up, so we need to cancel. MOM HAS CANCER!"

Now that I've dropped that bomb on him, all he could muster up to say was, "Umm ... OK. Don't worry, Crystal, we will figure it all out. Where are you? I will be right there."

He's my other safe haven and thank God he was on his way to me right now.

Why does everybody keep saying that it's going to be OK? How do they know? They don't! It won't be OK—it's cancer!

Cancer is something etched in your brain as a relentless killer. There is nothing good about it. It ruins lives and it takes loved ones away daily. This was something we never imagined would actually hit our family, and most certainly not Mom! Now, uninvited, it was here. It was now a part of this family and it was a part of my mom, too.

"Hello?" I said as I answered my phone.

I had now moved from the pool to the driveway. It was my sister-in-law calling to tell me that she loved me, she's here for me and that once again—you guessed it—"Everything is going to be OK." As I cried hysterically, I could only mutter the words, "I can't lose her!"

Naturally, the human thought process only reverts directly to the worst scenario possible when a diagnosis like cancer is thrown into the mix. I didn't know anything that was about to happen, nor could I even think straight. The thought of possibly losing my mom one day way sooner than I'd ever imagined, was ripping me to shreds.

As we entered into the longest weekend of our lives, suddenly nobody had plans. Nobody felt good, so we didn't want to make any plans, except to be there with her. We didn't know anything for certain, so there wasn't anything we could do except sit and painfully wait for answers while our minds spun out of control. We battled stomachaches and headaches. We fought with our own minds about what was going to be confirmed on Tuesday. We googled things we never fathomed googling before. We cried, laughed, split bottles of wine, and were terribly worried.

Tuesday slowly approached and she met her new doctor, who immediately made her feel comfortable in his knowledge and care. He confirmed that it was, in fact, cancer. He explained that surgery was a necessity to verify just how advanced it was.

"How soon can you schedule this surgery?" he asked her.

"How soon can you do it?" she responded.

Needless to say, she was in surgery the very next morning.

CHAPTER 5

UNDER THE KNIFE

"Beep! Beep! Beep!" the alarm clock obnoxiously chimed, flashing 3:00 a.m. ... time to get up!

It was the morning of surgery and before Mom got out of bed, she prayed. Even before her feet hit the ground, she'd already spoken to God. She never did anything without bringing it to Him first. She knew He'd take care of her, the hospital staff, and the hands of the surgeon. Because she knew that, she grabbed her overnight bag and headed to the hospital, confident and positive.

As 7:00 a.m. rolled around, there we all were, sitting nervously in the waiting room on the surgery floor. We tried to stay calm and optimistic, but that didn't last long before we started experiencing emotions we couldn't control. Dad paced the floor nonstop, took a couple of phone calls, made a few jokes to wear out the heavy emotions, grabbed a cup of coffee, and pretended to play it cool. My sisters and brother sat there trying to make light of the situation by staying positive and hopeful, too.

My brother, Rennie, is the type of person whom you absolutely need around in difficult times like these. He throws in a lot of very inappropriate comments and jokes that make you roll your eyes, wondering if he really came out of the same mom you did. But his very well-known presence brings you a sense of peace that often allows your mind to slip away for a bit, from what brought you there in the first place.

Currently, I was studying for a certification I wanted to get for my job. So I sat in those uncomfortable waiting room chairs and opened my five-inch three-ring binder to attempt to study. Yeah, right, that didn't last but all of five minutes and even then, I couldn't remember a word I read.

Going through difficult times, I think we all know how our minds can turn into our worst enemies. That morning, mine took me on quite the rollercoaster ride. I must have made about ten trips to the unisex bathroom around the corner in the two hours we waited to hear any news at all coming from the operating room. My nerves caused me relentless nausea and I felt like I had a twenty-pound weight lying directly atop my chest. My head was foggy, but I held back tears and put on a fake smile, pretending I was enjoying the corny stories being told, but they were going in one ear and right out the other. I prayed one minute and then thought miserably, why even pray? Because if God is real, then He wouldn't be putting her through this, damn it!

The original plan was for the doctor to go in laparoscopically to see if the cancer was contained in the ovaries. If it wasn't, he would have to open her up. Because Mom had delivered multiples, her organs inside were all jumbled up, so it was hard to find the exact location where the cancer was initially residing. The doctor had explained to Dad that once he made the decision that it was necessary to open her up, he would need Dad's consent to do so. For Dad to give his consent at the time of necessity, the doctor would call from the operating room to the waiting room and ask to speak with him right away.

I sat there in agony not knowing at all what was going on. Is she scared? What if she's terrified? What if she doesn't make it through the surgery? I tried to pacify my mind by people-watching in the corridor, but even that didn't bring any ease. I couldn't stand seeing some moms cheerfully walk by, pushing their daughters in wheelchairs to the exit doors. I couldn't help but overhear the desk clerks chatting away about their happy-go-lucky weekend, full of drinking stories. I regretted they were overly sharing. I tried to sip coffee and talk myself down from the middle of the anxiety attack I was experiencing, but I stayed mired in misery.

We glared at the patient TV, which let us know exactly where Mom was. Right now, her patient number was still stuck "IN PRE-OP," so we knew the surgery hadn't even started yet. I didn't think I'd make it that long just sitting there, battling emotions like I was, if she hadn't even started surgery yet.

"There's a chapel across the hall. Let's go say a prayer," my godmother said to us, knowing we were uncomfortable just sitting and waiting.

Katie, Meagan, and I headed with her down the stairwell to the chapel. It was dark inside, only being lit by the glow of dull wall sconces, and was eerily silent. I immediately stood there staring at the giant wooden cross on the wall, wondering if a quick little prayer was even going to help. Glancing at the clock as it ticked its way to 7:15 a.m., we stood in front of the altar, hand-in-hand. We huddled in a small hopeful circle and aired some of our emotions out loud. We were scared and just simply wanted to know why this was happening to her, to us, and to our family.

It was up to God to get her through this and praying made it seem a little more hopeful, because we felt we were doing something right.

"Please Lord, be with her as she lies on that surgical table facing her fate," we asked, hoping He was really listening. We asked that He guide the hands of the surgeon and lead the nursing staff to the correct instruments and tools needed to make this surgery a success. We asked that He be with us and calm our raging nerves. We even begged Him to help us remember that it was all in His hands and under His control, and to help keep our minds at ease and our emotions at bay.

"In Jesus' name we pray, Amen."

We shared quick hugs, threw out a few, "It'll all be okay," and headed back up the stairwell to the waiting room.

We waited politely at the door of the chapel while people passed by, very similar to waiting at the top of the subway stairwell in New York City, while the crowd never really seems to diminish until you rudely push your way back through. We made it through the foggy maze of this busy hospital hallway and sat back down. I glanced over at the patient TV and her patient number had changed to "SURGERY START" at the same time our prayer commenced, which was exactly 7:22 a.m.

Now, most of you may say that's just a silly coincidence and (no lie) that crossed my mind, too. However, instead of thinking that way, I at least tried to stay hopeful and take that as possibly a sign from God. Her surgery start was waiting on a prayer.

Now the real waiting game started. More anxiety flooded our chest cavities and we felt like our heads were in the direct line of multiple never-ending fog machines! Cold sweats and fear invaded as we tried to relax a little, taking deep breaths, resting our hands on our knees, and hanging our heads low. We were all in our own little town of worry, where anxiety was an understatement. We sat up, leaned down, crossed our legs, uncrossed our legs, and shifted our weight from one side of the chair to the other—basically not knowing what to do. We felt so helpless. Each time the phone rang, we looked at the desk clerks like startled deer in glaring headlights, wondering if it was about our mom. A few more calls rang out, but none about Mom, so a few more loud huffs of breath belched forth out of pure exhaustion and frustration.

Finally, the phone rang again.

"Okay, sir, I will get him. One moment," the desk clerk said, standing up after setting the phone down on the desk. Dad stood up before she could finish uttering those words and ran quickly to the desk and said, "Hello?" The rest of us sat on the edge of our seats, hearts pounding out of our chest, our breathing becoming very rapid and shallow. We glared with tunnel vision straight towards Dad. The background suddenly became silent.

"So, it's ovarian?" he asked.

"Wow, OK, and if the only option is to remove as much as you can, then we have no choice. Just do it," he consented right then and there.

"Wait, Doc? Don't forget; you MUST take good care of her. Do you hear me?" he asked sternly.

"OK, thanks. Bye." Click.

That was that! The long journey that was ahead had just begun. He walked back over to us and shared the news that we had already overheard.

"Well," he said, "it's ovarian cancer and he has to open her up from her chest down to the bottom of her abdomen, in order to remove everything that's covered with cancer."

I'm pretty sure I stopped breathing at that moment.

Dad went on with, "While he's in there, he will remove every organ that she can possibly live without in hopes of lessening the risk of the cancer spreading in the future. So ... here we go!"

Those words were not what I wanted to hear. However, none of this is what I ever wanted in the first place nor imagined was really going to happen. Life is so unfair.

Sitting in the hospital while your mother undergoes a full body debulking surgery is heart-wrenching and terrifying, to say the least. Everything going on in that operating room is totally out of our control and knowing that is painful.

As we waited, the clock hit 9:54 a.m. and her patient number flashes: "SURGERY COMPLETE." Whew! Now we could breathe somewhat! We sighed with relief, thinking the hardest part of all this was now over. There was almost a sense of excitement and joy in those next few minutes, like our worries had been taken away, because the surgery was complete. We seemed to have forgotten all the horror we just sat through this entire time.

At 9:58 a.m., the pastor of our church came walking through the doorway. We joined hands in one big circle of family, friends, and church members. Then Pastor began a powerful prayer that was so important, the ongoing hallway traffic paused along with us to bow their heads, too. After the Amen, we all dropped hands, and the traffic resumed as normal.

Mom's patient number flashed, "OUT OF O.R.," at exactly 10:01 a.m.

"Now what? What are we supposed to do? When can we go see her? How will we know what room they take her to? Is somebody going to let us know what our next move is going to be?" I had questions, but nobody knew how to answer them. A few minutes ago, we had hope during that powerful prayer, but now we were becoming impatient, anxious, and selfish, as if we were the only family in the hospital waiting to see our post-op patient.

"Sir, once the doctor has completed his surgical transcription and his mandatory post op procedures, he will come out and ask to speak with the family. Until then, please have a seat," said the desk clerk who clearly wasn't experiencing the same agony we were.

At 10:45 a.m., a good-looking man in green scrubs and a tight scrub hat came out looking for somebody. Clearly that had to be the doctor looking for our family.

"Heath family?" he said as he bobbed up and down trying to search over top of all the heads of everybody else in the waiting room.

That's us!

All twenty of us followed the doctor into a ridiculously small side discussion room, where we closed the door and crammed in to hear him out.

He started with, "Well, I'll start with saying how important Pam must be, because never in my career, have I seen this big of a fan club for any one of my patients, ever." He had that right!

"The surgery went well," he continued. "The cancer had spread from her ovaries to her abdomen, and I had to remove everything I knew she could live without, her ovaries, fallopian tubes, the omentum, and her appendix."

Good Lord, what did he leave? I thought.

"I need you all to remember though, cancer is microscopic. Just like throwing sand on carpet, I could only remove what I was physically able to see. Because there will inevitably be unseen micro-particles left that I wasn't able to see, she will need six rounds of chemotherapy to knock the rest out."

He had gotten a head start with her by placing a port in her abdomen directly under her rib cage. That is where she'd have intraperitoneal chemo administered to make the pathway to her abdomen convenient. He told us she'd start with that, but in a few weeks, Mom would receive another port placement at a second site in her chest and have to follow up with intravenous chemotherapy to maximize the results.

Trying to contain our excitement from the success he had with her surgery, we also nodded with his upcoming plans in agreeance that that was the best course to take.

"I want to remind you though," he spoke a little louder, "that this is most definitely going to be a very difficult road ahead. She will be in a lot of pain considering I removed multiple organs. I cut her open from her spleen down to the middle of her pelvic bone. The road to recovery will be long, so you need to be patient with her. My nurse will let you know once she's assigned a room, so then you may go in for a brief visit. Be cautious, because she has a tube down her throat as well."

Gasping, our eyes widened, because we knew she hated the possibility of having that tube down her throat, and was secretly hoping she didn't need it.

"Oh, she hated it!" he said as he went to exit the discussion room to leave us to ourselves.

After we thanked him for everything he had done for her, Dad shook his hand. Then, off we went to the cafeteria, hoping to pass the time and stop our hunger pangs.

After lunch, we piled into the elevator to head to the sixth floor, just to wait for Sleeping Beauty to wake up. Dad, Meagan, Katie, Rennie, and I went back as a family to see her first. She was sleeping, highly medicated, and completely out of it. Tucked in tight under those rough, not-warm-at-all hospital sheets, she was breathing from the tube placed down her throat. Dad grabbed one of her hands and I grabbed the other. As we tried to stay quiet so as not to wake her, I stroked her cold hand gently.

Dad whispered, "Hey, Pam, we're all here. You are out of surgery now. The doctor said everything went well. We love you very much."

Her attempt to reply was a faint moan, but she was unable to open even one of her eyes to acknowledge us. However, we knew she heard us and that she was aware we were right by her side the whole time and never would we be anywhere else but with her.

When 12:26 p.m. rolled around, the nurses finally took out her unwanted throat tube, which made her feel slightly better. When the pain meds started to kick in, her road to recovery seemed to have finally begun.

For the next couple of days, Mom struggled. Although she experienced extreme pain all over her body, her will to get out of the hospital and to go home to her "somewhat normal life" was extraordinarily strong. She wasn't going to let anything or anyone get in her way. She tried hard to do what the nurses said. They closely monitored the pain and managed it as well as possible.

She actually sat up in bed on Day Two. She also had her first "walk" (which was a few steps across the room) on her second day as well. She made tremendous progress in just a few days post-op. Day Three came and her will to be discharged had grown even stronger. She spent those days following the directions of her round-the-clock nurses and prayed to God to help get her out of there. She walked a whopping five-hundred feet that day! A normal hospital stay after a debilitating surgery like she had is a good seven to fourteen days; but because she did so well, she was sent home on the afternoon of her fourth day. What a fighter she is!

The following days at home were very challenging, to put it mildly, both physically and emotionally. Due to the severed abdominal muscles, it was exceedingly difficult for her to even get up and down and in and out of bed. Because she had a countless number of staples holding her stomach together, she had to sleep in a recliner just to be able to breathe and minimize the amount of pain with which she was living. She had to keep up with many different medications and had to try to stay awake for a whole lot of visitors.

Mom developed fluid in her lungs, which took several weeks to eliminate, causing her constant shortness of breath. Regardless of those setbacks, she believed there was a plus side to all of this. While debulking half her body, the doctor gave her a two-for-one and removed a hernia she had developed twenty-five years ago when we, the triplets, were born.

"Now I have a normal belly button!" she exclaimed to us with pure little-girl giddiness.

She never fell short of remembering the reason behind the surgery and often wondered what exactly she was going to face coming up very soon.

"What about the cancer? What is my next step? Am I supposed to start chemotherapy soon? Did the doctor remove all the cancer? Is there anything specific I have to do to prepare for the start of chemo? Can I just attend my post-op visits and then move on with my life? How long do I have to take these medications? Will I lose my hair? Am I now considered a cancer survivor? Will I die?" It wasn't just her being an inquisitive, devastated, and emotional human being, as even her mind was confused. Having unanswered questions like that made every one of us uneasy.

During those trying days of her recovery, we often found her watching the TV show, *Ellen*. She loved Ellen and to this day, I swear she'd seen every episode at least five times! The only place I wanted to be was by her side, and that's where I stayed! Together we googled cancer-related topics during each commercial break and tried to gain somewhat of an understanding of how this whole cancer thing really works.

Either she'd answer the overflowing text messages chiming through her phone, or she'd have me answer them and update her progress to all her followers. The only difference between her actions and mine during those long days was the fact that she'd actually bow her head to pray. Unfortunately, my faith wasn't in a very good place at the time, and I was way more than bitter. I was overly angry. (That's putting it mildly!)

God should not have ever put her in this position in the first place. I did not pray nearly as often as she did. She was so faithful at it, and somehow she stayed thankful and gracious through it all. I apparently had a lot to learn.

She looked forward to her staples being removed the morning of the 10th of September. Not only would she feel better without artificially having her body held intact by staples, but to her it was a forward step. She was moving along quickly until the doctor decided it was a good idea to kill two birds with one stone during that appointment.

Chemotherapy introduction spilled right out of his mouth without any hesitation of holding it back, or at least dropping the bomb a little more conservatively. She may have been good at keeping her emotions under wraps in her heart and mind, but she wasn't too good at keeping them from being written all over her face. However, she was better at that than I was, so much that she'd put her feelings aside just to remind me as she said, "Calm down, relax and be open to the instructions and advice the doctor is giving to us, Crystal."

I appreciated her trying to calm me down about something she was enduring, but that was too much to ask of me right now. I couldn't just calm down! How unfair life is, making Mom go through chemo. She had so many hopes of not having to do any of that, since over half her internal body parts were now gutted. But nope—why would we think this was going to go in her favor? Nothing had gone her way since cancer barged into our lives, so why would it start now? God, I hate cancer!

She tried teaching me in her gentle and smart-mom way, as she said, "I have two options: either I can become bitter and completely block out the entire conversation we just had. Or I can accept it for what it is, follow along this journey the absolute best way I can, and realize that understanding His recommendations and remembering it's all in God's hands. Really it's the better way, Crystal."

She was right. I hated ever admitting that when I didn't agree to something she said, but it was the truth.

She was determined to take the bull by its horns and conquer exactly what needed to be conquered. Although Option One sounded much easier to me, she didn't care if I agreed with her or not. She went with Option Two because she knew deep down, it wasn't going to end up being just about her. As much as she deserved to think of only herself in that moment, she didn't. That was who she was—she never thought of just herself. She knew not only was her husband and children going to need her around, but her grandkids definitely were! I know she didn't do it just for them, but she probably could have. Her grandchildren made up her whole world. The light in her days came from them. When they are old enough to realize that, they'll know just how much their Memaw really was a true legend.

She had never been one to give up and throw in the towel on the first round just after the bell sounded. She knew if it didn't challenge her, it wouldn't change her and, by God, she was going to change that. She was determined to give herself the chance to fight this awful disease; that had now been diagnosed as Stage 3 Ovarian and Primary Peritoneal Cancer.

The doctor gave her many pamphlets and informational handouts to read, along with instructions on how she would receive chemotherapy. He gave her hope through pep talks, not only as a doctor, but as a friend to whom she had given her trust, quite quickly.

This world in which we live plants in our brains that trusting somebody so easily that you've just met, isn't how it is supposed to be, but she didn't care. She knew right when she met her doctor that her trust was in him, but fully in God first. When you have a doctor who you have just barely met, who has already opened up almost your entire body and worked on it from the inside, you don't have much of a choice but to hand over the torch into the hands of that man sitting right in front of you.

Spilling out the way things are going to go, she sat there and extended her trust out to the doctor immediately.

After all, this was his expertise. This is what he gets paid the big bucks for, so he obviously knows what he's talking about, right? I held onto that thought, because internally, I hoped that was true.

As he laid the law down to her, she laid it down right back to him. My girl! She made it noticeably clear to him who she was and for what exactly she's fighting for. She was quite blunt with her truth.

"I have four kids out in that waiting room right now who NEED me. I will do whatever I possibly can do to fight this disease head on. I do not want you to sugarcoat anything, ever! I want you to lay it out there to me, as if I am your own mother. I can take it and I will take it. I'm tough, but I am NOT alone. I'll always have God and my family on my side."

He knew at that very moment that Mom was someone incredibly special, who was placed in his room that day for a reason. No matter what came up, he promised to do whatever he possibly could to give her a fighting chance at defeating this cancer. The doctor-to-patient connection transformed from "just another patient on the schedule" to something very personal and very dear to the hearts of them both. It was a trust and bond that only grew stronger with each visit. Trust me, there were a lot of those.

As she walked out of the exam room and down the hall after her appointment had concluded, she turned back and smiled at him, gave a nod, and left him with, "Hey, we got this!"

He smiled back at her, grabbed his next chart, and said, "Hey there!" as he closed the door behind him.

CHAPTER 6

CHEMOTHERAPY

I'm almost positive there's never been a better party or event planner than my mom. She'd go above and beyond organizing, planning, and executing to be well prepared for what was about to take place. Chemo though, isn't the type of event for which you can accurately plan. For her, it was the fear of the unknown.

Just knowing she had cancer was scary and confusing, but adding to what might lie ahead, chemo, her fear was amplified. She was anxious and understandably very nervous. She dreaded the fact that sooner or later, she'd have to face something she never thought she'd have to face. She prayed and prayed in the weeks prior, and she knew the morning of the procedure that, no matter the amount of worry she carried with her, it wouldn't change anything. She did what she knew was best and handed it over to God.

Originally, she was to wait three or more weeks after her surgery to heal before starting chemo for the first time, but she hit her first bump in the road much sooner than expected. She woke up with a fever the morning she was due for the port placement in her chest and, although she felt no symptoms of the fever, her conservative doctor was taking no chances. He put her on an antibiotic and sent her home for a few more days. It wasn't until after those minor setbacks had fully passed that he would even think about port placement.

Chemotherapy began almost exactly a month after her surgery. She received Taxotere, Cisplatin, and Taxol chemotherapy drugs. Her regimen would consist of IV chemo on Monday, IP chemo in the abdomen via port on Tuesday, followed by several liters of fluids on Wednesday, Thursday, and Friday. IP chemo in the abdomen would then be administered again that following Monday and concluded by the outrageously expensive—we're talking seven grand expensive—Neulasta shot injected on Tuesday. It was a long and trying seven days on chemo and twelve short days off. That went on for six rounds before she could attest to saying she hit full completion.

As the glass sliding doors whooshed open at the entrance to the cancer center, she walked into the lobby and over to the desk.

"Good morning! Name please?" greeted the lady at the front desk. Mom gave her full name and all the necessary information, completed the preliminary novel of paperwork, and proceeded to find a seat next to the window. Looking around, she felt too "normal" to be there. She felt out of place and, ironically, we felt the same. She was taken back to the chemo lab, which looked like a big room lined with pedicure bowls, except instead of spa bowls, it was picc-lines and IV bags. She sat down in one of those oddly comfortable chairs, laid her bag on the side table, and pulled out her iPad that she totes around everywhere she goes. She was determined to beat at least ten more levels of Candy Crush while she was there.

The nurses in the chemo lab were extremely nice and seemed genuinely friendly, when they offered her a drink and a magazine as soon as she sat down. However, no time was wasted, as they came to her side to immediately explain what would take place and how this whole chemotherapy thing really works.

"For the next four hours, your only responsibility is to rest and relax, OK?" the nurse said to her. Mom loved the sound of that, because quite frankly, resting and relaxing had simply never been a part of her life agenda. That type of thing had never made its rounds back to her ever since she birthed triplets so she was going to sit back and enjoy every minute of this.

Chemo that morning was given through an IV, since she didn't have her mediport placed yet. Sitting there overhearing the nurse's conversations with other patients in the same room, Mom pulled out her iPad, started level sixty-five of Candy Crush, and went straight into relaxation mode per the nurse's orders.

"What a breeze that was! I got to rest, actually beat twelve levels of Candy Crush, and I feel just fine with no noticeable side effects," Mom told me over the phone.

The next day she received IP chemo through the port in her abdomen that had been placed during her surgery. Having a port already placed there was not the least bit comfortable, but it was tolerable. She had been told it was an injection site, but it would hurt unless she prepared herself with a medicated cream to deaden that area before being accessed. She had no problem with caking on that cream prior to any chemo session—she was taking no chances! After receiving her pre-meds (IV bag filled with a concoction of anti-nausea medication, Benadryl, and Zantac), it was time to access the port. She took one large deep breath and ... it was nothing!

"Well, that was easy," Mom said to the nurse. "Another anxious moment put down just like that."

That was the hardest day, having two liters of chemo drugs pumped straight to her abdomen, followed by two bags of fluids, as she sat there watching her belly grow by the minute. Unfortunately, it continued that way for days. She went home that second night feeling incredibly uncomfortable. She tried to sleep, but lying flat made her miserable, so she moved to the recliner just to squeeze in a few hours of shut-eye before the sun came up on yet another trying day. This was the first time she verbally asked the "Is this really worth it?" question that will come up, no matter how strong a cancer patient you are.

It's the overwhelming changes of this new life that consists of fatigue and multiple aches and pains that unfortunately come up quite quickly. I watched as she moaned and groaned, trying to make herself comfortable but no matter how many pillows I stuffed behind her back or the number of blankets I laid over her, she wasn't comfortable at all. That killed me. I couldn't seem to help even if I tried.

Going through these types of days, it would be such an easy way out to throw your hands up and quit just like that, but you can't. That's life and unfortunately it keeps going, whether your hands are up in exhaustion, or they're folded in prayer. Your body and mind are being pushed to the brink, but you're resilient and you will bounce back.

Being stamped with a cancer diagnosis, you'll start understanding that bumps in the road seem to abruptly increase. Whether it's after an emergency surgery or at the start of your new chemo regimen, you'll feel like most days you just don't get a break.

As if debulking mom's entire body and pumping her full of toxic, cancer-killing drugs wasn't enough, she still had to deal with taking care of her dad (Grandpa), who happened to be preparing for his own open-heart surgery. The relationship between Mom and Grandpa was quite like mine with her. She always believed he hung the moon. Although stubborn at most times, ultimately she honored his word and always looked up to him. He was the kind of man who never seemed to be afraid of anything. He'd been through so much in his life with excessive lessons learned, that being scared or afraid of something just didn't seem to be in his makeup.

By the time I grew old enough to develop my own feelings about him, I believed that nothing and nobody could ever break him down. He was as tough as nails, but a big loving teddy bear at the same time, genuine and generously kind to everybody. He was the type of person who answered the door in his tight white t-shirt tucked into pants that were pulled halfway up his body and held together by his black belt stretching over his Santa Claus belly. Often he draped his blue velvet man robe over his outfit, wore big framed bifocals, and carried a mug of steaming hot coffee at noon, but his gentle deep voice always greeted you the same way each time.

"Hey, Sweet-art!" (Bless his bones, his sweet southern voice always hyphenated that word. He was so cute.)

He'd always start with a giant bear hug before you even stepped in the door, smashing your face against the side of his glasses case that were tucked into his shirt pocket. Then he'd kiss you, stabbing your cheek with his prickly facial hair, smelling like old men's cologne and Folgers. Gosh, what I'd do for another one of his Starbucks smelling, cologne overpowering face-smashing hugs. I sure do miss him.

Not only was he the patriarch of our entire family, but he meant the world to Mom. We had a family get-together at his house the day before his surgery and he seemed very odd. Usually he was up-and-at-'em and ready to go when the family came over, but I don't think I ever saw him leave "his chair," which was a recliner that every grandchild fought each other over endlessly, just to be the lucky one to get to sit in it.

"Grandpa, what's wrong?" I asked him, worried because he wasn't acting right.

"Oh, nothing, Sweet-art," he said to me as he turned to smile and grab my hand.

"Okay, I just want to make sure you're OK, because you seem tired or something."

But all he could do was lie to me saying, "You're always my little angel, nothing is wrong, or I would tell you," as he kissed my forehead. However, I knew he wasn't telling the truth. Something was definitely wrong.

Mom could see it, too, but she also tried to play it cool. She tried not to upset anybody else in the house, but it was obvious that Grandpa wasn't acting himself.

We were in between her first and second rounds of chemo at this time, when he headed into his surgery that next morning. He was still scared for some reason, which was definitely not him. Mom reassured him that everything was going to be okay and that he made the right decision to proceed. He had researched the best hospital and doctor for this specific surgery, and he shared with Mom his feelings of doubt, but even then, after her reassurance, his feelings didn't quite let up.

After Mom was diagnosed with ovarian cancer, he worried more than ever. After all, his little girl had to fight something that he couldn't control or cure. It was hard for all of us. It was an unsettling feeling for him to be going into such a major surgery while she was battling something that seemed to him to be much bigger. He believed, deep down in his heart (no pun intended), that this was the correct decision, so the show went on.

Sitting in the waiting room with the rest of the family, Mom included, we waited for confirmation of a successful surgery for him. The doctor finally approached the room and informed us, "He's out of surgery and everything went very well."

I wondered, *Am I the only one that feels like the doctors always say that, even if things didn't go so well?*

He told us that once he was all settled in his room in the ICU, we'd be able to go back to see him, two at a time. Unfortunately, many things went wrong during his hospital stay, especially those first ten days. You know, because everything didn't go so well, like in the doctors' script that they use to inform the family when their patient is coming out of surgery with no complications. Shocking, but my point exactly! He ended up having to be rushed back into surgery not once, but two more times after the first operation.

Meanwhile, his seventy-eight-year-old wife, Grandma, could not care for herself at home alone, by any means. Stubborn as all get out, she wasn't capable of being left alone even for a mere minute. She temporarily moved in with my parents, so her "overly strict" daughter could keep her under close watch. That meant, she was moving in with us, too, because at this point, I was still living back at home with my little family of four pending our newly built house. It was chaotic, if you really want the truth.

You usually found Grandma creeping out of the back bedroom at one o'clock in the afternoon in her white-and-pink flowered, paper-like cotton nightgown and her tiny size-five white scrunched up house slippers. She'd venture out to the kitchen wanting somebody to make her breakfast, usually a bowl of sliced white grapefruit covered in salt that she wasn't supposed to have. She was too busy pricking her tiny little finger to check her blood sugar that was supposed to have been taken that morning—like six long hours ago.

Mom would drop Grandma off at the hospital every day to sit with Grandpa, then she would visit in between every chance she was able. Being with both, whether there was anything specific to do or not, was comforting for Mom—sometimes stressful, but mostly comforting. It seemed to bring some balance into her quickly shifting lifestyle. She could sit and visit while her own problems seemingly faded away. She didn't think much of her life outside those hospital walls during visiting hours. She rarely discussed the chemo round that she had completed prior, and she didn't talk much of her journey with cancer.

Her disease didn't exist when she sat at Grandpa's bedside. Whether or not she verbally acknowledged that she had cancer, it always found a way of creeping back in to remind her. Maybe it was the devil knocking at the door, but to her it was an opportunity to remember that taking care of herself had to remain on top of the list.

One morning in November, Mom pulled into the hospital parking lot and proceeded to slowly walk to the elevator, and I mean sloth-status slow, because Grandma was in tow. You see, anything at all that included Grace, as we called Grandma, didn't exactly beat the clock. It was always quite a time-consuming adventure each time her petite little soul was forced to leave the house. Normally, parking and taking somebody up the elevator would only take a quick ten minutes max, but that wasn't the case with her. Not only did you park and take ten minutes alone to get Grace out of the car, but you had to make sure she grabbed all of her very minimal belongings. She'd most definitely need her gray zip-up jacket, her off-brand Yeti of iced dirt water (I mean, unsweet tea), and her beat-up old brown leather purse that contained God knows what. The only things known to man in that purse were the crumbled up old tissues she always saved to reuse (compliments of the era she grew up in that us millennials couldn't care less about), and, of course, her dead flip phone that she never charged unless Mom did it for her.

At this point, walking wasn't much of an option when the time clock was ticking as fast as it did those days. Grabbing a free, old creaky wheelchair that was conveniently placed at the front doors of the hospital (probably for people like her) was much safer and a lot more efficient for anybody with the honor of bringing Grace up for visiting hours. Thirty-five minutes in, you could finally drop her off, much like those daycare drop-off mornings when your toddler stalls, just to make you late for work. Mom was exhausted. She felt so run down because she had just used every bit of energy to push that wheelchair down the corridors just to take the elevator to the sixth floor.

"I don't feel so well," she told Grandpa. "I'm going back home to rest for a little while, but I'll be back later to pick her up and lug her back home." Mom sighed, trying to catch her breath.

Grandpa was sitting up in bed slurping applesauce. He replied, "OK, Honey," in his I-totally-know-what-you-just-went-through-getting-her-up-here voice.

Mom finally made it back down to the car, which was thankfully parked in the handicap parking spot right up front—perks of taking care of the handicapped, I mean elderly. Usually when Mom didn't feel well, you could see it on her face, but she tried not to make it known, to avoid burdening anybody around her. She was the kind of woman who, no matter what she feels like, is going to tell you, "I'm okay, I feel just fine! Don't worry."

But I worried, because I knew she wasn't OK; something didn't seem right, and I could tell. It had come over her all too quickly. I know because I happened to pull in next to her at the same time she was attempting to leave. She was slumped over the steering wheel, breathing heavily, her face clammy, like she was cooling down after a three-mile run. She looked at me like she truly needed help.

I yanked open the passenger door and yelled, "Mom! What's wrong?" She looked at me with helpless eyes, as I demanded, "Call Dad right now! He will come and pick you up!"

"Crystal, I'm fine, just give me a minute to rest," she told me, trying to bargain with me as I reached for my cell phone. After a few minutes of her slump party, I threatened that either she call Dad, or I would.

When she finally made the call, I grabbed the phone from her, because she wasn't exactly telling him the whole truth about how shitty she was very obviously feeling. "Something isn't right, Dad. She's all slumped over the steering wheel and she's sweaty, but the air has been on full blast this whole time. She seems to be very light-headed," I told him, worrying him now, too.

Dad, being the amazing husband he's always been, left work before we hung up the phone, rushing from there to drive her home safely. It was weird seeing her that exhausted. She wasn't able to concentrate on anything, much less drive herself five miles home.

I stood there in disbelief, watching as they drove out of the parking lot. It was right then that I realized this whole cancer thing was very much real. Not only had it stamped itself to Mom like an unwanted drunken spring break tattoo, but it had invited itself into this whole family, robbing Mom of all her usual activities and what seemed like endless energy.

It made me sad to watch her trying to care for herself and so many others at the same time. I felt like it made her feel defeated and nearly worthless. She doesn't have time to go home and rest, but she has to feel better. Dad needs her, I need her, my siblings and her grandchildren need her. My grandparents need her.

Who else was going to be the drill sergeant Grace needs to make sure she isn't skipping out on her diabetic medicine and throwing away the lunches she's supposed to be eating on time, so her blood sugar stays in the normal range. We didn't need Grace landing herself in a room at the same hospital, which she would do, if there was no supervision. I could supervise to an extent, but I'm not quite the Nazi to Grace that Mom was! She did indeed go home to rest for several hours and somehow, I was the one to pull the short straw to have to lug sweet Gracey-poo back home. Just kidding—I love you, Grandma.

Mom still needed to have her second port placement done. We secretly hoped that if the doctor forgot, then maybe she wouldn't have to continue chemo and this whole cancer shit would just go away. Hey, a girl can dream!

After several attempts to place the port into her chest, it finally worked the fourth time. Naturally, ups and downs happened every single day. For us, frustration showed up more often than not. For her though, she chose to take the higher road. She tried to understand why we were all so frustrated at the multiple attempts to place the port. She told us, "I'm thankful for having some much-needed time off, enough to regain the strength back that I'm going to need going into this next chemo round."

It gave her the opportunity to be where she was needed the most and that was at the hospital with her dad during all his unexpected surgeries. It had been a scary road, having to be opened up three different times, two of those unplanned, but now at this point, he was on the rehab floor and resting comfortably and on the road to recovery. Grace was behaving, taking her medications on time, and eating like she was supposed to be doing all along. Mom was able to visit and then get some much needed rest.

She started her second round of chemo with considerably more ambition and a strong sense of comfort, too. She said goodbye to the fear of the unknown, because she knew now just what to expect. She knew how to push herself to get through it and she knew exactly what not to do as well. She had finally settled into a routine that seemed to be easily tolerated.

In my family, we grew up extremely close to each other. There wasn't much we did without one another, even if we wanted to. Now that Mom was "sick," we vowed to never let her be alone through any of this journey without at least one of us being by her side through it all. Every appointment, procedure, surgery, office visit discussion, or chemo session, she was accompanied as if she had round-the-clock bodyguards. And in a way, that's exactly what we were. Somebody was going to always be there to protect her, even if that meant another pair of eyes and ears would be there with her to share her experience. When they say cancer doesn't just affect one person, it affects the entire family ... I can fully attest to that. It's the utmost truth!

With that being said, the day finally came when Mom needed to attend a session of fluids alone. Want to talk about feeling guilty?

"You guys, I'm totally OK with going by myself, really! I'll be just fine. You don't have to worry," she told us. We assured her that we knew she'd be fine, but we weren't OK with her going alone.

"All I'm going to do is drive over there, sit for a few hours, and pass the time beating more levels of Candy Crush. I'll post an update on Facebook and maybe I'll even take a nap," she assured us. She hadn't taken a nap in what seemed like years. She knew that no matter how bad we felt for not being able to go with her, she needed to be alone this time. She wanted to give us, her caregivers, a break. We took it, but hated it, remembering she was strong and deserved some alone time, too. It sucked, but we texted her the whole time.

CHAPTER 7

CANCER WITH A SIDE OF HAIR LOSS

*A*s you take on the unwanted nickname of "cancer patient," you will experience many emotions you never thought were real. You'll wonder if you're insane and you'll question whether you will ever feel "normal" again. You'll start to feel very scared, nervous, anxious, overwhelmed, sad, undetermined, questionable, helpless, hopeless, isolated, depressed and sad—just to name a few. The good news though is that you'll never be alone.

Truthfully, every emotion you face is completely normal and expected. It may not be the same reaction other cancer victims feel during their battle with cancer, but that doesn't mean it's not normal.

In the beginning, you'll realize that your journey is yours alone. It'll never be the same as someone else's and it will never go exactly by the books that you've started reading about other people on their road with cancer. Chances are, you'll go through things you can't even find on Google, and you'll experience some very trying times.

However, just think on this: along with those dark days you're going to endure will come brighter days filled with blessings that you can't even fathom at this point in time. You can choose to live your days how you wish, and nobody will try persuading you to make decisions on one way or the other, because remember … there is only one you. You only have one chance at life, regardless of the speed bumps you hit along the way.

Every human being is fighting some sort of battle and the only one who already knows how your battle will play out is the same one who will help carry you all the way to the end, and that's God. Now you can choose to live without Him if you please, but no matter what you choose, He'll still very much be there, whether you believe He is or not. That's called grace, and you should be thankful it's a real thing.

In the beginning, the emotional decisions seem more overwhelming than the physical ones. You'll feel forced one way or another into deciding how to respond to this menacing disease, and you'll have to choose whether or not to use the tools you've learned throughout your life up to this point.

Do you remember those Bible lessons you were made to sit through in Sunday School as a kid? Remember they were the ones where you weren't really paying attention, because you'd rather be outside playing. Did they have any significance that can now bring some enlightenment and advice to the table to help guide your current life situation? Was there a specific sermon in which you didn't fall asleep that didn't mean much to you as a kid, but now is significantly clearer to you why it's been in the back of your head all these years?

Regardless of what you come up with, decisions have to be made. Now is your time to shine and prove to yourself and the rest of the world that you can and will overcome this. This is not fake news, people—this is legitimate and it's simply the hard truth!

No matter with which cancer you've now been labeled, you'll fight it to the end, to the best of your ability and, honestly, you will be OK. If you're wondering—yeah, right, Crystal, you don't know if I'll really be OK or not. Well, pat yourself on the back, because you're intuitive and you'll go far in life. But I do know this, because there's a God in heaven who loves and cares for you, you'll be just fine. He will carry you when you feel like you just can't hang on anymore. Not only that, but you have to be OK, because there simply is no other choice.

Statistics didn't hide the fact that Mom could expect to lose her hair about ten to fourteen days after her first round of chemo, and it showed no mercy. Anytime you hear the word "cancer," your mind naturally associates it with hair loss. No matter how hard you try to prepare yourself for it, you just simply cannot.

Mom often wondered how her family would feel about her becoming bald. What would her grandchildren think of her? Will they look at her funny, but still love her? Will they think of her as the same Memaw they've always ever known? This was an emotion awfully hard to deal with, for her and for us.

During this time, my husband and I and our two young sons were living at my parents' house. To them, Memaw was the best person in the entire world. I cried many days, wondering what they would think about her and if it would hurt her feelings. I promised myself to do everything in my power to make it the easiest transition for both Mom and my kids. I didn't exactly know how to explain to them that Memaw has a sickness that was going to take away her hair. I didn't want them to believe that every time they got sick, they might lose their hair, too. I knew from the very beginning that this turning point was going to be a hard one, and I needed to explain to them what was coming and what to expect, the best I could.

As a mother, you spend your entire life trying to shelter your children from any harm, hurt, sadness, and worry. I knew what Mom meant to them and what they meant to her, so it was going to be my job to make sure they were informed as much as their little minds could possibly comprehend.

After days of pondering about what to say to them and questioning when the right time would be to say it, I made a plan. I decided to go to the local library and check out a book on how to explain cancer to young children. I hate reading and I hate the library, but this time was different—I was on a mission. I knew how important it was to find the perfect book—even more important than any book I probably didn't read. The book report I probably bombed way back in high school was most likely the last time I was even at this library. I wanted them to understand what was about to happen to her and what wouldn't happen to them, if they woke up tomorrow morning with a sore throat.

It was tough. I cried walking through the library, not wanting to believe that my reality had led me there in the first place. I walked aimlessly up and down every aisle overflowing with endless romance novels, which entirely overwhelmed me.

Sweet little Elizabeth from the front desk walked over to me, after realizing I looked obviously very dazed and confused. She asked me what book I was trying to find.

"I need something that can help explain cancer to children," I told her, but she looked at me like I was crazy, as if I had eight heads or something. "Is … there … even such thing?" I asked her, thinking there's no way there was. I kept feeling my head, making sure I still only had one and not truly eight.

She put her hand on my shoulder and said, "Well, ma'am, yes, there are books here about that. But you definitely won't find it in this section," she said, pointing to the few books I was thumbing through. *"The Great Gatsby* and *To Kill a Mockingbird* aren't going to do the trick," she said, slightly laughing, but in a nice, oh-she-must-need-some-serious-help kind of way.

She led me to the children's section, which only happened to be across the entire library from where I stood in my own puddle of tears. There she showed me a few books that might help. I scanned the shelf back and forth a few times, trying to hint to her that I just wanted to be left alone. I think she finally caught on as she said, "Well, if there's anything else I can do to help, please don't hesitate to ask. I'll be happy to point you in the right direction."

I appreciate you, you little angel, truly I do, but you already pointed me to the right section, full of the truth I was trying so desperately to avoid. I am forever grateful and if you're her boss reading this book; you should totally give her a raise! She was great!

I finally found, *When Someone You Love Has Cancer.* It presented all the important facts about what exactly cancer is, what can happen because of the medications you take when you have cancer, and how it can emotionally affect each person within the family. Everyone wondered why that was the book I chose to read that night. After reading it, I could see their minds racing and the confusion welling up on their faces, almost as blunt as the fact that Mom's hair had already started falling out. It wasn't my normal book to read, like *Dragons Love Tacos* or *The Pigeon Wants a Hot Dog.* I didn't want to scare them, and I didn't want them to worry. No matter what happens, she'll always be the same Memaw that they love to the moon and back.

Unfortunately, the statistics proved to be astonishingly accurate. The hair loss came in due time. Her doctor was right, because after her very first round of chemo, the unfathomable began, and it was exceedingly difficult and extremely emotional. Although she knew it was going to happen eventually, it was a hard horse pill to swallow. The hopefulness of beating the odds and keeping her hair, slowly dwindled away each time she'd blow dry it. Her bathroom suddenly resembled a snowstorm made of fine blonde hair.

She didn't stay down for very long, although she mentioned to Dad, "Well, one good thing about this is that we should be on time everywhere we go from here on out. I won't have any hair to worry about!" I love that about her, making light of such an emotional and devastating moment. That's the true will of a fighter—that was her.

Meagan had a conversation with Mom about losing her hair and she offered the advice of at least one way to look at it. She told her that it was the last thing she'd have to let go of before she could start this fight with a pure and clean slate! Losing your hair is very traumatic for anyone. Being a woman in the world today, it's quite difficult to shake off our cultural and personal attachment to our hair. It acts as our security blanket, and we go above and beyond to take care of it our entire lives. Losing it due to cancer is like pouring coarse salt on a gaping full-body wound. Many people spend their days worrying about what other people will think, how they will look, and so on. But that's normal, not just for people with a disease.

But grasp this—life now is vastly different for you. No, you didn't choose it this way and no, you didn't want it like this, but you *can* choose how to respond. This is a new chapter in your life's novel that needs a starting point. Before it can commence, the old one must conclude, and what better time than now? Move forward with grace and accept it for what it is. You aren't alone, nor will you ever be. No matter, you will have gut-wrenching feelings about the lost attachment to your hair. It's going to fall out and you cannot change that. The only thing you *can* change is your personal way of thinking. That alone will take you further than your own understanding at this point.

A few days later, after an even bigger blonde-storm in the bathroom, Mom decided it was time. Meagan, who was a hair stylist, came over with her razor and clippers. She shared an emotional moment with Mom and together they said goodbye to the last strands of her pretty blonde bob. They laughed and they cried—like, a lot! Not only was it hard for Mom, but it's emotionally devastating for a daughter to have to shave the head of her mother. She felt horrible for being the one to shave Mom's head, but oddly enough, she felt honored, too, because she was the one to help Mom close this chapter of her life and start a new one.

Mom described it as a feeling of freedom and empowerment. It gave her insight into a new way of facing life and what all it throws in your way. It became quite comical to her the first time she attempted to apply makeup to her face with a bald head. She looked into the mirror, completely confused as she laughed and called up Meagan, "How far up am I supposed to put foundation? I have no hairline as a guide."

Meagan laughed and replied, "Just high enough for your scarf to cover it!" It's moments like these that Mom now treasured in a different light.

Despite the initial impact of hair loss, the experience of losing your hair as a result of a treatment known to help kick cancer in the ass can be empowering as you take pride in your newly altered appearance and exactly what it symbolizes. The media tells us that women should have hair and that it should be long and wavy and soft, but not frizzy. It portrays a false rule that a woman's hair should never be messed up or out of place and it should never go gray. It will always be wrong to generalize a person solely on the appearance of their hair.

People form opinions on one's identity simply by their hairstyle. We're convinced that we should be young, healthy, and vibrant our whole lives, and that starts with our hair. Negatively, losing your hair in today's culture is often viewed as a "stamp of sickness." It's become an outward sign to the rest of the world that we're battling something out of our control, and to most, it becomes a sign of weakness. That's an incredibly false belief! Our hair translates into confidence, and when we have none, we don't seem confident, which leads to devastating isolation. Unfortunately, the society in which we live has caused women with hair loss to suffer in silence. You become self-conscious—just ask me about the time I cut my bangs with eyebrow scissors in the sixth grade. You end up socially insecure, because having to face uncertainty is tough.

Expectedly, Mom worried about what people would think of her and how they would react to her wearing a wig or bandana out in public. Our bodies are built with self-esteem included and being bald is a major letdown. But there are tons of options. Coping with hair loss during treatment and battling this disease, in itself, is a huge fight. Don't add to it, and don't let the world do it for you, because it will if you aren't careful. You're the only one who is able to control how to respond to this abrupt and unfair change.

There is only one way to genuinely find the answers to the right way of coping and that's solely with God. Simply pray, talk to Him, and explain that your feelings and emotions are taking over the best of you. Give it all to Him. Ask for help to keep you feeling positive about a disease that works very aggressively at tearing you down. You don't have to check out a book from the library on this topic, because it's in the Bible. It'll tell you that it's the devil working overtime, but on the flip side, it will also tell you in the very next sentence that God is there with an extended hand, waiting for you to grab hold. Do it—you'll thank me later.

With His help, those battling this disease can learn to reject the idea of being the "face of cancer." Although we can't deny reality, we can deny its ability to mold our beliefs and shoot down how convincing it is on who we are and who we are not.

In my opinion, my bald mother was the most beautiful person on the face of the planet. Her hairless head did not make me think for once, that she was helpless or sick, much less weak! It showed me just how strong she truly was. She proved time and time again that she's strong enough to walk down the street, regardless of what she looked like. I even told her to hold her middle finger up to the rest of the world while she's walking around, confident and brave. She wouldn't do it though. She said, "That's an awful idea, Crystal. I don't have to prove anything to anyone," she told me in response to my genius idea. But being proper is her. She was doing that even without physically holding her finger high in the sky. She proved her strength and that she can fight and win a battle about which I personally know nothing. If anything, it made me say an extra prayer for her throughout the day when I saw her. It also made me thank God for placing someone in front of me who can give me a reality check in my own life. I became truly thankful for all the blessings and feelings of gratefulness from this simple reminder that He's the only one in control.

Our culture sucks these days—just being honest. Hair loss is devastating to every person forced to watch it fall to the floor each time you pull out the hairbrush. It's portrayed as non-life-threatening, because they don't take the time to look further at the actual life-threatening disease that's causing all this in the first place. It's seen as "no big deal, just live with it." This is when you have my permission to indeed raise that middle finger, because until they become bald in their own bathrooms, the world will never be able to confirm that it's just not the case.

We feel powerless, because the one thing we usually do have control over is our hair. We can cut, color, and style it in any way shape or form that we choose, and we can use it to manipulate our identities. And although it helps contribute to our well-being, it'll never shape our whole being. It even goes deeper than that, forming the general sense of who we are, but trust yourself and your own internal guidance, which is your gut. Stop seeking external validation! Use your internal strength to influence the world's perception of you.

It may be disorienting to look in the mirror and not recognize the person staring back at you, but remember you are still the same person on the inside. Try celebrating who you really are and focus on those qualities. Seek out all the options, which are countless these days, like wigs, scarves, hats, head wraps, turbans, and caps. Honestly, it could be a lot of fun! All the other opinionated pieces of shit simply can't be three different people all in the same day like you can!

Fortunately for you, it's like playing dress-up times ten. I mean, let's be real. Nobody else has the chance to be Shirley Temple, Audrey Hepburn, and Marilyn Monroe all in the same damn day!

Just sayin' …

CHAPTER 8

SOCIAL MEDIA

To us, social media actually proved to have an upside! Who would have thought? For our life, it ended up being a platform for our updates that many searched for and expected daily. Most of the time, it took the place of a phone call to a friend or a letter in the mail, that nobody writes anymore. It overruled all the nosey emails and even helped avoid the emotions that easily welled up during an actual face-to-face conversation.

Writing can be very therapeutic, and half the time, it reached more people than we ever expected. Mom's journey was never hers alone. I've already explained our family's take on this whole thing, but it also engulfed many others the same way. It consumed not only our community, but hundreds of people out of state and even out of the country. Whether Mom updated her Facebook page or my sisters and I did it for her, everyone was intentionally and voluntarily informed as much as possible.

Many are aware that social media isn't always a positive outlet, but that comes with the territory. Many times, we acquired unwanted opinions that we didn't care to receive and at times, some of our readers left comments on those updates that weren't so nice. You know, somehow everybody suddenly becomes an expert at exactly what you're going through. Some posted "concern" that came across as purely fake, while others threw out the words, "praying for you" when praying was never a thing in their daily lives in the first place.

Any post, whether it was celebratory or struggle, at times turned into ammo for other assholes. There isn't any need to explain further on the actions and comments made from a few family members and friends. They weren't being held at gunpoint and being forced to read those updates. It was awesome, totally kind—no, actually, I'm lying—it was nauseating and just pure disgusting!

Battling a giant like cancer makes it difficult to focus on *normal life* and all the other challenges you have to face outside the disease.

You try your best to forget all the petty I-just-want-attention-so-here-is-my-not-so-professional-opinion-on-how-to-do-it-the-right-way drama that comes along with having family and friends who feel the need to throw it out there, since they've never had cancer or anything like it. A lot of emotions are involved, and much of it is behind the scenes. Just because you've been stamped by this disease doesn't mean life itself stops, fortunately and unfortunately. Sadly, it will always include hurtful comments and shitty advice from the inexperienced peanut gallery.

Here's the problem though: as a daughter, you become extremely defensive and suddenly you form this steel shell of an exterior that you use as an outward sign of strength and a tough attitude. But on the inside, you're broken. You let it get the best of you and you try to walk away, but there are too many emotions weighing you down. It causes you to make decisions that otherwise, you wouldn't normally make. I allowed relationships with certain family members to diminish, and I lost some friends along the way, too. Sharing even the slightest part of your life on public social media becomes everyone else's information and Spa Day conversation topics. Fortunately, we chose that route and thankfully the good greatly outweighed the bad. You take the bad with a grain of salt and you use it to run faster towards the good.

Pam Heath's wall of posts became pinned to the top of hundreds of news feeds. If it was a popularity contest on Facebook, she would have blown the rest of the world out of the water! I'm exaggerating … a little, but it definitely seemed that way. She began to update after every challenge she endured and every milestone she hit, but her followers wanted more. It then became a daily accountability task, because if you didn't see a post from her on any given day, then "something was wrong."

No matter what her posts contained, they always ended with two important things. One: she never forgot to thank her family, friends, and all her prayer warriors out there following along with her. She made sure to include all the ones who wanted to be included and reminded them that the prayers they're praying for her had been working. Two: she never, not once, ended without thanking the Big Man upstairs! She knew He was the reason she'd made it this far and she knew He'd be the reason she was going to finish it. She remained true in her personal relationship with God. Her faith was unbreakable.

I take that back—actually each of her posts consisted of three things. Humor was always in there somewhere. Mom believed that getting through some of your darkest days is much easier with a laugh or two. She always, without a doubt, reminded us that somewhere in there is a silver lining. You may have to dig a little deeper to find it – or if you're anything like me, which I hope you are not, you might have to dig a lot deeper to find it, but it's always there somehow.

"Life is what happens to you while you're making other plans," she'd say entirely too often. I couldn't help but laugh each time she'd joyfully say that with a smile because, well, shit, she's right! Here she was making plans to have one more baby, but nope. Life was over there, like "Yeah, right, watch this. Hold my beer" when it threw her triplets.

Being roommates with cancer, you might wonder how joy can be found in almost every situation that you're up against. This was a hard one for me and, at times, it still is! Mom assured me on multiple occasions throughout my life that every situation or experience into which we're put has a reason or lesson and, often, some type of joy that follows it.

I didn't quite believe that one. For example, I asked her, "How can pushing a port placement procedure back four different times have some sort of joy attached to it?" To me, it didn't—it was frustrating. To her though, it did! "It gave me the opportunity to be more present in the lives of the ones who needed me the most. It gave me a few extra days to rest and recuperate, to align my thoughts accurately, and to regain enough strength to fight through my second round of chemo," she told me, watching me roll my eyes at her, because once again she does have a good point.

"Yeah, yeah, that was a good one, but your hair—what about losing your hair? There's nothing good that came from that and you were so sad," I threw back at her, convinced I was right this time. "How can a lesson, much less joy, come from something as traumatic as that? Do explain, and I'll wait."

She'd already expressed this several times, but clearly she had no problem repeating it once more. "Well, for starters, there's absolutely no reason your dad can get mad at me for being late somewhere because it won't be my fault. He has more hair now than I do, so when I'm sitting in the car honking at him to 'hurry up we are going to be late,' I'll be the first one to laugh saying, 'I told you so!' " She was all too joyful with that answer, seeing a silver lining in there somewhere, and clearly bragging that she was right again.

I swear she's an angel.

Understandably, there was plenty of sympathy to go around, especially when you read her posts about losing her pretty blonde hair, but she didn't need your sympathy. She didn't *want* it. Yet somehow, she was the one bringing everyone in the sad squad up from their down feelings about her ongoing and challenging battle. She reminded us that inevitably having an obvious downside always comes with the not-so-obvious upside at the same time. Check out this charmer:

> *I want to thank you all for your continued support in every way shown. Keeping my spirits high, like you've all done, is such a HUGE part of my success. You make it easy for me to be silly, laugh, and lighten my burdens, even though some of you have seen the brave side of me showing my bald head!! Lol! And I must say there has not been a freer feeling I've ever experienced than standing under a hot shower with NO HAIR!!! You girls out there that have been there know just what I'm talking about! IT'S AWESOME!*
>
> *So, as I continue down my path to recovery and healing, I send out all my sincere love and thanks to you warriors, known and unknown!*

> *~From Me to You~*
> **Fighting this battle like a GIRL, wife, mother, "Memaw," daughter, daughter-in-law, sister, cousin, aunt, great-aunt and friend!**

And there you have it ladies and gentlemen, the truth that lies within an angel from God.

After all, Mom was certainly still a normal person. She just became a warrior of a battle that most people, fortunately, won't ever have to fight, but she was not normal because she was actually a friendly, genuine, and well-known person, who was badass at displaying the perfect example of living life to its fullest, no matter what's thrown in her way.

If anything, posting about your journey of vulnerability, struggle, and wins can show others that life is real, and it can even gain you hundreds of extra prayers—they can't hurt! For many others, cancer is viewed as a personal disease that should be kept under wraps and to yourself. I get it, there's nothing wrong with that!

Others might feel that airing that laundry to the world will only put the sympathy and burden on others, and some may not want to let the general public in on their personal battle that they're learning to cope with and fight against. Again, honestly that's totally cool. But for Mom, as an individual in control of her own life and feelings, she saw it as a way to let the concerned know the plan, to gain support and advice from fellow fighters and experienced mentors, and to inspire others silently walking in those same footsteps. She used it to welcome more genuine prayers that always aided her along the way. It was the biggest reminder to her that she was never alone and never would be. It lessened the feelings of isolation, minimized feelings of being overwhelmed, and definitely strengthened our support system by what seemed like millions of supporters.

Cancer doesn't come with a guidebook or tutorial on what to do next. Well, neither does life for that matter, so it's discouraging for anyone who has to bear the raw emotions that come along with a detrimental disease that attacks your own body. If you're newly diagnosed with some form of shit like cancer, whether it be ovarian, non-Hodgkin's lymphoma, malignant melanoma, metastatic breast cancer, or colon, lung, pancreatic, prostate, or whatever other kind of cancer is lurking out there—hell, even if it's a UTI—I challenge you to a new outlook on your journey ahead, just like Pam did.

When the extensive list of emotions you may have never felt before now, actually start hitting you, try documenting your struggles and celebrate your wins. If you aren't a computer nerd and you don't even know your login credentials for social media, grab a journal. Date it with today's date, log your feelings, bookmark it, get crazy with the highlighters, and brighten not only that page of Debbie downers, but your entire day. Rewire your mind to force all the positive thoughts forward and shove away all negative thoughts—that the devil is so kindly giving away for free—and push them to the back, where hopefully you'll never be able to reach them again.

But if you are a computer geek like, oh, ninety-nine percent of the rest of world, log your winding road on Facebook and post away! Because if you get too annoying and overly posting, well, there's a small "UNFOLLOW" button conveniently placed at the top of your page. Don't worry—it's their fault, if they don't click it.

Look up your diagnosis under the hashtag tab on Instagram and connect with others learning how to do life like you. Google will simply not cut it. It may mend your wound very temporarily, but it most likely will dump the entire saltshaker on that wound, if you aren't careful. I think we can all agree that at some point in our confusing lives, we put our faith on the opinion of Google. I am just as guilty as the next person sitting there mumbling under their breath that they "should not be looking this up on Google."

I get it! I've worked in the medical field for many years, and I'll admit, doctors and nurses are the worst. Somehow, even knowing that, my fingers continue to type into that little box even when the voice in my head is shouting at me not to do it. I googled a sore throat once—according to Google, if I didn't get to the doctor's office right away, I was going to die! It would be a slow, painful death that would end in misery because my throat will close and all breathing will just stop, boom, gone. Sounds pretty legit, but good news, people: it's going to take a lot more than Google's non-licensed opinion to put me out for good –I lived! In fact, I didn't even go to the doctor. I chugged a few glasses of warm salt water, drowned my misery in an ungodly amount of water, and here I am, still very much alive and kicking.

The internet, starting with social media platforms, is spiraling out of control with negative and unpromising stories and fake facts pertaining to your survival chances. And those chances go way down if you listen to the illiterate douchebag that invents a blog post, with intentions of only making himself feel important since he bombed the United States Medical Licensing Exam. Same goes for the magazines claiming, "Drink this and you'll lose twenty pounds!" The same can be said for the horrifying experience that your all too friendly neighbor, Ellen, shared with you one day when you both happened to be walking to the mailbox at the same time. Cancer may affect the way you live your life after the unfortunate and devastating bomb that it's dropped on you. However, it can't affect or take away the ability you have to make your own decisions. It can't control that then, now, or in the future. Keeping yourself mentally strong and stable is equally as important during your body's physical fight.

Social media can be a double-edged sword, and it'll make you question whether it's more harmful or helpful. In some ways, it's most likely both. Ultimately you are the one in control of what affects you, because there is no right or wrong choice or decision here. There's nobody on the other side of the computer screen who will ever have the power of deciding your own fate.

Mom's Facebook account became her voice, with hopes of generating more awareness for the public, which was constantly begging for it anyway. It offered and accepted support, advice, encouragement, and even reality. It gave her the opportunity to make connections with people with whom she otherwise would have never connected with who are battling cancer just like her. It never stayed at the "just another cancer patient with a documented journey" status. It evolved into a community with concern and support and only heightened as time went on. Mom strongly believed that it was a resource that she'd been given the opportunity to utilize in a way that positively brought awareness, comfort, and most importantly, glory to God, whose love she was publicly spreading.

Here's where we revert back to the decision-making process of this whole shitty deal. Use it, or don't. That's totally up to you. No matter your choosing, it'll all be A-okay! The truth is this: just because you don't know how to work your desktop computer or you haven't jumped on the smartphone train (although you probably should, but now you're just way too late), either way, it doesn't mean you're going to die faster. And just because you could probably earn a degree in technology knowledge and that's the only way of life for you and you can use a computer like a genius, it doesn't mean you will live longer. Sorry, but sometimes the truth doesn't go one way or the other and that's what makes life difficult.

But that's just it though—it's the truth. Only God has that power to decide, and social media fortunately has absolutely nothing to do with it. It can simply be an easy way to lay out all the hard feelings you're trying your best to fight alone, and it can be a mega support system that you literally had no clue had been there this whole time. It's your life, your decisions, so make them wisely. But don't forget what truly matters and who is really in control. That's neither you nor me, and it's definitely not Zuckerberg, who is making millions off each post you make, just sayin' ...

CHAPTER 9

COMPLICATIONS

*M*om was gearing up and preparing for her third chemo round when exhaustion steadily became almost unmanageable. She had a hard time getting through each day, and naturally being the upbeat, energetic, silly, and fun Memaw that she was, that seemed to decline as cancer worked overtime in robbing her of that.

"Can we please go to Memaw's house!?" the grandchildren asked every day after school.

They never skipped a beat! School was out and it was off to Memaw's we go! It was never, "Can we go to Memaw and Papa's?" it was *all* Memaw! After all, to them, everything was hers! They believed the only things Papa owned was his jeep and his boat—everything else was simply "Memaw's."

They'd raid her overflowing fridge of snacks, take no time in pulling out every toy on the premises, and even at times ended up in the pool with their clothes on. Her house was like heaven to them, as long as she was there! But after a while, even those daily play dates exhausted her and she was unable to keep up like normal, which was so rare for her. It was definitely not in Memaw's job description.

Mom was given the opportunity for a blood transfusion after she completed her third round of chemo. "It'll help boost your energy levels," she was told. At first, I hated that idea. It's always irked me, knowing that somebody else's blood is pumped into your veins. Is it really possible to filter out another human's blood completely and efficiently enough to run through hers without any more complications potentially trying to hinder her progress? It just seemed unsafe to me, and I tried convincing her not to do it. Although, I'll admit, I wasn't the one feeling so tired all the time like she was.

"Crystal, it's just an option right now," she tried explaining to me. Her eyes were tired, her body wasn't performing like usual, and I could tell this blood transfusion option, to her was moving up that list fast. The doctor assured her that he'd never present her with something he didn't feel would benefit her, and she trusted him. He laid out the risks and benefits associated with that minor procedure, and she believed the pros most definitely outweighed the cons. With any decision she had to make, she took the time to think on it and pray about it—she never made a decision right away.

I appreciated that about her. She's smart! I hadn't gotten that far in my life because my decisions are always made on a whim, which is most likely why most of them probably aren't the smartest decisions I've made! She pictured how her life would continue to go during those afterschool play dates, and that alone made the decision for her. She agreed to try it out after she completed her third round of chemo and had her first blood transfusion.

Thanksgiving was just around the corner and the majority of that holiday depended on her job duties. She wanted to be normal and be able to mingle and spend time with the family, plus nobody can make the dressing and stuffing like she can. After she received her transfusion, the fear and worry diminished as a feeling of accomplishment took over. She knew God had led her to that decision for a reason. She was so thankful that just a few short days later she had the energy of a sixteen-year-old concertgoer, who was determined to cook a fantastic Thanksgiving feast here in a few days.

The long four-and-a-half weeks that Grandpa spent in the hospital were very tiring and trying times. He was finally released two days after Mom completed chemo. She knew she wasn't in good enough shape at the time to stay with him and tend to his extensive post-op care like he would need. Her brother, my uncle "Bubba," assumed the role of caretaker for a few days in her place. Mom dropped Grandma back off at her own house now that Grandpa was there full time again. Unfortunately, after one day in, Grandma was taken away by ambulance.

"She isn't talking to us, Pam. She responds in gibberish and it's like she is staring right through me," my worried uncle said to Mom over the phone. We sped back across town to their house and found Grandma perched in her recliner with no recollection of what was going on around her and completely out of it. My mom and uncle made the decision to call 9-1-1 just to make sure nothing serious was happening to her now. Grandpa followed as they took her out on the gurney, making it almost to the front door, where he leaned over the dining room table and began to cry.

"I've never seen him like this" I said to Katie, who agreed with me. We kept assuring him "Grandpa, she'll be just fine. She's probably just tired, so once they get her to the hospital, they'll check her out and she'll come back home." But he didn't believe that for some reason. Mom made her way back inside after seeing Grace off in the ambulance, to reassure him again. He sat slumped over in a chair at the table, with worry and fear written across his scruffy cute face. When Mom leaned down to hug him, he whispered in her ear, "I don't think I'm ever going to see her again."

"Daddy, don't say that. Mom will be just fine—I think she's purely exhausted. Let's get you back in your chair to rest and I'll head up to the hospital to be with her. I'll let you know how she's doing," Mom said, trying to soothe him. This is what we tried so hard to avoid by keeping Grace on a strict schedule, back in Grandpa's hospital days, which was just a whopping one day ago.

Multi-tasking from her chemo chair that had become like a second home, Mom did her best keeping up with the whole family. She'd coordinate Grandpa's post-op appointments and check in with the nurses on how Grace was cooperating during her hospital stay. She made sure to rearrange the family's schedules so Bubba could still get in some much-needed time at work, while triaging Grandpa's needs over the telephone as best she could. Quite a lot was going on all at once, especially having those chemo drugs pumped into her body at the same time. However, for Mom, that was her job, so it was a way out of dwelling on her own struggles and remembering where she actually was at the time.

"Mrs. Heath, you are all done for today. I'll call your nurse over to flush out your port and have you on your way," said one of the sweet nurses in the chemo lab.

"Yes! Another day down and another bag of chemo! Now I can go home," Mom exclaimed. After she left chemo, she decided to make a quick stop at the hospital to pop in on Grace. She reported back to us that Grandma was doing just fine, because she had round-the-clock supervision and was being forced to do everything correctly. Although it was a good report, she and the doctor both agreed to keep her there one more night, so Grace would be able to rest fully. She made a call to Grandpa on her way back home, letting him know that Grandma was doing very well and that she'd be discharged tomorrow. "Daddy, how did your appointment go today?" she asked.

"It went well, Sweet-art. The doctor wants me to continue following my post-op instructions and taking my medicine, but he said I seem to be doing great and healing up very well like he anticipated," he answered in his tired voice.

"Well, thank you, Jesus!" Mom replied, feeling confident and happy with his report. She could now rest with a peace of mind, knowing that both parents seem to be on the mend, especially now that she has nothing that needed her attention for the rest of the night. God is good!

CHAPTER 10

GRANDPA

A s 4:59 a.m. suddenly ticked over to 5:00 a.m., the house phone rang. It was still dark outside and entirely too early in the morning for any phone to be ringing! Anytime you hear the phone ring while it is still dark outside and it's not your cell phone alarm, it usually isn't a good sign. I immediately woke before the end of the first ring. Sitting straight up in bed, I waited for another ring to rule out the fact it was an intentional phone call, hoping it was just a dream or simply the wrong number. It rang again, so this time Mom reached for the blinking and disturbingly loud house phone sitting in the phone holder next to her on the nightstand and answered it.

I have always been a light sleeper and being in bed just across the house, I heard all this. That morning I had already laid wide awake for what seemed like an hour, as the steam crept out from under the bathroom door. I listened to the ongoing hum of the entirely too lengthy shower that my husband was taking. It was impossible to sleep when he got up to get ready for work in the mornings.

Most mornings I waited in bed until he left and then would either drift off back to sleep for a whopping thirty minutes longer, or I'd go ahead and beat the alarm clock and get up. I'd absorb the feeling of being a productive mom by packing lunches early, organizing back packs, and showering myself way before the kids woke up. This particular morning, the ringing house phone suddenly overshadowed the humming shower. My heart started to beat faster, I got a cold sweat, and stared at the ceiling too long without blinking, just knowing something wasn't right. I felt like I was frozen and physically unable to move, waiting to see if I heard footsteps on the wood floor coming across the house to our room.

A few minutes passed and when I didn't hear much, I figured maybe it was an accidental call, no big deal. My parents' house was big and flooded with echoing hollow wooden doors that didn't keep any footsteps quiet. Dad's closet was just outside his room and the squeaky door to it echoed louder than anything else in the house. Just as I tried to calmly close my eyes, assuming nothing came out of that phone call, I heard a few loud abrupt steps, then the squeak of Dad's closet door. That only meant he was up hours earlier than normal with unexpected plans.

I jumped out of bed and jogged my way across the house, knowing he was in there looking for clothes to throw on to go somewhere. "What happened? I heard the phone ring, so what's wrong? Why are you getting dressed? Where are you going?" Following my loud one hundred questions and not caring that my kid's bedroom was right around the corner, Dad took a deep breath. He had a very concerned, worried, and sad look on his face, knowing that telling me the news right there at 5 a.m. in a dark cold hallway was not a good idea.

"Your Grandpa just died," he said.

You know that feeling of the initial onset of shock that leaves you wondering why you can't think straight or even cry like you should? That feeling hit me immediately. My heart suddenly weighed more than my body, my head quickly filled with foggy useless thoughts, and I found myself screaming loudly, "What—are you serious? There is no way! Where is Mom?" That probably wasn't the best way to handle the emotional shock of the news I was just given, considering my kids woke up, climbed down from the twin bed they were sharing and ran out, demanding that I tell them what I was talking about and why everybody was awake and hanging out in the dark hallway.

I was still in my cheerleading shorts and old t-shirt. Papa smelled fresh of deodorant mixed with body wash and Jo Von Musk aftershave as he threw on a shirt and fastened his shorts. My emotions quickly took the back seat at that moment, and I became the calm, cool, and collective mom, telling them, "Nothing, we were just getting ready for work early. Now go back and lay down a little longer before I have to wake you up for school."

Knowing that time for school was approaching soon, they had no problem with going back to bed. As soon as their bedroom door closed, I obnoxiously darted past my dad to the bedroom to find

Mom. She was in the bathroom on the phone, staring into space with a very dazed look on her face, carrying on a conversation that included, "Okay, well, I'll call the coroner right away. We are getting dressed and will head that way now. Call your brother and let him know. I'll see you in a few minutes. We'll be there as quickly as we can. Love you, too. Bye."

She hung up, lifted her chin, and looked at me with eyes I'll never forget. They threw out a million words before the next blink. She was shocked, deeply saddened, filled with worry, concern, and questions. She didn't know what to do or what to say. She looked at me as if in that moment the world was ending right then and there.

I grabbed her neck, hugged her ever so tightly, and told her I loved her. I said I was going to put some clothes on and go with her to his house. I ran full speed to my room, barging into the bathroom where my husband, Sean, was just stepping out of the shower and wrapping himself with his towel. I very abruptly, in such an uncool way, blurted out the news quickly, "Grandpa just died! You have to take the kids to school, because I am leaving."

He, too, was thrown into an initial shock that had just hit me a few minutes prior, because he knew what Grandpa meant to me and how much love I had for that man. He now had to carry out the morning routine, pretending nothing was wrong and that Mommy just had to go into work early, so now they "get to ride to school in Daddy's big truck!"

The three of us left together quickly. I jumped in the back seat, stripped of any words, and just sat in silence, listening to the emotional feelings Mom and Dad were expressing in the front seat. We sped across town to Grandpa's house to take care of something we not only had ever been through before, but also had not expected to happen anytime soon. Dad offered the advice of reality and what exactly we needed to do in this situation in a timely manner.

Mom couldn't gather her thoughts, which left her speechless for most of the ride. She just stared out the window. When she did chime in, I could hear the tremble in her voice. I saw fear and tears in her eyes reflecting off the side view mirror and, for me, the worst sight in my life was to see her so sad. Someone with whom I was extremely close had just passed away, and the thought of depression was only a short distance away from hitting me. I could see Mom's heart breaking and that tore me up. Not only had a good person like mom been given an unfamiliar battle to fight just three months prior, but now she has been given more bad news and this time it is about her father!

Mom was devastated. She would never have been able to put into words what her dad meant to her. Not only was she in shock, but she still had to go to the Cancer Center that morning for a steroid shot that she normally is given after completing a round of chemo. Yeah, chemo. Remember? Mom still has cancer. She is still fighting this, on top of the very new whirlwind of Grandpa's sudden passing. Quickly approaching through the acute reaction of traumatic news, Mom remembered Grandma was still in the hospital resting from pure exhaustion, with absolutely no idea that this was happening. My grandparents, as I have said previously, did very little, if anything, without one another. The fact that Grandma was in the hospital recovering from spending every day for over a month visiting Grandpa in that same hospital and knowing that she was expecting to go home to him that very day was heartbreaking. She had no idea that her husband had just passed away. This was going to be an almost impossible message to deliver. Needless to say, it did not go over well. It was more like watching a movie where you sit clenching your hands over your mouth, holding back tears, and thanking God you aren't the one experiencing the horrifying scene unfolding right in front of you.

That morning, Grandpa's house was very chaotic and sad. The sun was just starting to come up. For the first time ever, half my family was at their house before the crack of dawn. Walking into another movie scene and trying to figure out what to do next was not something with which Mom was familiar. Making phone calls and desperately trying to rack our brain to make sure we didn't leave anybody out was what made that next hour fly by. The coroner gave us a timeframe on when he was coming and what exactly we needed to do to be ready for the arrival of the god-awful dreaded sight of the death gurney that would carry Grandpa out of his home forever. As we awaited the arrival of the hearse, we took turns whispering in his cold stiff ear our goodbyes and promises, and throwing out as many "I love you's" as we possibly could.

For me, seeing Grandpa lying there, lifeless and cold, was a dreaded sight. He, too, was my world. Growing up, I had a personal relationship with him that was so special. Many days before his passing, I spent my lunch breaks with him at the hospital. Whether he was awake and munching on the bland hospital food or soundly sleeping with his mouth wide open during my thirty-minute lunch breaks, it usually didn't matter, as long as it was spent with him. I loved him tremendously and most of the time just being around him was plenty good enough for me. After all, I was his "little angel."

Suddenly that morning, all the end-of-life stages went out the window. I didn't look at it in that sense. I saw my loving Grandpa lying on his back on the bedroom floor and this was my last chance ever to cuddle with him! That was one of my favorite things to do when he was around. It felt very much like home. I felt safe and loved just being under his big arm, and curling up in a ball with him was something I always treasured.

I found myself not socializing or crying with the rest of my family that morning. Instead, I nuzzled my way up under his heavy, cold, wrinkly arm and laid there with my head towards his. I whispered many things to him, told him I loved him at least a million times (as if he didn't already know that). I made him a promise that I'd always take care of Mom, and thanked him for just being him. I closed my eyes and for a few minutes, everything that was happening went away.

I went right back to my happy and safe place and drifted off to memory lane. I heard his sweet but deep voice, rubbed my face up against his prickly cheeks, sniffed his unique scent, and replayed every memory my head contained of him and I together. It was just like one of those flashbacks you see in a movie when a person stares into space and suddenly, the scene changes to something very sunny, beautiful, and vibrant with colors—a scene filled with laughter, chirping birds, and butterflies.

It was almost always followed with the sun beaming down on your face as you hear the faint, but echoed voices bringing your fondest moments back to life. The place where all your worries and problems don't exist for a while, and then suddenly they do. As with every flashback scene, there comes a cold quick snap back to reality—the kind of reality check that knocks the breath out of you. It brings back the sadness and disappointment, as if you are a kid again finding out Santa Claus isn't real. Those types of feelings change your life forever.

"The coroner is here and he's coming through the bedroom glass sliding doors, so clear the way and move back." This was the very last moment I had with him, so against my will, I was told to move away from him. I thought about it for a mere 2.5 seconds and then just simply said "No!" I heard the creaking of the gurney across the bedroom and the gentle voices of the coroner and his assistant letting us know what they were going to do next.

I chose to lay there and figure out a way that they could take him with me still attached to his side. "I don't want to leave him. I'm not ready. I can't get up right now," I tried to warn them. As my siblings and cousins turned their heads away with streaming tears, I looked up at Mom, because in that brand new moment, I felt she was the only living human being who still held up my heart and soul.

"Crystal, please don't make this harder on me than it already is. Please give him a kiss and get up—he has to go."

My heart went from broken to shattered, hearing the sadness in her voice. I never dared make Mom upset with me and would not intentionally do something that made life even harder for her. Thinking what is best for her, I chose to get up and let them take him away from our lives forever.

The rest of that morning, as everyone tried to find their composure and steer through the shock and fog that filled their heads, Mom had to leave to receive her steroid shot at the cancer center. Having to draw yourself back to your own personal reality, a shitty one at that, remembering you must take care of your own body and fight a disease, while trying to wrap your head around the news you just received, never makes a good combo. However, she knew it had to be done.

Back at the house, the rest of us nervously waited for Mom to finish her session and the start of visiting hours at the hospital where Grandma Grace was. We went back and forth about what should be said and who should say it. We discussed if we should inform the nursing staff first, and throwing horrid reactions out on the table about how we all thought Grandma would take the news.

Finally, someone mentioned it was time to go, so we all loaded up to support the three bearers of the worst news in Grandma's life. When we got there, Mom met us and informed the nursing staff about what was about to take place, in case they needed to intervene with not only Grandma, but her roommate.

Mom and her two brothers walked into the room and closed the door behind them. We stood in the hallway waiting, as if we were going to be able to go in and visit once they came out. That was a moment only the three of them could explain. Not a single family member in that hallway would ever pay to relive. They discharged her a short time later and my Uncle Bubba took her home.

As we drove back to our house and tried to go about our daily lives as if nothing ever happened, Mom went inside and collapsed, thinking. *How could all this be happening? My dad and I had a deal. I would fight hard to overcome this cancer, and he would get through his surgery and rehab, but now he's gone!* She felt like she didn't need to hold up her end of the bargain anymore. Why should she go through all this pain now without him? What good was it going to do? Her unpleasant thoughts took over too much of her mind at that point.

She went through a very rough patch, as the days painfully passed. Thanksgiving was just two days away. She had to plan a funeral and get her mother, her family, and herself through this. Her whole life, she had always been her dad's strong one and she knew the rest of the family would be looking to her for strength.

At this point, Mom was out of strength. She didn't want to do this anymore. She wanted so badly to fall asleep and wake up to the life she used to have. The stress and grief got the very best of her. She couldn't eat, she broke out in sudden painful rashes, and her skin became so raw from excessive daily peeling. It seemed that she had absolutely no strength left. We were already mourning the loss of our family's patriarch, so no way were we are going to sit back and watch something happen to the matriarch!

All our family and Mom's friends rallied around her, encouraged and prayed for her, and demanded she get through this. At that moment, Mom heard her dad say, "You're a fighter. You've never quit anything, so you can't stop now." Right then she thought, "I didn't start this fight, but I have to finish it!"

We got through Thanksgiving just trying to survive. We gathered together again as a family, this time ... minus one. It was a very difficult holiday, but somehow we made it through. We loved on one another and cried together. In a circle holding hands, connected to every family member there, we prayed over our family and blessed our food. As hard as it was, we thanked God for the blessings we had and tried to convince ourselves we were still thankful for many things in our lives.

Although that dark, lonely hole was very much present and extremely raw in every heart in that house, I remember silently thanking God for letting me still have my mom. I had just lost Grandpa and that hurt so bad, but I still had my mom, which meant life was still left in me and my world. Dishes clanking, foil unraveling, goodbyes being exchanged, and tears being wiped, we concluded our Thanksgiving dinner and went on our separate ways home.

In the foreground of chaos was the funeral planning that somehow was squeezed in, so the time came to lay Grandpa to rest. With her heart ripped out of her chest, Mom realized she was quickly losing it. Burying her father was by far the hardest feat she'd have to conquer yet. Even on the morning she was diagnosed with cancer, she did not cry nor was she scared. Today she was scared and she cried a lot.

By now most people would have thrown their hands up and given up right then and there. Others may slip into depression and chose to succumb to mental and physical breakdowns that come along with tremendous loss. Mom had every right under the sun to do just that. Nobody would have judged or questioned her intentions, but instead she chose another path. This is when the blessings keep coming.

She looked at the faces of her mother, her brothers, her husband and children, the sweet faces of her grandchildren, and her nieces and nephews, and right then she knew exactly what she needed to do. Her daddy was her pillar of strength, but thankfully she had decided it was time for her to take over that role for the rest of the family. He instilled more fight in her than anyone could imagine.

There were many times during this difficult day when she questioned herself and wondered how she was supposed to get through her last three chemo sessions without his encouragement and support. Little did she know, she had just gained more strength and tenacity to fight this battle head on, since she now had the most special guardian angel watching her from above.

Just like him, she doesn't make promises that she can't keep. Although she didn't start this fight, she promised him that she *will* finish it.

CHAPTER 11

UNWANTED SETBACKS

*R*ound four came and went in the beginning of December. Mom had several very bad days and, times, her faith and her strength were tested beyond measure. She took to social media again and updated her fan club on the eventful last few weeks we'd had. She so graciously asked for prayers for her upcoming session. The aches and pains that she had been experiencing were still present, but thankfully they had not gotten any worse. The rash on her hands was being controlled with medicated lotion. The neuropathy in her hands and feet was pretty bad, but bearable. Hey, after all, she was surviving on Campbell's creamy tomato soup and Publix Dutch apple pie yogurt!

"How bad could life be?" she said in a post. She went through a phase of losing her taste along with much of her pride. It's tough learning to live with the side effects of chemotherapy. You either find a way to get along with it and keep going or you choose to try another chemo medication on your diminishing short list of options. Mom said she would rather stay bald-headed for the rest of her life, than not be able to taste anything. It was truly awful. She could still smell everything and visualize how good it should taste, but when it entered her mouth, there was nothing. Tasteless. Bland. Just plain miserable!

Taste changes during chemotherapy are quite common, although Mom was not aware of this ahead of time. Although she did understand that chemo fights the bad cancer cells, but in turn, it sacrifices the good. She forgot there are cells on her tongue. It didn't even cross her mind she had to say goodbye to her taste along with everything else she had recently said goodbye to. This was probably the worst part of chemo so far.

She tried to Google what to do and how to manage it so she could still eat and keep up with her normal life, but nothing seemed to help ease this side effect in the slightest. The internet was flooded with advice and opinions from one website to the other. She tried maintaining good oral hygiene, increasing her fluid intake, and trying to eat smaller more frequent meals throughout the day hoping her taste would come back, but it didn't budge. She experienced painful mouth sores that made the sweet and tart foods, such as oranges or lemonade, too excruciating to tolerate. She invested in a medicated mouthwash that seemed to ease the pain temporarily, but the symptoms always came back when it was time to eat again.

Finding the right foods that tasted somewhat appealing, as opposed to no taste at all, was a long process of trial and error. Instead of eating normal dinners like lasagna, chicken, or vegetable soup, she opted for Wendy's frosties and fruit salad milkshakes from our local ice cream diner, hoping that surely not every type of food was going to be a complete waste.

Mom did what she had to do and attended her chemo sessions on time. She found herself sitting under her soft teal blanket in that cold chemo lab, putting on and pulling off her cheap dollar store readers while trying to catch up on Facebook. She passed the time by trying to beat the next level on Cookie Jam, which was a new game she had started to play, because Candy Crush was making her too frustrated. Instead, she'd minimize that one and start something else that would make her feel like she was winning something.

She received her chemo followed by two days of fluids, which made her feel just as full as she had on the day she gave birth to triplets. You know, that feeling of being nine months pregnant, completely miserable, and way beyond over it? Yeah, that's what it felt like—constantly. Or the feeling after eating at a buffet and then trying to carry on like normal, with a stomach feeling like it was bursting at the seams, not to mention the popped buttons on your jeans. Her body puffed up and swelled, but she took it like a champ. She knew it was necessary, which meant she'd put aside her pride and put one foot in front of the other instead.

If you have been through cancer and treatments, you know just how difficult the road can be. There is so much more to it, so it's way too easy to fall off the wagon and give up before you even start. There will be many days when you feel like you can't continue, and on others when your mind takes control of your heart. When you experience a tragic loss or gigantic bumps in the road seem to pop up out of nowhere, you are faced with yet another decision that has to be made (I told you there were lots). Even the most positive and upbeat people out there have moments of self-pity and despair. We aren't perfect—we are human and you must aid in your own pathway in life.

They say cancer doesn't just affect one person, but it affects the whole family. That statement is as close to the truth as you can get. For Mom, that meant it affected not only her family, but her friends and our entire community. When your days become trying and dark, somehow God throws signs of grace and mercy back in your face. She posted an update on her GoFundMe account one day. Although it was filled with the many negative sides of battling cancer, she didn't forget to always end it with something positive. She had a knack for that. She promised her readers that although it wasn't good news or a very upbeat message this time, she would try her best and be back in the game very soon.

Receiving simple acts of kindness and thoughtfulness such as cards, phone calls, text messages, and words of encouragement and support play a bigger role in this fight than most outsiders will ever realize. During a life-threatening battle, when fighting to stay alive, hearing and seeing others who care enough to go out of their way to remind you of their love, thoughts, and support can offer you just enough energy to fight the fire flaming inside your battered beaten-up soul.

Those are blessings from God. Regardless of the cancer trying to ruin your life, those small signs remind you that you're much more important, not only to yourself, but to many others around you. You play a role in this world and others are always watching in awe. On those days of sorrow and pity, make a pact with yourself to find the good in something. It is always there. Those acts throughout our community encouraged Mom to continue fighting. It gave her the hope and stamina she needed to push through the pain. Remember, David fought and beat Goliath, but it wouldn't have happened without God and the army standing directly behind him.

CRYSTAL BELL

To some people in the world you may be small, but to others, you are the world!

CHAPTER 12

MERRY STRUGGLES

*C*hristmas was slow coming that year as we tried picking our lives back up after an unexpected cancer diagnosis and a tremendous loss in the family. Christmas in our household was always extravagant, to put it mildly. It was a time of ugly sweater parties, cookie parties, and we reveled in the fact that it was definitely OK to drink too much eggnog since it only came around this time of year—nobody counts calories at Christmas time anyway. If you do, well, pat yourself on the back—maybe you'll be the next Jenny Craig, who knows? We had countless family traditions and Christmas movie nights in our pajamas. For as long as I can remember, we were the self-proclaimed Griswold's—no, literally, it just fit us.

A few days before Christmas every year, we started this tradition of The Griswold Family Movie Night. We'd come in our pull-out-of-the-back-of-the-closet-once-a-year-and-hope-they-still-fit-you pajamas, pour a glass of hot red wine (don't knock it till you try it), cram together on the couch, and press PLAY to *Christmas Vacation*. Those were fun times, yet chaotic and ... well ... memorable. The way that night went every year was more like trying to take a quiet and peaceful nap in the middle of Times Square. You plop down with the intentions of watching this movie—the one you've seen oh, ten times a year for as long as you can remember. Regardless, there's always that brother-in-law who recites every word before it's even said on the actual movie, no matter how many times you tell him to shut up.

If it wasn't that, it was the kids rolling around on the floor with nonexistent attention spans, bored out of their minds, because this movie contained no eye-popping vibrant colors that their usual cartoons did. Laughing slightly, because it was so far from quiet in the room, it becomes frustrating when you realize your wine is either empty or there's a fly floating in it! Dad never sits on the couch, so he and his sidekick of a son are sitting in dining room chairs behind the couch, cracking inside jokes on Mom or carrying on their own farting competition, which becomes louder than the volume of the movie that you haven't paid attention to yet! And, not to mention how there's always that one person who can't stop complaining about how hot it is in the house and how somebody needs to turn the air down now! (That one was usually me.)

Memorable at this point is probably the best word I can use to describe those holiday living room mishaps, but they were such a good thing. During the chaos of our mulled wine-Christmas movie-kid tumbling-fart competing-pajama party, we would forget most of the problems that currently were part of our lives outside that steamy hot living room.

We didn't think about how Mom still had cancer. The scarf on her head has become so normal, we no longer even noticed it. She forgot about all the tasteless chicken wings and Christmas cookies, because the only thing she had to worry about was keeping her wine glass filled up to deal with the beautiful chaos that was filling up her living room.

The rash on her hands—well, she didn't have time to fret about that. She was constantly grabbing children from under her feet and placing them in her lap with high hopes of them gently falling asleep there, only to lessen the noise by mmm … maybe a tad. Dad was lost in laughter so much that remembering his wife was battling something beyond his control just didn't come up during that time, especially sitting next to Rennie. You were never serious if you were even anywhere near his funny and inappropriate presence. It just worked!

I remember sitting there, not really even able to hear myself think, but realizing how lucky I was to be in a family this dysfunctional and fun. We made memories no matter the situation and we always cherished those as ones we'd carry with us forever. In my not-so-professional opinion, I believe those are times God perfectly places in your life to teach you to step back a little and take a deep breath. He proves how there is indeed so much more to life than a sickness that tries defining your life story. His perfect placement of these memory-making times, I guess you could say is like a godly type of prescription that you actually *want* to take because the bottle is labeled in big bold letters CURE ALL WORRIES, exactly when it's needed the most.

My point is this: life is forever evolving. Inevitably, we'll all be thrown curveballs at some point, but it's our decision to swing at the right time. Cancer itself will never define you, nor make up every chapter of your book. It may feel like the majority of the time it's defining your path in life, but it's not. It's just a roadblock that you will eventually push your way through. It's simply a piece to the puzzle, but it'll never be the whole thing.

During a life fight, whatever it may be, eyes are always watching and hearts are depending on you. For me, Christmas and Mom came together, hand-in-hand. Every year, she never ceased to make it better than the last, and for that I am forever grateful. So are my kids, who have the best of the best, thanks to her and Papa's wallet. I depended on her to make the holidays worthwhile, and I looked up to her to always feel good so I could be happy and enjoy them, too. I get it—needing her to constantly feel good for everybody else's sake sounds very selfish of me. But that's not how I see it. To me, it's admiration. Watching her fight something bigger than I ever understood in its entirety, and remaining the same person through every aspect of our lives means she's a hero—*our* hero—**my** hero.

It proved how strong she was to endure the deep-down emotional and physical pain, but still laugh with her family as she swore up and down something didn't taste right and she must have left something out of the lasagna, because it just wasn't her best one this time. If she wasn't throwing herself under the bus about something nobody else even noticed, she was dancing around the house with the grandkids. Memaw was always known for spraying the whipped cream can in the mouths of the most hyper kids on the planet, who at this point have no hope of coming down from their sugar high, especially because we still have over half the movie left to watch. She had been given a specific job to do and she worked it exactly the way it had been intended to be worked. It makes it hard not to thank God for those silly times that will stay in our memory banks forever.

It's too humanly convenient to thank Him in the good times and curse Him in the bad—I'm especially guilty of that! I fully realize thanking Him is just too difficult to do, because in hard times you feel defeated, like there isn't much good left to be thankful for. I knew deep down that I was still very much mad at Him for "giving" my mom cancer. How could He do that? There's no good reason to single her out for all that pain and suffering! I get it, but I've learned that giving Him thanks and feeling grateful even in the bad times, is what makes you appreciate His power and the good that comes out of it.

She always stressed the fact that there's a lesson in everything. I found that very hard to believe, but she was right. Like, does a football player feel grateful for the endless days and nights that he spends running sprints or pushing artificially weighted fake men across the football field all hours of the night? She would have told me, yes. He sure will when he gets drafted into the NFL and reflects on the cruel road it took him to get him there, Crystal. Or, how about the hours you spent in sweaty workouts that don't show on the scale in your bathroom? She'd say yes to that, too, because you'll be thankful when the doctor says you can come off your diabetic medicine, because your blood sugar is in the normal range now, all because of the hard work you've put in. So she has a point. I used to complain to her about how unfair it seemed having to put money away in my 401K while I'm struggling just to make ends meet, but her response was, "When you retire one day down the road, you'll be thanking God all the way to the bank, my dear." We can all learn such a valuable lesson from her positivity.

Now that Christmas Eve has arrived, the husbands are off playing in their yearly anticipated golf game. We're left to do all the wrapping and baking. Here we go again, but there doesn't seem to be much good in this one, Mom … (insert all the eye rolling emoji's).

Being a wife and mother, there's no time to spare come Christmas Eve. I'm the epitome of a full-blown procrastinator, so I still had every motherly duty left on my list, all while tending to the kids whose Daddy didn't take them along with him to the golf course. "I'm locking my door, so fend for yourselves until I come out," I'd yell to the boys while I lugged out my wine glass and all the excessive amounts of wrapping paper rolls I spent too much money on and about eight tape dispensers. In my house, Santa doesn't stay up until 2 a.m. wrapping toys. No way. Not this Santa!

Sitting down on Christmas Eve and starting to wrap presents, I had this weird thing, like it was a fresh start. My Christmas presents this year were going to look overly professional, considering the fact I always sucked at wrapping. Like somehow, I was going to wrap gifts like I was one of those ladies at the department store's free gift-wrapping counter. I was determined.

About six presents in, it wasn't looking good and by this point, I was out of wine and totally over it. I texted, "Katie, can you come wrap my presents? I'll pay you!" But she never came. Now I had no choice—I had to do it. This time, I had the whole wine bottle in my room and my gift-wrapping time was extended by a good three hours. Needless to say, I always ended up in there forever and still didn't finish it all. Santa was bringing some unwrapped gifts again this year, kiddos. Katie and Meagan would never do it for me, because they were off doing the same thing and tying up all their loose ends. Mom—well, I didn't even ask her. I already knew the answer to that one. She's most likely in the kitchen baking away and preparing food for the next day, feeling like Betty Crocker and all. She'd be dancing around the overflowing countertops, singing to blaring Christmas music like she was auditioning for *American Idol*, with the windows open and sneaking in a few lukewarm sips from her coffee mug that's been sitting under the Keurig all morning because there's "too much to do" to be able to finish one hot cup of coffee all at once.

She always stressed herself out trying to prepare for any holiday or party. She never thought it was funny, but it was quite comical to blow her phone up with the chimes of the ongoing "Heath girls" group text thread. "I can't get anything done around here because my phone won't stop going off! People don't realize how much I have left to do," she'd say, but honestly, we knew exactly how much she had left to do. However, it was way too funny to see her get all worked up about it and yet, she still answered her phone.

With her balsam fir Yankee candles still burning, you could hear *Jingle Bells* blaring out the kitchen windows, which were open, gracefully inviting in the slightly crisp scent with a hint of warm Florida winter air flowing right through them. Finally, she could breathe! Her baking was done, she was showered, and had just sat down to finish her morning coffee at 3 p.m., when the guys came rolling back in "a few beers down." They had to rush to get ready for the same church service that we were "leaving for in fifteen minutes."

Church on Christmas Eve was something we didn't even think about. It was always a part of the holiday tradition. And speaking of tradition, among the most treasured was the reading of '*Twas the Night before Christmas* before anybody was allowed to go home that night.

Following church, we'd meet back at Mom and Dad's house to eat—you guessed it—lasagna. Then we would sit through the book reading before anybody's departure. For as far back as I can remember, that same old paperback book with my name written on the inside cover in my childish scribble, was always read to us as children by Mom before we were allowed to scurry off to bed, trying our hardest to fall asleep.

As our families grew, it transitioned into our children's tradition instead. However, the two things that remained the same were the old beaten book and the storyteller: Memaw. It didn't matter how tired you were or how close Santa was on the Santa Tracker app. Not until Memaw read the book was your Christmas Eve complete. "Merry Christmas to all, and to all … a good night," she'd exclaim at the end of the tale, smiling at all her grandbabies staring up at her intently. Kiss-kiss, "Memaw loves you, now go straight to bed," she'd demand, loading them up in their car seats.

"Phew!" she'd sigh, walking back inside and telling Dad her duties were done for the night. Each year she grew more and more tired—but Mom was traditional. It was important to her, so that's just how it went.

The cherished family traditions carry over to Christmas Day, too. Before the sun rises, my boys are up and at 'em, ready to go. I try every year to pull a "mom," telling them, "Let's just sleep another hour." But to them, absolutely not! Instead, they'd ambush our California King bed, demanding we get up right now! I'll admit that genius idea of Mom's never sounded good to us as kids either.

Right about now that sounds like the perfect plan, but that has yet to happen. Sean turns on cartoons as I finally roll out of bed, making them wait until I brush my teeth, put on deodorant, change my clothes, and maybe brush my hair. They hate if I say, "Daddy has to take a shower." We'd lollygag around, trying to make ourselves a tad more presentable than we would be if we just jumped right in, straight out of the sheets. Just as their excitement is about to burst, I'd pull another "mom," saying "Just wait till I set up the video camera on my iPhone (once mom's ancient camcorder) and put breakfast in the oven."

"UGGGHH!" they always shout in unison, like it's the first time they've ever heard that one. Before they're allowed to come out, I have to line them up in birth order, just like Mom did to us, except for me; that line is half as short, considering I only have two kids as opposed to Mom's four. Finally, they come barreling out with pure giddiness to see what Santa brought them.

Our Christmas mornings are filled with overwhelming excitement, entirely too many presents, and always that surprised look on Daddy's face when he sees just how many presents Santa brought them this year. I may or may not go a little overboard every single year. Sorry, babe! Although, he never seems to let the dollar signs overshadow the joy and happiness of these spoiled kids. He's such a team player. Don't get me wrong, but there are times his face shows he is just as stunned as they are at their overly expensive gifts that Santa somehow fit in his sleigh, but his widened eyes, to them, just means he's thrilled at what all they got. It's a win-win!

Just as the sight of our wood floors disappear under mounds of wadded up wrapping paper and stacks of brand-new shiny things, the doorbell rings! "There's Memaw!" the boys shout as they race to the door. There always stood Memaw, Papa, and Bubba (my brother, who also assumed the role of "Bubba" to my kids), with 7-11 coffee in hand, coming to see everything that Santa brought.

Once again, Christmas and Memaw came as a packaged deal. She was there to make sure memories were being made and she wanted no part in missing any of this! It was always such a huge deal to her, not minding at all that Papa was fine with just being told by the boys later on what they got—but not to her. She had to be there for herself to see them so excited and happy. (And it was only until after Rennie got married that he was dragged along with them.)

Their morning was never complete until Memaw had come to see what they all got. They'd shout, barely containing their excitement, until she showed up at their door. The day though was never fully complete until they opened Memaw's presents, because "Those are *always* the best presents, even better than Santa's!" they voiced out loud every December 25th. Extravagant and over-the-top, hers put ours to shame. Those dollar signs that Sean sees on Christmas morning never compared to the dollar signs Papa sees, that's for sure!

It's so ironic how Memaw's flooded stockings of goodies were too heavy to hang on her metal stocking holders, too. Now they are laid out nice and neat on her couch, just like theirs are at home. In her house there has to be a "fake" Santa who hands out all the presents, while the rest of us crowd around the couch and coffee table, anxiously waiting to see what else we have to fit into the truck and make room for at home.

Usually, Mom appointed Dad to be Santa—he was outvoted without his consent and there just wasn't ever anything that he could do about it. He's the type of Santa who passes out gifts as fast as he possibly can, which ended up taking forever because Mom's Christmas tree had an ungodly number of presents stored underneath it. The gifts would start piling up on the day after Thanksgiving, and continuously grew from then. By the time Christmas rolled around, it was almost impossible to pull out any dining chairs from the table because the gifts were extending out so far you could barely walk through the room. The kids jumped and leaped, screaming with pure excitement at all her gifts they just received, as we sat around, truly enjoying the time together as one big happy "Griswold" family.

These traditions and memories are etched in our hearts and will be carried on with us for as long as time goes on. The love, laughter, and smiles are something that can never be taken away. It's easy to forget the negative burdens in our lives, while we focus and grow on the good. Nobody let Mom's cancer diagnosis ruin the holidays and quite honestly, I think for a short while, it was forgotten, even by her. Getting caught up in all the holiday cheer makes you realize that the struggles aren't ever what truly matters.

Our lives contain much more than the tribulations trying to shape it. It's not the disease or side effects that you carry with you down the road, but the memories and family time that stay alive. Although that Christmas specifically was emotionally harder than any other one we have had, because we did have something so special to us that was ripped away just a very short time ago. But what joy and cheerful spirits that we did have left in our hearts is what kept the holidays going, not only for us as adults, but for our children who are resilient and showed us that it is still possible.

As the day ended, we finally had time to sit down and reflect on the day and all the spoiled kids who just added to their abundant and plentiful life stock of toys! During the hustle and bustle of a chaotic Christmas, our minds ran faster than the kids ran through the house. It isn't until time slows down that our minds start to grab from other parts of our lives, reminding us of things we'd rather not be reminded of. But that's life and, unfortunately, it happens.

We sat down, talked and laughed, and became emotional about this being the first year a huge loss had left a void in our hearts. Mom inevitably wondered if this would be her last Christmas that she'd be a part of. She cried, missing her daddy so much as she kept replaying those memories in her head. She tried to hold it in, but we saw it. Together, we tried to cheer her up and remind her not to think that way and assure her that this was most definitely not going to be her last Christmas. But honestly, we secretly wondered the same thing. It very well could have been the last one for any of us—not just for Mom. Unfortunately, she just happened to be the only one with a cancer label attached to her, which was known for many deaths. That's what made it harder—much harder.

As we sat, deep in our tired and emotional mind games, we heard a knock at the door. *What the?* we all thought, looking at the clock and wondering if someone really did just knock on our door this late on Christmas night. Dad got up and answered it, as we all tilted our heads toward the front windows, trying to catch a glimpse of what was out there.

"Pam," he chuckled, sounding surprised, "You have to come see this!"

For a split second, we looked around at each other and then jumped up in unison to race to the door. There stood six people, dressed very pristinely, and smiling until the last person hit the doorway before they began singing—Christmas carolers?

OK, let's take a quick pause right there. We live in Florida, and we had never seen real life Christmas carolers. Aren't they supposed to come with snow or something? That was pretty much a nonexistent sight down here in ole' sunny Florida. But there they were ... angelic voices singing better that any church choir I've ever been made to sit through and quietly listen.

We huddled together in awe, trying to hold back tears. It was emotional, but in a really good way. Their songs were followed by warm hugs and tears from both parties. We were so thankful for the generosity they brought to our front door, because it truly concluded our Christmas in a way that we could have never imagined. Maybe for you, Christmas carolers are a normal yearly occurrence, or maybe it just sounds cheesy and totally non-emotional. But for us, we didn't live in a winter wonderland where Christmas carolers have to shovel snow just to show up unannounced, singing in their long winter parkas. "Wow," Mom sighed, "that was definitely a sign from Daddy!" She felt that he came before the night ended, just to let her know that he was OK and that she would be, too.

That sparked a renewed spirit in Mom and was just what she needed to push on further. Being a witness in that moment, one could only describe it exactly the way Mom did: "God sent six angels to knock on my door tonight to sing carols that sounded like they came straight from Heaven, just to remind me that Dad is always watching!" It brought back the joy we felt had been taken from us, leaving us with a touch on the shoulder from an angel, so we could walk away in awe and smile. The fight in Mom's soul had just been restored and it seemed stronger now than ever. She needed that for this new upcoming year that was only a few short days away.

Angels are everywhere. They may be people still living on earth, people in your small circle of friends, or even members of your very own family, sitting in the same room you are. Angels may be pets or even a neighbor down the street and, in many cases, they come as complete strangers. Whoever it is, I believe they surround us each day we're still fortunate enough to walk this earth. They have jobs just like we do, and when they're taken away from here, that doesn't mean their love stops and it definitely doesn't mean that their jobs do either.

CHAPTER 13

THE HAPPIEST NEW YEAR!

"*H*appy New Year!" The ball dropped as we clanked champagne flutes all around to our joyful and hopeful promises of a brand new, only ten-seconds-in, year.

Our mind is a very wise part of our bodies, as it does a great job (or maybe for some, a not-so-great job) when we need it and it's our worst enemy, when we need it the least. It is funny how the last sixty seconds of one year can change your whole outlook on life, as we enter into the first sixty seconds of a brand new year. Suddenly you feel empowered to do good, and it offers more positivity and hope to be able to conquer the world that you didn't do a very good job defeating previously.

For some, those New Year resolutions don't last but a few days, if that. For others, they turn into a new way of life. But for a cancer patient, it means another milestone is crossed, another chance at life is given, and a new fresh start is in the books. Specifically, for Mom, it meant she was only six days away from the start of her fifth round of chemo, and that was a big deal considering she was told in the very beginning that she'd only need six total rounds. January 6th through the 14th was strictly intense chemo, but she was determined and much more than ready to be done with all of it.

Recovering from her fifth round, she was gearing up and preparing for her sixth and final week of treatment, which was scheduled on January 27th. Unexpectedly though, on January 24th she received a phone call from her doctor. "Mrs. Heath?" Mom's heart sank. She was so close to the end, but now she could feel her hope and determination slipping away, just from hearing a few words on the other end of the phone. "This is the doctor's office. We wanted to tell you that you only need to come in one more day, Monday the 27th because after that, you will be completely done with all your chemo."

She was distraught—happy by all means, but totally caught off guard. That wasn't what she was expecting. She responded quickly, "Wait! What do you mean? So I don't need to go through my last round, but just one more day and I'm completely finished? Is this a joke or are you serious?"

The nurse explained to her that because she had been doing so well and her report from the last PET scan came back with no substantial evidence of cancerous lesions, the doctor felt he had no reason to put her through even just one more round.

"The end is just a weekend away!" she shouted gleefully as she hung up the phone. "Thank you, Jesus."

The chemo lab in which Mom had spent the last six months had a very unique way of concluding your last and final treatment. Once finished, you "ring out" before leaving for good. It was a bell that she passed each day as she walked through the doorway with a small wooden plaque above it that reads:

> Ring this bell
> Three times well
> A toll to clearly say,
> My treatment is done
> The course is run,
> And I am on my way!

Many tough days, Mom had sat there tearing up, watching as others completed their rounds by ringing the bell. She longed for the day she would be doing the same and when it would be her turn. The day was here, Monday, the 27th day of January, as the final bag of chemo dripped slowly into her veins.

She could feel the tears welling up in her. It was finally Mom's turn to ring out. She walked over to that bell, full of pride, rang it loudly three times, and let out a huge sigh of relief as the tears of accomplishment flooded her cheeks. Her treatment was OVER and now she was in REMISSION!

When a cancer patient hits the milestone of Remission, it's a huge reason to celebrate! Mom felt relief that the grind of chemotherapy was over, an accomplishment, because she was still standing. She could finally celebrate making it over this huge hurdle. The feeling of accomplishment only comes to those who have fought hard to get to where they are. Most don't understand the true meaning of it, unless you've been there emotionally and physically. Suddenly, life means much more as you end a road paved by something as tough as fighting cancer and just learning to survive.

We felt guilty not being there with her at that appointment, but thankfully Meagan was able to attend it with her. She was present to share that prideful moment of joy with our hero, Mom, as she rang the bell on her way out for good. I know she wished we could have all been there with her at that moment, but she understood when we said we couldn't.

She knew other responsibilities hadn't allowed us to be there, but little did she know those "other responsibilities" were anxiously awaiting her arrival back home. The excitement Meagan felt in secret while driving her home after her appointment was hard to contain. She knew what was waiting for Mom and she couldn't seem to get there fast enough. Trying to carry on a normal conversation during what seemed like a very lengthy drive home made it hard not to spill the beans. Pulling around the corner into the driveway, there was something beyond special waiting for Mom, a surprise moment and a true testament of the joy felt by her success.

"They're coming in hot!" we shouted, witnessing her car pulling into the driveway on two wheels like they were rounding Turn Four in a NASCAR race, just aiming straight for the finish line. Standing there in the hot Florida sun in the middle of the driveway was every one of her close family members and friends. Each person dressed in teal (like her blanket), taking part in holding up the huge homemade sign that screamed in big bold letters, "YOU DID IT!"

With anxious hearts and smiling faces, beaming with proud feelings for Mom, she reached for the car door to get out as we all stood there like statues with smiles etched in our faces. Seeing the emotions flood her face was a sight that could speak a million words, yet was inexplicable at the same time. She was trying so hard to fight off the tears and the shock that she felt upon seeing her huge support group glowing with pride. She wasn't expecting that, but now the fact that nobody "except Meagan" was able to go to her final appointment with her made total sense.

As she stepped slowly out of the front seat onto the driveway, a bag of post-chemo must-haves on her shoulder, bandana wrapped around her perfectly shaped bald head, she was taken aback by an influx of emotions that hit her like a brick wall. She gasped very loudly, gripped her hand over her mouth in awe, and began to cry tears of joy and overwhelming happiness!

This exceptionally prideful moment was caught in one of the most iconic pictures ever taken. It was almost as if she was told to react in the way she did, as she looked at the very staged, much practiced, group of family and friends holding up an over-the-top, vibrant shining homemade sign that anybody could have read all the way across the boulevard. There is a saying that a picture is worth a thousand words. This is the type of picture that defines that cliché. In fact, we all knew, Mom included, that plenty more than a thousand words could have been said to describe that moment, yet I don't believe it would ever be humanly possible.

Mom wasn't somebody who liked to be the center of attention and would much rather fly behind the scenes to make sure everything was under control. But today, it was all about her! This was a moment much more worthy and deserving to ever be told in any fairy tale. Today, she was the forefront of the world's attention and rightfully so! She had courageously earned that position, whether she wanted the attention or not.

After we exchanged multiple hugs and tears in the driveway, we decided maybe the hot muggy Florida sunshine wasn't quite the place for a party. We made our way into the fully stocked, well-prepared, and perfectly arranged get together inside. Hours ticked by as we mingled around the kitchen like we had just invented our own middle-of-the-day, middle-of-the-week, celebratory cocktail party. With finger foods galore, we shared stories and endless laughs, truly soaking up everything about this day. At one point during her celebration, we gathered around in a large circle outlining the entire dining room. We raised champagne flutes, wine glasses, and beer bottles as Mom started to cry.

"After my last chemo day today, I came home to the most AWESOME SURPRISE of teal balloons, a big sign, and beautiful smiling faces of family and friends! I was so overwhelmed. And as I said to some of them tonight, and to many that were not there, whether it was a glance my way, a card, a phone call, a visit, a bracelet, a blanket, a meal, a comfort box, a monetary donation, a necklace, a head wrap, a ride to and companionship to chemo, an email, an inquiry, a Facebook message or response, house calls and meds from a favorite doctor, weekly texts, clothes to make my port access easier, notes of encouragement, all the prayers, chocolate bars, Christmas caroling, a chemo bag of goodies, your availability to me at the drop of a hat, or a hug on my darkest days ... you will NEVER know what this has meant to me and how much you all have touched me in a way beyond words. I THANK YOU and LOVE YOU ALL FROM THE DEPTHS OF MY HEART! When I started this journey, my first prayer to God was to thank Him for all my blessings, and I asked him to please give me the opportunity to fight this fight. My prayer was answered! I fought and I won! But there are some people who were with me daily and saw my ups and downs, my tears, my pain, my bald head, my rashes, my swollen legs and feet, my puffy eyes and face, and my clumsiness, as well as my strength. They listened to me rejoice and they listened to me cry and complain, but they've never left my side and that would be my husband, my children, and my mom. You are all my heart and soul. I would not have been able to do this without you! Thank you and I love you all dearly!! God's blessings are abundant. God is good."

Fighting against ovarian cancer or any other kind automatically comes with ups and downs. Some may have fewer than others, but they'll always exist. It's important to feel both. The downs will help you appreciate the beauty in the blessings God has given you. The ups allow you to openly celebrate those same blessings. In a way, they're connected, as both help to merge your human being into the thankful one God intended when creating you.

This celebration was the "up" to a very "down" life-experience. Putting aside what doesn't significantly matter currently, and having learned to focus only on the present, is when you can genuinely celebrate life's accomplishments, which come in many forms—known and unknown. To Mom, it came after finishing a very hard, painful, overwhelming, emotionally exhausting, and unexpected turning point in her life. Just like most situations though, life will never remain the same. Some days may seem never-ending and emotionally too hard to handle, because the sun will always set on a once bright and shining afternoon. But on the flip side–the sun will always rise again, forcing away the darkness of a dull night.

Now that Mom was finally in remission, something much anticipated and very hard to achieve, she was jumping right in to enjoy her life again. Free of chemo, medication side effects, and now ... free of cancer! She had both her ports removed because she was determined to never need them again. Finally holding the reins, she'd gained back her "normal" life. Thus far, her year had been going so well that she planned a celebratory cruise vacation with Dad and her best friends as she celebrated her fifty-fifth birthday, along with many family members' birthdays. She even broke a thirty-year personal record and finally went on a week-long vacation, just her and Dad to the Florida Keys. No kids, no grandkids, and no problems!

For me, her remission was a joyous feeling of relief. All this time, I had struggled with my own issues of faith. I cursed and stayed mad at God, wondering if He really is up there and if so, why was He letting all this happen to her, while He just sat back and watched. Now that she was able to ring that bell, hear the doctor tell her she was now in remission, to see the smile on her face, and watch the tears of joy fall down her cheeks, I decided maybe God wasn't so bad after all.

Over the next several months, things fell back into place. We felt like we finally had our old happy life back before cancer became a part of it. The struggle she endured of losing her hair and taste buds thankfully were now coming back. "Hallelujah, I have hair and now

I can eat!" she said. Life was good again. She fought it, she won, and now there wasn't much more that we felt we couldn't handle that we didn't just conquer. After all, she kicked cancer's ass. It should have known that it messed with the wrong family!

CHAPTER 14

JOY, SHORT-LIVED

*E*very three months, Mom followed up with the doctor for a quick "everything is going okay" checkup. She'd get bloodwork and tests to make sure her CA125 levels were still good, and then go on her way. She sat in the exam room feeling confident, coming up to her ninth month of remission.

After an abrupt knock on the door, the doctor barged in and said, "Pam! How are you?" He entered in, greeting her with his normal southern voice and smile, but wasted no time getting down to business. "Your cancer antigen level is elevated from what it was in May, so we need to do a CT biopsy in a few weeks to follow up and make sure it's nothing to worry about," he told her.

She felt discouraged after hearing that, considering all this time everything had been going so well without any news of rising cancer levels. She had adjusted nicely back into what she considered normal life. But now, was something going wrong again? She left a little bummed that day but nonetheless still carried great hope and positivity.

Every year in October, Mom and Dad made a trip to North Carolina to the home of their long-time friends, John and Vicki. Their home was snuggled up in the mountains, surrounded by nature and pure serenity. It's a small town cozied up in the northwestern corner of North Carolina and overflowing with wineries. It was the place where she always went to escape all her worries. Something about being there reminded her that life is so much bigger and beautiful than the problems she was enduring. It gave her a sense of peace within and never failed to leave her with a rejuvenated soul. As they entered the front gate and drove past the landing strip of this very wealthy and pristine golf club, it was a ten-minute trek up the mountain via some very winding roads before pulling into the driveway of "The Meating Place" (John and Vicki's international meat company).

In October, the weather in the mountains is absolutely beautiful. It's nothing like Florida weather in October. The vibes are different. Something in the air there makes its way into your body, turning you into the happiest version of yourself. Your mind thinks clearer and you're more open to taking in the natural beauty God planted there. The birds chirping and the faint sound of the stream water, snuggled back behind a shady remote cabin sounds like heaven to your ears.

In fact, they made trips there so often that the master bedroom on the bottom floor of this mansion was named, "Pam and Rennie's Room." It was furnished more than even my own master bedroom in my not-so-mansion like home in the middle of a small town in central Florida. Next to the king-sized bed were wooden nightstands topped with pictures of Mom and Dad, lit by beaming autumn sunshine through the grand window overlooking the mountainside on the back of the property. They settled into their room, put away the few new things they had brought with them to add to their specific sides of the closet that stayed stocked with their belongings year-round, and made their way upstairs to do what was normally on the agenda—plop down on the cold leather couches with a glass of red wine in hand.

"Ah, life is good! What do you want to do for dinner tonight, Vic?" Vicki is mom's best friend, the kind of friend that you meet and instantly realize she's totally your soul sister that completes your world. Often attached to the hip, they didn't do much without one another. Their sister-like relationship was one that exceeds the definition of true friendship and, honestly, even sisterhood. They often made trips to the mountain house, just the two of them and the dogs, doing nothing for a week or two but relaxing on the couch with their iPads, and binge-watching Netflix with bottles of red wine from the cellar downstairs and a crockpot full of White Chicken Chili.

This time, the husbands tagged along. I'm sure they didn't come up just to attend the annual Woolly Worm Festival that went on downtown every fall that they seemed to enjoy *soooooo* much. This was a festival set aside for the third weekend in October to determine which worm will have the honor of predicting the severity of the coming winter. Sounds more like a weird spin-off of Groundhog Day to me, but this quaint little village nestled between the Carolina's largest ski resorts always made a big deal of their fuzzy worm weekend.

Things got a little weird from a bystander's point of view, because I never personally attended the festival, but from what I understand a "wooly worm" is a real thing. In fact, so much so that wooly worm races really happened as these tiny creepy crawlers inched their way up a three-foot length of string. So Dad and John, I feel for you! But Mom and Vicki never cared if they were there with them or not—they were still going to the festival!

Quite honestly, if I had to guess, the guys found a beer tent or something similar and most likely never left it until their wallets and arms were needed to pay for and carry the overflowing bags of handcrafted wares and t-shirts with furry worm-like creatures imprinted on the front, for all the grandbabies back home.

Finally, after suffering through a ridiculous amount of time spent walking around this outdoor farmer's market worm race event thing, the guys left to go swing the sticks at the golf course, while Mom and Vic sat around the fire pit at the local winery down the road. I guess you could say it was more like a reward from having spent time and hard-earned money on homemade knickknacks that the grandkids would most likely lose within a week, but, hey, Mom was happy.

This vacation was just what she needed and she didn't have a care in the world! Occasionally back at home, I'd get a Facetime call from her as she sat on the back deck of the house gloating about how beautiful it was there and how it was "just too bad" I was still home in Florida. I'd throw in a quick "That's so pretty, Mom! I hope you're having a great time and drinking some wine for me, since you didn't invite me on this trip with you."

Those phone calls always ended with, "I am! Love you! Bye!" They never lasted more than a few minutes because ironically, she would say, "The service is so bad here, you're breaking up, so I have to go!" I knew what it meant to her to be there, so I'd hang up laughing at the fact that she still thought I actually bought that excuse.

One phone call came through while she was off in mountain country that wasn't necessarily what she was expecting so soon.

"Mrs. Heath? This is the nurse calling. I just wanted to follow up with you on the results of your biopsy we took a few weeks ago." Ironically, the night before I had come across one of her Facebook posts asking for prayers as she nervously awaited this specific phone call.

The nurse dropped the bomb as she said, "Unfortunately, the cancer has returned." After hanging up and staring at the faces of the other three anxiously staring back at her, she said, "Well, I can't say I'm surprised. I was well aware of the chances of a relapse and now the time has come for me to start chemo all over again."

After hearing the news of her relapse, I didn't quite know whether I should be mad and upset or remain hopeful and optimistic. I was confused and angry that this was happening to her again. My mom is my hero, she fought her cancer when it was unwillingly given to her, and she had made her way through it just fine. I don't understand how it can be "gone" and then just "show up again." Did the doctor verify that he had the right patient's chart? Couldn't the nurse have waited until she was home from vacation? What about the chemotherapy drug company – did they personally try these drugs themselves to determine how effective or ineffective the medication is that they promote? *If God really is good, then He wouldn't be letting this happen to her again,* I thought as I sat down on my bed listening to Mom break the news to me on the other end of the phone.

"Crystal, don't get yourself worked up like this. It is what it is. I have some time and different options this go around. I'll make a decision on what I feel is the right choice of a treatment plan. I don't have to do anything right away, so I'll continue to enjoy my time up here in the Smokies, and we will figure it out when I get home. Whatever it may be, just remember–we got this!"

She had a good point, but even then, I felt so mad about it. Why was I the one being consoled in this situation, when it isn't even about me? The person fighting cancer is the person on the other end of my cell phone reassuring ME that everything will be okay. This didn't seem right and wasn't how I thought it should be. I should be the one consoling her about this situation, but instead it was the opposite.

In conjunction, I started fighting with my own guilt. I didn't want her to have to worry about me worrying about her. The devastation came back around and this time, I felt like there was no reason to smile, knowing this was our life, yet again. I felt like if she couldn't be well then neither should I. Why does everything keep happening to her, of all people? It was so unfair that coming up to her ninth month of remission, it just decides to come back all over again. I felt so bad for her and I wanted so badly to be able to fix it, but how I felt wasn't going to fix it.

It became very hard for me to carry on with life without succumbing to all the negative thoughts and feelings I had for this cancer battle. You know, the feelings that come like a zit on your face at the worst possible time and takes forever to fade away in the slightest? Yeah, those feelings. I couldn't feel happy about anything, knowing she was going through cancer all over again, thanks to its shitty reoccurrence.

I may have been totally bad company to have around, but one thing good that I did still feel, no matter what happened, was that she was MY mother. Here I am, daughter-of-the-year, with the ugliest grinch-like facial expressions glued to my face. There she was gallivanting around mountain country totally living her best life, in full vacation-mode. She didn't seem to mind the bad news bomb, the resurfacing feelings of worry, or even the amount of Dad's money she just dropped at that worm festival. She was going to live life happy, no matter what.

Mom took to her Facebook page that night to update her growing number of fans about her recent news. She let everyone know who had been thinking, praying, and reaching out to her that unfortunately the cancer had returned. However, she wasn't the least bit surprised by it or even worried at this point. She expressed that she was truthfully a tad bummed that she could no longer claim the title of an "Ovarian Cancer Survivor" any longer, but she promised that wasn't going to knock her down.

She went on about how she'd had the best summer and fall season and how she had enjoyed every minute of it spent with family and friends. She was still looking forward to the upcoming holidays and made sure to thank everybody for the ongoing love and support. She told them that she strives daily to pay it forward and bring it all back to God–who in her eyes was always good! She even reached out to her followers asking for prayers for a very dear friend who had recently endured a tragic accident, putting herself on the back burner like she always did, just so she could put many others first.

I think we are all guilty to some degree of expediting ourselves to the very forefront of selfishness and to intentionally at times put others behind us. We're all selfish humans by default. Although we know we shouldn't be that way, we just are. I learned back in my childhood Sunday School classes that God's intentions are the complete opposite of that. Mom did just that, and perfectly.

On the other hand, me—well, let's just say I wasn't exactly the poster child for that type of Bible billboard. I begged and bargained with God, pleading that if he'd answer my prayers and rid her of all the pain she was feeling, I'd do my best to always spread His word of love and miracles. I thought that was the type of prayer I was supposed to pray.

News Flash: not when your words don't match your real feelings. He sees right through that. After all, I was only going to carry out my end of the bargain if He carried out His! When that prayer wasn't even acknowledged, must less answered, it led me nowhere—that is, nowhere good. That dark tunnel I was trying so hard to find a way out of only got darker and longer as I battled resentment towards God.

Trying to put on a front out in public, and most importantly in front of Mom, was just as difficult as it was wasteful to try and understand why all this was happening in the first place. She could see right through me, so I wasn't fooling anybody. I didn't want to be negative or down in front of her, because she needed me to be supportive and understanding. However, I was awful and totally not cut out for that role. I wasn't solving the world's problems or hers, and most importantly, I wasn't solving mine!

CHAPTER 15

MOM IS BACK!

hen Grandpa was alive, he had the makings of what we'd call a "computer nerd"—naturally, I must add. He spent hours upon days on his ancient desktop computer, which was eventually upgraded as the years and technology evolved. He researched our family tree and every other topic that crossed his inquisitive and knowledgeable mind. To him, it didn't matter if he was reading about an odd medical condition or a very interesting genealogy find that he might add to our family tree. At the time, he was the only one in our family who was even the slightest bit interested in it, but it was all important to him. Nobody really knows if he ever got very far in that family tree, but with the number of hours he put into it, I'd always hoped we would at least find out if we were related to somebody of significant importance, like Thomas Edison or Alexander Graham Bell.

He perched himself in his "computer room" (in reality, simply a hallway leading to the master bedroom), which was tucked away on a dark and cluttered desk that was only lit by the dull orange glow of the oldest desk lamp you've ever seen. He was focused intently on the screen as he adjusted his also ancient and oversized trifocals, reflecting the blue glow of his Windows 98 computer screen.

Grandma made sure to steer clear of him while she followed her weekly task of "oh, just working in the yard," standing there in her pink scrunched terry cloth tube top, downing pure pickle juice from the vintage, army-green plastic container she always stored at the back of the top shelf in her fridge. If you haven't tried it, I highly recommend it—you'll thank me later. You could most likely find her lounging in her recliner, catching up on her rerun episodes of soaps or chatting on the phone, usually with Mom, about every irrelevant and useless topic, just to be able to physically talk to anybody who would listen.

That was a very typical day in the household of Grandma and Grandpa. As irrelevant, useless, and quite boring (if we're being honest) as it sounds, I am thankful that the seemingly odd trait of Grandpa's research techniques was organically passed down to Mom. At times, she too could assume the role of a pure "computer nerd" and spend an ungodly amount of hours on her laptop researching information that she'd claim was "just paying the bills." She figured that if she claimed her time as such, somehow it would validate the exceedingly long hours she spent on her electronics each day.

"Okay, I'm out of here, heading to work," Dad would say as he kissed her forehead.

"Have a great day," Mom would throw in as he rushed out the door, leaving nothing behind but a scent trail of his Jovan Musk aftershave. She was already plopped down at the kitchen table bench seat, opening her continuously charged laptop to start her "bill-paying" process. That seat marked the spot where she would spend twenty-three hours of the day working. OK, not really that long, but that's definitely what it seemed like.

Occasionally Dad would stop back by the house for lunch and ask, "Hey, how's it going?"

Her response usually was, "Yes, I am still in my pajamas sitting at the table, paying bills!" He knew that wasn't necessarily the truth, but he let it be for the sake of avoiding a very frustrated and unneeded conversation from the world's hardest working homemaker. But when he showed back up at six o'clock from work and asked, "What have you been doing all day?" He knew her response wasn't going to be so refreshingly honest, but rather annoyed on her part.

She would spit back, "Rennie, I have been paying bills all day long," but only as a coat of sugar, just to suffice the tension growing in response to her countless hours perched at the same spot at the kitchen table.

Now, let's get one thing straight. We all know that paying bills does not take anywhere near the length of time it took her and most definitely, not all day. In fact, it may take an hour at the most. That is, if you aren't with the times and don't have them already preset to "auto-pay." But it doesn't take twenty-three hours of the day. Again, kidding.

I get you, Mom! You're doing other things and it's just easier to blame it on the monthly money you're dishing out for an expensive family of six. *I feel you sister! Totally a good try!* During the months of her remission, we settled back into our "normal daily lives" without having to worry about the thought of cancer consuming her body anymore. What we didn't realize was that the hours of "paying bills" were really hours of researching medical options for every scenario she believed could pop back up at any time. Thankfully, she spent many days preparing for the road that she knew was ahead. When she was told her cancer had come back, while the rest of us were in shock and disagreement, she was sharing with us how she had already come to terms with its reappearance and pleaded for us not to worry, because she had put in many hours of research and was already prepared for this unfortunate reoccurrence. Now those ridiculous twenty-three hours of "bill paying" made much more sense.

So where does she go from here? That was a question I asked myself twenty-million times over, but unfortunately, it was a question unable to be answered at the time. She did know whatever course of treatment she decided she was going to take would be the one she was intended to take and would go all in, ready to fight. Her trust and faith in God are what steered her down her next path. She quoted Matthew 7:7, "Ask and it will be given to you; seek, and you will find; knock, and it will be opened to you." She expressed, "I am a very faithful believer in God, and I will continue to pray for His healing and seek His peace and comfort during this ongoing journey." I on the other hand, wasn't exactly that way in this situation, but it was most definitely refreshing to see such grace fill a tiny five-foot-two human body that goes by the name, of "Mom."

She was always one for options and knowing each one in depth well ahead of time—that's how she worked. She was already leaning towards the next steps she'd be interested in taking, but before she set them in stone, she decided a "vacay" would be best. Her idea of a vacation wasn't exactly my idea of one.

But instead of sitting at the pool bar in Cabo, she sat in the waiting room at MD Anderson in Houston, Texas, which is the number one ranked cancer center in the United States, and she had every right to be all up in that. She wanted to see what the doctors out there had to say about the future treatment options she had been given back home. She most likely feared that there was a cure that just happened to slip through the cracks during her multiple research sessions and she just couldn't continue on, knowing there may be another option out there that she could potentially take part in.

During her trip to Texas, she gained much more confidence in her doctor here and was at ease with the decision she was leaning towards back home. The doctors at MD Anderson told her they would treat her in the exact same way as her typical oncologist at home was urging her to accept. That made her decision much easier. That was great news! This time it came with an extra cherry on top, as she was told that with this new treatment, she wouldn't lose her hair! "Hallelujah, Amen!! Life is good!" she shouted from the rooftops.

For the next twelve months, we had our old mom back. Memaw was "normal" again and life seemed so great. Although she was back on a monthly chemo regimen, it didn't seem to rip away any of her life quality, which gave our faith a little boost upward. Truthfully, at this point, I liked God! He was on our side, so I figured, "What the hell? I'll give Him another shot at it."

That seems so wrong, but it was the only thing that made sense to me. I know there are times He doesn't seem so generous and working towards my advantage, but right now Mom was Mom, so I rolled with it. Those feelings felt right with each good memory that emerged from our daily lives. We had many blessed and happy days when I actually smiled and looked up just to say, "Thank you." I enjoyed feeling like a normal daughter again, because nothing seemed outwardly wrong with Mom anymore. That was all the comfort I needed to tend to my own little family.

An unexpected gift of greatness came as Mom, for the first time, lived a full day without any cancer thoughts crossing her mind. To say she was thankful for that day is quite the understatement. She was so excited and felt extremely uplifted and proud the next day to remember that she hadn't even thought about it once! Detrimental diagnoses and traumas do a damn good job at stealing almost everything of yours at that time in your life, but this day was different! Cancer is good at consuming not only your body and its vital organs, but it's good at consuming every bit of your thought process along the way. Not today, cancer, not today!

Mom believed the non-thoughts weren't a coincidence, but merely a blessing sent from the skies. I believed it was a much-overdue reward for fighting her ass off all this time. It was a milestone crossed that left her with the reminder of how many moments can seem so small to some, but so big to others. Be thankful, because those moments don't come so often to the majority.

Those times bubbled over into the holidays, and we were able to enjoy another chaotic *Griswold Family Christmas* movie night, which I have previously invited you in on. We soaked in all the celebrations. Then there were the days when she was able to attend more surprising lunch dates with the grands at school. They were her pure joy. Her energy and self-confidence were back and being able to truly live life again made her ongoing fight worth every minute of struggle she'd been through thus far.

Living with her during these extravagant milestones, I felt blessed that she was able to spend each day with my boys, Jaxon and Tanner. To them, she was life! She fulfilled every meaning behind that word, and life outside of Memaw never really existed. I thank God to this day that "living back with your parents" wasn't anything like it's chalked up to be. Just be sure not to ask Dad, as his opinion will almost certainly be the complete opposite! Some call it luck, but luck isn't the word—I'm blessed.

Now ease down on your image of a fairytale, because our life didn't exactly match *those* standards. There were many times I selfishly didn't want to be there, especially the nights my marriage twisted up a petty argument—truly unable to yell at each other for fear of somebody else in the house hearing that nonsense.

Here's an insight for you—I never had the luxury of having another person on my side of the battlefield during those bouts of ridiculousness. The person I wanted on my side was Mom all the way, but she always chose another side—Sean's. Dad stayed out of it, like every time, and Mom always felt the need to voice her unasked-for opinion in agreement with my husband.

I mean, shouldn't your mom stay on your side? I know, it's a simple and usually inevitable scenario, but she didn't care how

I thought it was supposed be. Regardless of the topic, Mom only went after what she believed truly mattered and whatever was a very valid point. I'll go ahead and spare you from digging deep into my "bigger person panties" and disregard the may-or-may-not-be-honest statement of, "I was usually always wrong," but she did at least throw me somewhat of a tiny bone in the midst. She'd never admit to Sean that she totally backed him up on current and prior disagreements, but she did just that. Thanks, Mom, but you truly did a horrible job at hiding your pick.

On the downside of Jaxon and Tanner's two-year-long sleepover with Memaw, there was a specific little girl that didn't get nearly as much time in. Neither Maddie nor Memaw were even the slightest bit OK with that. Maddie was her first granddaughter and was very special to Mom. "I'm here to have lunch with Maddie and check her out early," Mom would say. "OK, go ahead," said the sweet lady at the front office of her school. Mom had to be kind of slick walking through the hallways of the school, knowing any second Jaxon could spot her and she'd have no choice but to check him out, too. "Memaw!" Maddie screamed with excitement as her class arrived at the lunchroom in a single-file line. They spent the rest of the afternoon together, just Mom and her "May-Tay." The love and joy of life overflowed as the two giggled and laughed together. Memaw was in her element and Maddie was on top of the world.

"I am never afraid when I am with you, because you are my Memaw and I love you very much!" echoed the sweetest little angelic voice you've probably ever heard. As if that remark alone isn't sappy and full of the purest love ever, she ended it engulfed in Memaw's arms. As Mom wiped a tear from the side of her cheek, she couldn't help but think what a special moment that was. It could have very easily melted her heart, if that was ever physically possible.

These are the moments in life that go far beyond defining what is worth fighting for. This was just one glimpse of the blessed times Mom was able to share with Dad, each one of her kids, and her grandkids. Life didn't matter when she was with family and, quite frankly, it took the back seat every single time! These are the times that make you feel bad for questioning the goodness of God, because it's honestly always there.

Even as I sit here and write this on paper, it makes me feel bad for doubting His love. Deep down, sometimes deeper than others, I know God is good. I know how lucky I am, and I know that life is flooded with blessings. On the other end of that thought, Mom is good, too, like really good. She doesn't deserve anything bad happening to her, especially cancer! Period. Case closed. End of story.

CHAPTER 16

ALL GOOD THINGS
COME TO AN END

I am unwilling having to defend the bullshit phrase, "All good things come to an end." It absolutely sucks, because unfortunately it's true.

Exactly twelve months into our joyride through a wonderful and happy life, the devil creeped back in without knocking and we weren't even given the chance to turn him away. The "perfect chemo drug"—if that's not the biggest contradiction you've ever heard—finally just quit. It gave up on her and on us, just like that!

Then, like clockwork, the chemo also became ineffective, her body stopped accepting the benefits of something that had been keeping her cancer at bay, and allowing her to have her life back. The treatment just gave up, almost like how I decided to just give up at that moment. Thanks, cancer, you literally are awful.

No wonder I doubted God as much as I did. He wasn't playing fair and these games were senseless. Didn't He know how much He'd already put her though? Now, she's knocked down once again? I'd had enough—I threw my hands up and tossed in the towel, the same way the unreliable chemo treatment behaved. War had officially broken out in my head, and I was running full speed out of those trenches. Unfortunately, I started down an even worse path that headed me towards being the perfect poster child for depression. While I was busy "Forest-Gumping" it down this sickening and very winding road with no end, Mom was busy making extremely difficult decisions, truly worth the depression.

Wouldn't you know, she was given yet another option of chemo. Now, don't get me wrong, folks—I was thankful. I mean bring on all the options, but I had doubts and discouragement again. I was wondering if this was going to give up on her, too, like straight failure. This time, it was an oral pill she could take at home. She could continue to travel and maintain her way of life, instead of being tied to the chemo lab every three weeks.

I started wallowing in my own self-pity, believing I'd make everything better by feeling bad for myself and for her. On top of it all, she told me; "Crystal, I'd be crazy for not taking this option. But if I am going to do this, you need to take a huge step back into your own life."

Yes, ma'am! Now I just felt like a sad, scared puppy with her tail between her legs. I stopped moving one foot in front of the other and watched as the day came when she made her final decision. Agreeing to start this new chemo came with good news. This drug would not cost her a dime! "What a Godsend," Mom exclaimed. Behind her back—kind of like her agreement with my husband behind his back during our arguments—I agreed that it was a God-sent gift, but in no way, shape, or form was I going to openly admit that. Nah, I'm good.

Just as she began this other "great chemo drug," our hope started to head back up the same mountain that we had already climbed a million times by this point. We reached the top quicker than expected and the only option now was to go back down.

Sadly, the aggressive side effects, including hair loss, came right back. Mom did her best fighting through the chronic fatigue and found many ways to totally rock the bandanas and wigs, which happened to turn her into quite the fashionista. She did her best keeping her faith front and center, her head held high, and kept her attitude positive, which took her farther than most could ever say. She followed up with her many doctor appointments to monitor the progression of the chemo benefits and the cancer, only to find out that no matter what she was doing to try and avoid the cancer progression, her antigen levels continued to rise.

It seemed as if what she was doing (or what she was told to do) was completely pointless. Mom quickly felt that she needed to remind me on many of my negative days that there is still good, which definitely outweighs the bad. She was molding me into what she believed I should be as a Christian. I did what most daughters do—I rolled my eyes and half-listened to what I thought was an unimportant topic of "God and how good He truly is."

Many times, I wondered how she could be so positive in such negative, completely unfair situations. Like, how does that even work? I must not have been given that talent, because I had zero understanding of how that was even possible. Although she was told her cancer was progressing and maybe it was time to stop this chemo regimen, she continued to pray. She was told it could possibly take two to four months to really kick in, so she sat back and gave it another fighting chance instead of throwing in the towel.

Mom was asked to be the 2016 honorary speaker at the Relay for Life. Speaking in public wasn't typically a comfortable situation in which she liked to put herself in. But digging deep, she knew if there was even just one person out there listening to her story who she could help, this whole cancer thing would be way worth it.

She accepted the offer and began to write down her experience up to this point in time. There were many days and nights we made sure to avoid the living room, because we knew whatever it was that we needed or wanted to say wasn't as important as what she was in the process of writing. It most definitely wasn't worth getting our heads bitten off at the same time. So we let her have her space to revisit all the good days and the bad, so she could accurately write them down on paper to share with the world.

She started off jotting ideas down in the memo app on her iPhone and quickly realized there was more to it that had resurfaced while she racked her "chemo brain." Now, she took to her laptop to create the finished product. Saying many nightly prayers and adding a few more sleepless hours to her nights, she put aside her nerves and discomfort to prepare for an honorary night much anticipated by many cancer patients and survivors.

She felt very honored to speak and, as her family, we felt extremely honored to be there to hear her genuine testimony. I will admit, it was a little uncomfortable for me to see Mom so nervous about something. However, once she put on an outfit covered in teal, gently combed and placed her blonde wig on her perfectly shaped bald head, and praying once again, she headed for the event. As several family and friends gathered at a local high school football stadium, beaming with anxious smiles and covered in teal also, we showered her with love and plenty of support.

For me personally, I thought how amazing it was that other people could gain even the slightest glimpse of how special my mom really is. To ask her to speak at this event about her fight made me love her even more. I was so excited to hear her speak and even more excited for others to hear her words of truth about her honest struggle.

Standing in the hot humid sun, gathered, talking, laughing, and pitching her some encouraging advice, she was finally called to take the stage. Thank God for the big white tent that covered not only the stage that day, but the chairs for the audience as well. We were able to sit there and enjoy her speech, instead of feeling our skin melt off or burn to a crisp from the 95-degree weather of a typical Florida spring. I want to applaud the people who put on the Relay for Life, because not only were they extremely accommodating, but they were thinking of how the guests and their families could sit and enjoy the inspirational story of one person with cancer, while the rest of us avoided potentially inviting skin cancer into our own lives. It was as if they were mind readers or maybe they just knew how unprepared Florida people can be coming to an open, unshaded football field without sunscreen. There really are angels everywhere, I tell you.

Before I even had time to talk myself down from having a nervous breakdown for Mom, whom I knew didn't like public speaking, she started promptly with her speech.

> *First of all, I would like to thank you for inviting me here to share my journey. I hope in doing so, it will bring some much-needed awareness to ovarian cancer.*

OK, sidenote really quick: I have to say one of the best parts of this night by far was the sight of Dad bending down just in front of the stage with his phone—you know, the same phone that he still doesn't have a clue of how to text on, but totally figured out how to use it to record her entire speech! Crouched down the whole time, knees giving out, legs trembling, hips stiff from being in the same position through her long, very slow-paced and much practiced speech, he didn't miss a moment. It may have been all the love and pride he felt for his wife that persuaded him to record a ten-minute speech on his phone, or simply the conversation he would have landed himself in on the way home that night, if he hadn't recorded the whole thing. He won't ever admit it, so we may not know that answer, but what we do know is the picture that was captured that night of Mom's speech is worth a million words!

While Dad was suffering in a very awkward position, the rest of us were in plastic chairs under the shade, with legs crossed and constant smiles on our faces as we listened to her voice a very tough life story. Some of us, I won't say who, became teary-eyed with growing admiration for our amazing mother. To stand on stage in front of a crowd of people gleaming at you as you bravely share some of the worst and most vulnerable times of your life, is an incredible testament of courage and utter tenacity. That takes a lot of experience, struggle, and pride to stand all five feet of her and willingly invite the world into the darkest depths of her personal life. For that alone, I am extremely proud to call her Mom.

As she concluded her speech, a sigh of relief and accomplishment sounded out. On the other hand, Dad was preparing to get up without looking like a baby giraffe just learning how to stand on its own feet. The grandkids were finally able to run around and talk without getting stared down by their parents or being shushed by other onlookers. They took off like they had been sitting there against their will their entire lives.

As we tried desperately to wrangle up the kids who were running wild and free from the white tent, Mom stepped into a convertible car at the beginning of the track. She rounded the track on the back of this convertible with her very own chauffeur, gracefully waving to cancer patients, survivors, and family and friends of people who had passed on from this disease and people yet to be diagnosed. They proudly clapped, whistled, and cheered her on as she was paraded around like the most famous celebrity you'd ever seen.

I felt overwhelmed with joy as I watched my very own deserving mother live in this moment, being celebrated by complete strangers! To hear her put into words the way she looks at this long journey and to see the smiles and hope on the faces of everybody surrounding her, made me prouder than I could ever possibly express out loud. Through the tears and raw reminders of how this disease has affected our lives and most importantly hers, for the first time in a quite a long time, I thanked God for making her MY mother, the most beautiful, inspirational, strongest, and endearing person I will ever know!

I looked up to see this bright glow around her as she rounded the fourth and final turn of the track. She approached her entourage of family and friends, waiting for her as she cried tears of joy and waved like the prettiest southern belle that's ever existed. It was a moment in time that every guest there will quite possibly never forget. But in case our minds and memories ever give out, we do have the most amazing pictures to show for it.

Up to this point in her life, her story has been nothing short of a roller coaster ride. Every cancer patient experiences both ups and downs differently. The question is what do we do with them? *Let it keep us down or do we learn from the downs to keep us up?* Those are wise words from an angel.

CHAPTER 17

LIFE'S TOUGH, BUT GOD IS GOOD

The world continues to spin, the clocks continue to tick, and our footsteps continue forward. Life goes by regardless of how you decide to live it. We had been praying hard, staying positive (or at least trying to stay positive), and hoping for the best.

It came time for Mom's normal follow-up visit that she had to attend after a few months into a chemo regimen. The results she received that day, "weren't exactly what I had hoped for," she told me. "But then again, I've said that before," she voiced with a hopeful smirk on her face. Her cancer antigen levels had significantly increased now and the PET scan revealed the ever-so-dreaded metastasis. Her body had developed four new lesions that were completely blocking out any chemotherapy drugs pumped into her veins to keep that from happening. Once again it was like clockwork. Que the flooded feelings of fear and anger, which showed up in due time. This was a place we had been before and had no desire to be back in. Then again, that's life for you.

"This makes me so mad! Why isn't anything working? I don't understand it, Mom. This is so unfair." I cried out to her.

She gently and calmly replied with her hands around me, "Honey, it's not up to us to question any of this. Being a cancer patient for over three years, it prepares a person for the good *and* the bad. The bad seems to be the norm most of the time, with the good being a total surprise. You can always look forward to the good." Well, she wasn't wrong.

"OK, Pam," said her doctor, "we have some more options up for discussion and we need to decide on another road to take from here." Mom always felt a very calming trust with him, and she knew he was placed there for a reason. Undergoing the care of an oncologist naturally comes with an uneasy feeling of somebody else being in control of your life besides just you. There's a trust that doesn't come as easily to some people as it did for Mom but she knew God always has a plan and the people in and out of her life have been put there for many reasons, mostly unknown.

"Let's hear it," Mom replied. He went over some different chemo drugs and then suggested she go back to some she had tried in the first few months of her "cancer life." He explained that back then, those were the ones that had sent her into remission and now they knew a lot more about that specific drug line from what they did before.

"They just might work again," he said to her. Having recalled the severe side effects of these two medications, Mom was very unsure about openly allowing herself to go back to that. He knew her so well and could read her like a book. He could tell by the look on her face that she wasn't a fan of this idea whatsoever. He went on to mention another drug option and then finished with music to her ears: "You could also take a break from therapy if you want. I will not try to talk you out of it, but if you do go with that option, I don't suggest it be a long one!"

Those words were refreshing. She felt at ease. The tension of the on-the-spot decision making went away right then. She expressed to him how special this upcoming month was to her and she'd love nothing more than to take a break. Not only was it her birthday month, but she had two trips planned. One consisted of a seven-day cruise with friends and the other, a highly anticipated mystery weekend trip with her daughters.

He understood and quickly replied, "Well then, we will hold off until after that."

That decision was a no brainer, but she still had her doubts. Although she had made her decision, she still went home and pondered it for the rest of the afternoon. "I could take a six-week break and get to feeling better, then take these two trips, and make plenty more memories with my family and friends. Or I can start this new chemo round and feel like crap while attempting those two trips that I may or may not feel up to attending when the time comes," she reasoned out loud. Not only that, but there was only a twenty percent chance of these new chemo drugs working anyway, so her decision came easily this time around, or at least that's how I saw it.

All through her journey, she stayed consistent about the importance of maintaining her quality of life. What is life even like without any quality in it anyway? I agreed with her on that. She believed that her main purpose in life was not to fight this deadly disease, just to come out like a shriveled-up prune, lifeless but with a beating heart. That idea never sat well with her, and it was never even an option in her old book of tricks. There was so much more depth and meaning for her. She didn't always feel like she had control over most of this, but she knew not ending up as a dead dried out fruit was something that she could control for the time being.

She chose the break. She knew in the back of her mind that the PET scan she would have to get at the end of this break would be worse than it was right now. Inevitably it would not improve, but it took three months for this current one to be as bad as it was, so six weeks was a time frame she wasn't going to worry about. "To me, memories are way more important," she told us. I can't disagree with that. She has a very valid point there and somehow, she's always right. Yes, Dad, I went ahead and "took one for the team" and admitted it for the both of us.

As she previously stated in her in speech, "Every cancer patient goes through ups and down, but it's what we decide to do with those ups and downs that matter. Do we let it keep us down, or do we learn from those downs to keep us up?" I would not have the relationship with God that I have, had it not been for this situation. I thank God every day for the troublesome times, because it's the peace they produce that far outweighs the trials I endure. Our purpose is not to get lost in the dark side of our journey, but to be a beacon of light so that others can find their way. She continued to stay positive because she believed her optimism played a huge part in taking her this far. It lessened her pain and made her mind and heart stronger. She refused to let it take her will or destroy her faith. "Life may be tough," she said, "but God is always good."

May couldn't come around quick enough. Mom didn't have to attend chemo for the next several weeks and it was getting closer to the surprise trip we had planned for her. She started to feel so much better as the days went on. Her excitement built quickly, and she could hardly stand the fact that we had planned something for her that she wasn't previously let in on. We told her early on not to ask us for any details, because we would not budge. She learned to live without questions for quite some time. She hated every minute of it, but took it like a champ.

The morning finally arrived and we were ready to hit the road. Meagan and Katie piled into the car and picked Mom up on the way to grab me before hitting the highway. "Crystal, are you ready? We're here, let's go!" I heard as they came barreling into my house.

"Hold on, I'm coming!" I yelled as I rushed around my bathroom trying to find anything else that I might have forgotten to pack in my oversized suitcase (which was completely unnecessary for four days, by the way). I flipped the lights off and ran out the door.

As we got on the road, it didn't seem to be going quite as planned. We weren't even ten miles out, and Katie was already being way too serious about her driving responsibilities. Meagan, groaning and curled up in a ball, was very sick to her stomach. "Just calm down, everybody," Mom said, and here I am in the back seat, worried about when we will stop to get mimosas!

The dust settled and Mom attempted to entice us to drop hints about where were going. In no way were we going to give in after five months of surprise planning five minutes into our trip. Cracker Barrel was only about twenty-five minutes away, but even that seemed like it took a whole day to get there. "Grandma" Katie is an overly cautious driver, if I'm being honest. Meagan and I were in the back seat bursting with excitement and doing eye rolls about our quite dramatic (but safe!) driver of a sister, who was born with Mom's dramatic traits. You know how they say, "Like mother, like daughter." Yup, that was most definitely the case during this five-hour car ride, for sure!

Moving along down the highway at a ridiculously slow pace, we finally stopped at breakfast for Mom's first surprise. We played it cool as just another mother-daughter breakfast. We couldn't contain our excitement much longer. "We're here!" Katie shouted as she put the car in park. Thank God! Not that it's probably lunch time by now or anything. It was then that Mom decided to put her lipstick on in the passenger visor mirror. You know, right now was a good time, because she didn't have nearly enough time to do it on the way.

As we piled out of the car, I had to exit through the trunk, which was closer to my seat way in the very back of the car where they stuck me. Walking up as she stuffed her lipstick back into her teal purse, completely oblivious, Mom finally noticed her best friend, Vicki, perched down in those famous wooden rocking chairs out front, like every other Cracker Barrel on the planet. She was shocked to say the least! She had no clue her best friend would be joining her and her daughters on such a special trip. She wondered how on earth Vicki was able to keep a secret from her for so long, when she normally wasn't a good secret-keeper at all. They didn't keep anything from each other, but this was fun. I'm proud of you, Vic.

After a few plates of pancakes and glasses of mimosas, we went on to our destination and arrived at the cutest, most modern chic loft in Savannah, Georgia. We had a blast! Savannah was one of Moms favorite places to go and now we had the next four days together to enjoy and forget the rest of the world's problems. And we did just that!

Cancer was rarely ever brought up, if at all, which made the weekend so much more special. It was as if everybody and everything was normal again. We were just there to celebrate the birthday of the best mom in the world. Those times and trips are memories you can't really explain or put down on paper and, in most cases, you probably shouldn't. These are times that make you remember what life is truly about. We shared so many laughs and stories, had a classy rooftop brunch, walked down River Street with cocktails in hand, shopped for things we didn't need, got dressed up for a fancy dinner at Ruth's Chris Steak House, and then shared tears about life in our quaint Loft on Congress. Our girls' weekend was a success and Mom was worn out by the time we rolled back into reality, kicking and screaming.

In life, there are moments that come and go that teach you to take a step back and reevaluate what is truly important. It makes you realize your priorities, not only as a person, but as a mother and a daughter. There are times that humble your heart and spirit and make you think deeper than you are used to doing. They make you realize that living with cancer isn't what defines you. It is simply a detour you've had to take unexpectedly—we all have them. Allowing ourselves to let each diagnosis steer the way we live our lives would mean there would be no such things as vacations or good memories. Our days would be filled with aches and pains and sorrow and self-pity. I guess these are the lessons Mom has always tried to teach me. Keeping faith in God is the only way. I'll admit, it seemed a whole lot easier just to wallow in my own sorrows than it was to enjoy life and try not to remember all the unfair trials thrown into the mix.

"Like, why can't we just have happy days every day? Then the world would be perfect. Maybe then I would have more faith in the man upstairs if everything went my way!"

"That isn't what life is all about, Crystal. You aren't getting the big picture." Mom totally called me out. I ended up walking right back into the darkness every time a chemo drug stopped working and a new one dripped into her veins. Maybe it's because some of us are so blind to the blessings the whole way through, just hoping that this is "the one" that will make our life perfect again. Maybe it's the disappointment I feel knowing in the back of my head there is a possibility it won't work, like all the failed drugs in the past.

We won't even go into the fact that, out of everybody in the world, God picked Mom to have to fight off such pain. Being a daughter is a hard job, because there isn't anything you can do to help someone like your mother in situations entirely out of human control. It's extremely painful to watch, without the ability to make it all better for her. I wasn't getting anywhere with the worries I toyed with in my mind. Placing all our faith in God is the answer to all Mom's troubles, so I figured I might as well keep trying it, too. I guess it can't hurt any worse than it already does.

Every bad day has an ending as a new one begins, and my self-pity party was dwindling away. There were no favors coming from my sulking sessions, so I knew I needed to pick myself up and try even harder than I thought I already was. If not for me, at least for Mom and my children, and my poor husband, who had to live with me—God bless him. We went through the days aiming for normality and worked hard at keeping her spirits up on the days she felt low.

I'd tell you that the kids wanting to go to Memaw's house every day of the week was an exaggeration, but it wasn't, and I was OK with that. I, too, felt like my days weren't complete without a hang session with her, so we did just that.

"Hey, guys! How was your day?" I'd ask my kids as they climbed into the car.

"Can we go to Memaw's house?" they'd both respond in unison. It was hard to ever say no even if we had planned on going out that evening. Going to her house was important and it was each day's highlight, so time had to be made for it. If they weren't in car seats, they'd probably jump right out of the car the second we pulled into her driveway, but they had to wait until I parked. They kept begging me the whole time to hurry and get them out, so they could go tell Memaw about their day.

Before I could even ask them to help throw their goldfish trash away, they were gone. I trailed in behind them, after picking up goldfish crushed in the creases behind their car seats.

"Hey, Mom," I'd say as I walked in, exhausted and annoyed that I had just cleaned out the whole cracker isle of the Publix grocery store that had been smashed into the seats of my car.

"Hey, honey!" Her voice was such a breath of fresh air. Not to mention, it totally put me at ease when she'd hand me the already poured glass of Pinot Noir that she'd made me before I even got into the kitchen.

Each afternoon, we'd sit out on the front driveway while the kids pulled out every toy stored in their garage. We'd sit out there for what seemed like hours, sipping wine and talking about our day, with the kids' laughter echoing in the background. The only reason we ever had to conclude our little gatherings was because the boys left all eighty-five toys laying around as the sun set. "The mosquitoes are coming," they'd yell, running into the house and leaving us behind. We were forced to go inside, because leaving the kids alone in Memaw and Papa's house without supervision was never a good idea.

Those nights we'd rush inside, chaos and all. After a few threats of, "if you don't get in the car right now, we won't come back!" they'd finally leave Memaw and Papa with sweet sweaty kisses and head out until the next day when we could repeat that all over again.

That was the absolute perfect ending to Mom's days. The last thing she thought about in the middle of all the ruckus was having cancer. At this point, the wigs and bandanas were the normal. She held onto every good day she had and embraced every dirty little handprint left on the walls. She never minded when the kids left their shoes or shirts behind, all thrown around the living room, because that just meant we had to come back to Memaw's house again. Laughing at the fact that their parents pulled away with their kids half-dressed made Mom feel so truly blessed for each moment we spent with them. Mom soaked it all in and loved every beautiful mess they brought in with them, just to leave half of it behind.

For the next six months, Mom fought like hell as we stood right beside her. She had good days and bad, but for the most part, life seemed okay. Being the prepared and proactive person that she was, she had heard about a clinical trial at Moffitt Cancer Center that she may possibly be a candidate for. After her extensive research, she scheduled a consultation with the doctors there. She was currently on chemo, but that never stopped her from exploring additional options.

We started our trek through the holidays as we normally did and began to enjoy the crisp air Florida occasionally gets for about two days in the fall. Going into November, right before the holiday rush, Mom attended another PET scan and bloodwork appointment. By this time, the reality of it seemed normal. But as we all know, normalcy doesn't last very long when you're expecting to stay there.

"Pam, this chemo is no longer working," the doctor blurted out with no time wasted. It came as no surprise to her.

"I just don't understand," I said under my breath, trying to reason with myself as I shook my head held low, trying to keep her from overhearing my questionable and confusing reasoning about this unfortunate news.

"Crystal ... " she began. Well, shit she heard me. I looked up at her with eyes squinted and anger written so blatantly on my face and spit out, "How is it that we are praying as hard as we can but what we are praying for just won't happen?" I went on ranting, "Why do people keep saying to pray when something bad happens, but rarely those prayers ever even work?" I had so many questions for her, for

Him, for all of this. All these doubts and questions repeated in my head every single time something didn't go in her favor. Like, I really don't get it. I don't pray for much.

She tilted her head with a sweet smirk on her face, as she tried to respond with a sincere reason that would somehow make its way through my thick mind. She wasn't the least bit upset this round of bad news, because she knew her body and she had prepared herself for any type of outcome.

She expected this to happen, which is why she had previously visited Moffitt a few months back. For her, this transition brought extra hope. She knew all along that this would most likely happen and what better way to accept it, than planning it all out the way she had. Filled with so much grace, she jumped right into the next option she'd chosen. She amazes me daily.

She was preliminarily approved for a clinical trial, but of course she had to go through countless tests before receiving complete approval. "The nicest place to be is in someone else's thoughts, but the safest place to be is in someone's prayers," she said to many worrisome friends and family members following right along with her.

She was embarking into the unknown with this trial, which was very scary, and not only for her. "This is NOT going to get me down!" she wrote. "God willing, this might be the answer to some relief from this cancer, and maybe even a remission," she continued.

To me, as her daughter, I saw hope in that post on social media. Part of me admires her strength and positivity, but the other part of my being had such a broken heart. I know how hope is just an emotion that, at times, can play very unfair tricks with your mind, leaving you feeling completely defeated. I continued to pray during the nights I thought about it, because that's what Mom always does and if she does it, then so should I. It was a hard pill to swallow. I prayed, wondering if I was even praying correctly or if what I was praying for was even fair to ask God. I spent many nights praying so long that I fell asleep before "Amen" and had to pick it back up the next night. Maybe that is why it wasn't working? What if I don't even know how to pray? Then there definitely was no way He was going to answer me if a simple prayer isn't something I'm even capable of.

When you feel that lost and sad, blame comes way too easily. I searched constantly for things to blame her sickness on. I tried to think of every scenario and unfortunate event out there that could be the horrid culprit of cancer taking over her body and her life. In doing so, it led me nowhere, except to utter insanity. I went back and forth with the whole prayer thing, and I toiled with my own emotions, blaming myself for not being able to fix it. I even blamed myself for being a triplet, thinking that giving birth to multiples is what caused all this in the first place. I got mad at the doctors for not curing her like they're supposed to do. I gave up on God all too often. He seemed to be of no help anyway.

It was a long road that didn't seem to have any ending in sight. My world became darker each day. The smiles and happiness almost didn't exist anymore. Watching her battle cancer caused me to go the wrong way, without any strength to stop it and turn it around. What I didn't realize at the time, was heading down that path meant I was going alone. It meant I was separating myself further from God, which in turn, meant I'd be further from Mom. I started fighting my own demons in my head. Calling in to stay home from work became excessive, to say the least. Taking all the bad parts of life out on my family became a daily occurrence, because all the good was overshadowed by the traumatic events playing in Mom's life.

My husband and kids suffered in a different way, all because of my actions. I started buying stock in bottles of wine to down, just so I wouldn't think about it. OK, not really that much, but you get it. I depended on the vino to put me to sleep every night. I convinced myself that life just didn't mean much to me anymore. The only life that meant the world to me seemed to be dwindling away according to cancer's schedule. I didn't feel there was much left that was worth anything on my end. In my heart, I knew that life with my husband and my children indeed makes life worth living to the fullest, but I failed at holding on to that realization. I knew I was supposed to stay upbeat and positive, but that was a lot harder to do than the "Peanut Gallery" ever realized.

I spent many days at work (when I did go) in a bad mood, with lots of tears. I was short in my conversations. I suffered from headaches and depression with which I didn't know how to deal.

Every lunch break I got was spent on the phone with Mom, putting on a front about how "good" my day was going. I didn't have the heart to throw my issues at her while she was being held hostage by cancer, which was way too big to compare to my minuscule issues that I believed were a big deal. How dare I turn this around to focus on me? Unfortunately, without truly realizing it, that's exactly what I was doing. I was selfishly making life about me and my so-called problems. I was being the opposite of how a daughter is supposed to be and I was making things harder on her the whole time! Being the cause of her emotional pain was the absolute last thing on earth I ever wanted to be!

As I lay on the cold white tile floor of my bathroom, one hand gripped to my iPhone while the other held tightly to the tissue I was overusing to wipe away my tears, I waited for those three little dots to come across the screen of my ongoing text thread labeled, "Mama."

Mom, I'm so scared, I can't lose you!!

I texted her as I sat there behind that locked door in a tight ball, drenched in my own salty tears. She texted back,

Crystal, you have to help me stay positive!

My heart sank. It wasn't until that incoming text message that I finally realized I am truly making her battle worse. Do you want to talk about living with guilt and feeling like you've disappointed the entire world? Try being the reason of worry and concern in your cancer-fighting mother's heart. If that doesn't straighten your ass up, then there's probably no hope for you out there.

Thankfully, Mom always had a way to turn my head around full circle. I sat there feeling so ashamed of myself. At first, I didn't know what to say or how to respond. I was still trying to process and accept the very accurate truth behind her reply. I typed to her, "I'm so sorry that I texted you while I'm this upset. I don't want you to change your positivity, especially because of me." I sat there staring at the phone, not wanting to blink, just to be sure I wasn't going to miss her response when it chimed through from her end of the phone.

It's crazy knowing how much internal anxiousness shows up when somebody who means so much to you hasn't responded to your last text yet. Questions flooded me. What is she going to say back? What if she doesn't even respond? Did I make her so upset that she felt taking a break from our conversation was much needed? *Great, Crystal, look what you've done now!* I felt so bad.

Five very slow minutes ticked by, so I gasped before the incoming "ding!" could even finish ringing out. She finally replied, "You can talk to me anytime about anything, honey." she said. Right then, I felt an overwhelming calmness that only Mom could make me feel. It was a sense of peace and ease that naturally only stems from a mother, *my* mother. I felt like I was off the hook, like somehow I had another chance at continuing to help her fight, instead of adding to the unbearable weight that seemed to be dragging her down even more as the days rolled by. I just wanted to hug her right then.

"I am squeezing tightly—can you feel me?" she asked. "Yes, Mom, I can!" I replied with a smile. She went on, "Tighter and tighter!"

As the conversation came to an end, I left her with the truest of my words, "I love you so freaking much." The response she left me with that night is one I will never forget. "And I love you more! Always remember, you and I share the same heart, Crystal!"

Night made.

Mom went on to host another Thanksgiving feast at her house. A chaotic household of thirty-four just meant she'd received that many hugs all in one day! She was thankful for the company, the laughs, and all the love. That stressful but blessed day was exactly what she needed to refuel her mind before starting another round of treatment. She continued to ask for prayers from her followers and reminded them that their prayers are a huge part of her success. She thanked every person from the bottom of her heart, wished them all a very happy Thanksgiving, and gave all her thanks to God before resting her head that night.

Anytime Mom was to start a new chemo regimen, I suffered with stomachaches the night before. These aches were caused by those unwanted nerves that always found their way to the surface at the worst times. The uneasy and confusing emotions rolled back in, as did the chest pain. No matter how hard I tried to execute the mind-over-matter theory, it just never really seemed to work right for me. I tried to talk myself out of the nausea and insomnia. Trying to pray only went halfway before my thought process went right back to my awkward comfort place of worry.

The next thing I knew, it was a brand new day filled with fresh feelings of hope and excitement, thinking that this just might be the answer to our prayers and hoping it would diminish all the concern, worry, doubt, and negativity. I was asked to post on social media for all her followers awaiting an update on her journey. We always had an outpouring of uplifting comments and prayers to fall back on when things started to get rough again.

After seven long hours, eleven vials of blood, six EKGs, one flu shot, and three study drug capsules swallowed, it was a very successful day at Moffitt Cancer Center. It was now time for the trial to begin. Feeling anxious but hopeful, Mom's "Thank you, Jesus" moment of the day was finding out that the study drug capsules she had to swallow were not horse pills. She hated those! Now that she discovered they were tiny little things; she was one happy girl.

To a cancer patient, you learn to take what you can get. Sugar coating is for the birds and riding on a high horse through the process just simply isn't desirable. You see life in a way you've never seen it before. You start to become grateful for certain things that most of us take for granted and don't realize they are hidden blessings. It's hard to put yourself into the shoes of a cancer patient and share the excitement behind things that seem so small to us, but the size of a pill can change your whole damn day!

As horrible and unfair it is to have to duke it out with a disease that is so relentless, thankfully there are hidden gems in the lessons and trials that you face. Being the daughter of a fighter caused me, on many occasions, to take a step back and come to realize life's true matters. It's not at all about what car you just pulled up in or the square footage of the house you just built. Its true meanings are greater than the width of your wallet and more beautiful than any fake look you just had added to your natural God-given body parts.

God graciously gives us blessings each day, and expects us to respond as grateful and thankful believers. They're intentionally placed there to keep us grounded and remember who is ultimately in control. They come as reminders that show up when we need to be reminded the most. When we feel ungrateful and sorry for ourselves over whatever battle we're in, recognizing these blessings from God is the only true cure. A good hair day (or in most cases a good "scarf" day) can make or break you during such vulnerable times.

Cancer fighters see the light so much brighter, but that comes with dull days, too. Mom found many ways to turn her mind around and to widen her smile a little more. She was all about inspiring others along the way and making any situation tolerable and conquerable.

If you're one who needs examples to understand, well, here are a few from Mom's bag of tricks:

+ Match your eyeshadow to the color of your scarf for the day. Have some fun and venture out from the comfort zone of your usual boring makeup routine.

+ Maybe it's time for the old lipstick tube you shoved to the back of your vanity drawer to come on out and accentuate your ever-so-changing wardrobe.

+ Are your feet swollen with fluid? There is no better time than now to throw on your sparkly, normally-not-okay-to-wear-out-in-public house slippers and just rock them!

+ What better reason to give yourself a relaxing spa day or a much-needed pedicure? I mean when your feet are swollen, half the time you can't reach them anyway, so let the little Chinese ladies do it for you! Go all out and take advantage of the negative!

+ Have you ever wanted red hair or long hair? What about a short blonde bob or luscious thick curls? Fortunately for you, you can. You can even have all of them in the same day if your little heart desires! You know those really sweet and caring women who run the local wig store you never batted an eye at until now? Go see them—they're there for you!

  ◆ If you really want to spice it up, conquer the world as Ginger from *Gilligan's Island* with soft red locks for the morning.

◆ That night before your dinner date, throw a wrench into things and show up as Shirley Temple with those beautiful blonde ringlets, feeling like a brand new woman!

It's hard to live as a person battling cancer ... harder in more ways than one. Now is the time to love it and live it the right way. You can live the life of several people in one particular day and rock the looks for which most women pay loads of money for. In the end, it all works out—right?

CHAPTER 18

POSITIVITY GOES
A LONG WAY

The clinical trial began with a bang. Everybody, Mom included, felt amped up and energized. We were ready to go! This trial felt different than the rest. I personally felt a sense of great hope. The statistics showed positive success in patients like Mom. The fact that she was able to get into this trial really had me feeling reassured that this is the answer. Of course, like with anything else, it came with doubts and risks, but we had dealt with those in the past and came through, so this time was no different in that sense.

During this trial, Mom pushed on strong, putting her positivity and inspiration to good use. Regardless of the strenuous hurdles she had to jump just to get through life, good always came out every time. She received several messages a day from people watching her journey and following her closely. Messages like:

+ You are such a strong willed and energetic woman, I have followed you for years, you got this!

+ You are powerful in words, strength and spirit!

+ You are so amazing, and I love your faith!

+ Pam, you are amazing to me. My regret is not getting to know you better in high school because I missed out! You inspire me to be a better person and to have stronger faith. I pray for you all the time. God is bigger than cancer!

+ You're an overcomer! Our miracle. Always praying for your strength. Love you and everything about you!

+ I am so thankful for our very brief run-in yesterday. Your smile is infectious and as always you are amazing, you got this!

✦ My hands are lifted beyond the clouds! May God bless you and give you the desires of your heart. I have loved you from the moment I met you!

Those are just a few comments that flooded her timeline and inbox over the course of this challenge. Reading them gave her the will to keep going. That positivity vastly spread not only to the community, but to many others who only knew of her or didn't even know her at all. As for me, reading those words expanded the admiration I had for her. It was so inspiring to witness the honest, genuine, and kind words from others about how amazing and strong MY MOTHER was. She was already my hero and now, even though I didn't know it was possible, I grew more thankful to have her as my mom than I ever had before.

As always, life doesn't seem to go quite as planned. She hit times where her lab work didn't come back good enough to start another cycle of chemo. Regardless, her line of sight to the finish line never diminished. She was okay with the fact that something didn't work out at a specific time. There was always a light glowing in each dark room she entered, which was a trait I had a hard time matching. When she was knocked down, she didn't stay there long.

She wasn't able to start Cycle Two due to her neutrophil numbers being too low. Although she missed it by half-of-a-point (and yes, you read that right), she accepted the fact that the doctors must follow strict protocol. She was susceptible to infection at that time and was given another week off before they drew blood from her veins again. As far as the way she felt about that, she didn't mind having an extra week off. She hoped that over the course of those seven days maybe she'd find some relief from the queasiness she'd endured as an annoying side effect from that study drug, the one that she hadn't complained of yet. She continued to rely on her faith in God and the prayers of other family and friends surrounding her. Per her usual routine, she promised to keep the world updated, as they had so often requested.

She battled many rough days and shined during the good ones. She maintained normalcy as best she could, mainly for her grandkids whom she swore blessed her life more than anything else ever did. "I'd keep my natural human selfishness under wraps just to allow my grandchildren to take the limelight," she'd often exclaim.

I've always heard that being a grandparent is truly a rewarding life blessing, but most of the time it's not totally understandable until you become one yourself. You know as well as I do that we've all heard, "Being a grandparent truly is life's biggest blessing. You can love on them and then send them home!" Am I right? I know you've heard that a time or two. Thankfully, I am not a grandparent yet and, quite frankly, I hope that day doesn't come anytime soon! However, I am a parent, and if it's anything like the feeling of your own children having a grandparent like her, then I will gladly welcome that blessing with arms wide open when it comes.

Growing up, my childhood was what I would have considered perfect. Maybe not at the time, but looking back now, it was damn near flawless. My grandparents were very much present in my life and loads of my memories involve them. I had friends who weren't as lucky to go through life with their own grandparents. I had a hard time imagining how life could be so good without them. As you become a parent, naturally you realize you want better for your own kids. God blessed me with kids who have the most perfect grandparents, and I still can't thank Him enough for that.

Mom went along with the trial for several months and for the most part felt great. She made sure to continue her tradition of that annual trip to North Carolina with Vicki. What better way to start the New Year than snowed in with her very best friend in her stunning house in the mountains? She even made a special visit to her brother in North Carolina, and embarked on the "Key West Express" for a memorable weekend with two of her best friends and their husbands. She continued to spread ovarian cancer awareness in every way she knew how. She attended all the grandchildren's events like baseball games, dance recitals, and school award shows. She even organized and put her house up for sale, dealt with her brother being diagnosed with prostate cancer, shared a missing person's awareness for a hometown woman, and then requested prayers for a tragedy-stricken family that she didn't even know!

You see, God asks us to be selfless, not selfish. Most times it's easy for us to be selfish and think of only ourselves, but what good does that really do? Does it even change anything at all? Battling cancer seems to be a good enough reason to me to put yourself first and fight for your own life. I don't consider myself selfish, but being in her shoes, I am quite certain that I'd quickly become that way. However, that is where I was blessed with a mom like her to teach me those lessons. According to the Bible (Philippians 2:3 to be exact), we are to "do nothing out of selfish ambition or conceit, but in humility consider others more important than ourselves."

Maybe that's why Mom always shined so brightly to others who barely knew her. Also, that's possibly why God had blessed her so much during her lifetime. Yes, I did just say that God blessed her, regardless of her cancer diagnosis. Trust me, at times that's difficult to verbally admit. Admitting to that has taken me a long time, and comprehending that there are still blessings in disguise outside of the anger and sadness has taken even longer. Those selfish and uncontrollable feelings can fiercely turn into a spiraling depression if you aren't careful. But Mom was a blessing to the world.

CHAPTER 19

NURSE MOM

*I*n March of 2017, Dad was slapped with the "old man" label after being told that he needed a total hip replacement. Keep in mind that Dad is someone you'd often see walking the boulevard most early mornings, headphones in, with a random wave to any car that passed by honking. He's always been a very active man who takes his health seriously. He was told at a young age that his cholesterol level was extremely high and that if he didn't change his diet right away, he wouldn't make it to the age of thirty.

He didn't have a choice but to completely flip his life in the sense of the foods he chose to eat and the amount of time he put into exercising, because he had triplets to raise and a wife's wrath to deal with if he didn't help. Eventually, the diet change and daily walks became his lifestyle. But now many years later, he's been told he needs a brand new hip, which kind of threw a wrench into things at the time. Shit happens, but the pain he was in proved that it had to be done.

The night before his surgery, Mom called on all her ever-so-loyal prayer warriors to help in lifting him up in prayer for a successful and uncomplicated surgery. I have to be straight forward— this situation was less stressful for me to handle. Leaning on God came easier, truthfully without any question. I just knew God would get Dad through this "minor" surgery because this wasn't like any of Mom's surgeries in the past. His life wasn't on the line, so I thought replacing a hip was "no big deal." It may have been the fact that the focus, for once, was shifted away from cancer. Did it mean that Dad's hip surgery wasn't nearly as important to me as Mom fighting cancer? In one way, yes, but in another, no, not at all. It was less serious because, let's be honest, it was just a hip. This surgery came with minimal recovery time, so a few days in the hospital and he'd be on his way—bionic, but good as new!

Mom still hadn't felt very well during those last few weeks, but with Dad as the focus of our attention and time, she somehow courageously pulled it together. We sat there in the waiting room carrying on conversations about only God knows what, but I was happy. Glancing over and realizing Mom was sitting there with us, I became so thankful that she wasn't the one on the operating table this time. It was a comfort and a peaceful feeling that I hadn't remembered still existed until now.

After a few hours of Rennie's X-rated jokes, Dad was out and doing well. We crammed into his room to visit, taking videos of him high on anesthesia, and rolled our eyes at the stories that the nurses told about what went on between him and all the medical staff this whole time. We tried to stay decent and quiet considering there were many other patients we needed to respect, but we did a horrible job at that. "Ssshhh" Mom would say in between outburst of obnoxious laughing, before she just gave up at the hopes of staying quiet.

Then Dad blurted out, and very loudly I must add, "to the window, to the wall! As the sweat drops down my ..." and well, I'm pretty sure you know how the rest goes. He's quite a jokester and extremely outgoing and blunt, so most of the stories won't go farther than those hospital walls. Even though, unfortunately, the picture etched in our brains of his bare ass shining out the back of his hospital gown as he learned to walk again will haunt us forever. He mooned the whole recovery floor, and I'm almost positive he's proud of it. I know Rennie was!

I looked over at Mom so I could join in the embarrassed, blushing, eye-rolling girl group of the family, but all I saw was her gleaming smile directed his way. Her laugh made me so happy, because even though Dad's ass was most definitely a problem, the rest of her problems and struggles didn't exist right then. She was living in the moment—so caught up in all the "Heath-Family Chaos" that she glowed with pride and true happiness (and well, probably true humiliation, too).

Within a couple of hours, after a few unforgettable scenes, and stomach aches of laughter from the entire east wing of the hospital, Dad was discharged and taken home. Mom went into full nurse duty as she aided in his round-the-clock needs while he perched himself on the couch for the next week. She enjoyed (or maybe not) his constant company for a full week at home, but either way, she loved caring for him, making him meals, and demanding he take his pills in front of her, so she could witness him not throwing them away.

Let me give you an insight: he's a man who absolutely hates just sitting around doing nothing. He can't stand being told just to "relax," because to him, that was extremely boring. I did visit him a few times during that week, but I eventually stayed away, because he was completely lame the longer he sat around and I had no desire to catch the wrath of his boredom. I felt for Mom because she was forced to watch old movies with him—he'd recite every word to since he'd already seen them a thousand times. However, she was by far the best person to put up with him.

Hospitable to all his visitors, she did a great job taking care of him. When we'd call to check up on him, she'd say, "He's doing just fine." It felt so normal, and in a weird way, I liked it. I liked that he was doing well so quickly, and that Mom was well enough to take care of him like she always had. She had it under control. It gave us a glimpse of the "old life" we had well before cancer barged in. I liked it, I longed for it, and I begged God to just leave it that way.

CHAPTER 20

LIFE TRIALS

*A*mid Mom's clinical trial, I was still "technically" working my full-time job in ophthalmology. I say technically, because I was never there. Being in the medical field comes with limited time off. I've never been a fan of having to ask somebody else if I can take time off to do what I want, when I want to do it. It was such an annoying concept.

With what Mom was going through, it made it more difficult to show up for work to take care of my own patients. If it was up to me, which it clearly wasn't, I would have attended every doctor's appointment she ever had, although I did do my fair share of trying to be there. She'd tell me every single-time, "Crystal, I'm fine. It's going to be boring there anyway, so just go to work. I know how to contact you if necessary."

I had to keep myself somewhat grounded, remembering that I was a mom, married with young children who weren't old enough at the time to benefit from free grade school yet. We still had to dish out money for daycare, too, which seemed to be the only reason for slaving away like I did, or at least like I thought I did.

I've never been that person who "lives" at their job. I was there during work hours, but only because I had to be. I'd casually show up about ten minutes late, with Starbucks in hand, assuming that was the "norm" (they should have been used to that by now). Coffee first was my rule of thumb, or else I can't work. However, a whopping two minutes past my clock-in time, I'd get a text from my boss asking me if I was coming to work. Pulling out of the drive-thru, I'd respond with, "I didn't think I had to come today since I just left there yesterday," but she never thought that was funny. At least not until I walked in the backdoor and she was finally able to pick herself up off the floor, because I really did show up to work.

At this point, I had been at my job for seven years, which honestly was about six years and nine months longer than any of my previous jobs, but after seven years I felt it was totally time to retire. I told you the workforce just isn't my thing! I always dreamt of the moms who were able to drop the kids off at school, attend yoga class, hit the grocery store, and throw dinner in the crockpot. Maybe even straighten up the house, fold a load or two of laundry, and plop down on the couch with a glass of wine when Daddy and the kids got home. That seemed like a perfect day in my book, but it was way too far away from my reality at this point, so I stayed on the payroll.

I'd show up and clock in, thinking I was ready to get to work, but I really wasn't there. Physically, yes, but mentally, no—not at all. I knew my life outside the walls of work wasn't grand by any means, but I couldn't control my emotions. I even forgot how to put on a fake smile to my patients coming into my office, because worry was the only thing written on my face and clearly something was wrong. I became angry, resenting everything (including my job), because I felt like nobody had a clue what it was truly like. I was so selfish, like somehow, I thought they should be paying me to spend time with Mom, instead of being stuck in an eye doctor's office for eight hours every day.

Didn't they feel bad for what I was going through? I thought that all too often. I mean, I believed I deserved to keep my same job position at the same pay rate and just not be there for the time being. Unfortunately, that's not quite how it works in the medical field. For a little while, I tried to live that way. I started calling in to work at least once (sometimes twice) a week, because I figured telling them I was "sick" meant there was nothing they could do about it.

Instead, I'd spend the day with Mom, because you can't do anything when someone wakes up sick—right? Wrong! They labeled me with the "unreliable" employee stamp that nobody really wants in a career, but sadly, I couldn't blame them. I was very unreliable and, depending on the day, would totally determine my presence. It wasn't fair to them when I didn't show up and it wasn't fair to them when I did, because I simply didn't care about anything but Mom. She encouraged me every time about going in to work and, although I valued her opinion, that's just not what I wanted to do.

Lying is hard, even when your intentions are good. It's even harder when it's about something you can't control. I felt lost, falling into deep sorrow and depression as I saw her fight against cancer. My lies and fake excuses haunted me, when they started becoming real. I called out of work more and more, but now these times, I was truly sick. I'd wake up with stomachaches and headaches and feel so shitty that now I couldn't even spend time with Mom either.

It was an all-around miserable time when those "days off" turned into sick days that I had to spend alone in bed. I was spiraling out of control, without any strength to get my shit together. I finally applied for FMLA at work, as a safeguard, which was good and bad. It was good in the sense that I could now "plan" my days off and, no matter how many times I wasn't at work, I couldn't lose my job because of it. Plus, my boss couldn't yell at me now, since she knew I was technically "allowed" to call in sick. It was bad because that gave me an even more legit reason to take advantage of the system, which justified my absence and the days I longed to be with Mom.

"I have to go to Moffitt in the morning and since you can take some time off now, would you want to go with me?" Mom asked.

"Um, yes!" I chimed in, making her realize that her request was totally a no-brainer. I woke up the following morning feeling so happy and all of a sudden not sick, which was super weird. I felt fine! The sun hadn't even come up yet when my alarm went off. Most days, I'd hit snooze about twelve different times, but not this morning! I felt happy and optimistic that this drug "progress report" was going to come back with great news, and I felt motivated and excited to spend the day with just the two of us. It hadn't been that way for a long time, since you know some people have to work their life away. I was ready to go well before the crack of dawn!

I came barreling through Mom's front door like I always did and saw her rushing around the kitchen searching desperately for her coffee creamer as her mug overflowed with decaf coffee under the Keurig. Awkwardly talking to the dogs that were standing directly under her feet, they just kept staring at her, knowing that she was about to leave and there was a pretty good chance they weren't going with her. I couldn't help but stand there and laugh at the beautiful mess she was. It was totally chaotic, but it was cute when she'd insist, "If we don't leave now, we are going to be late!" However, "late" was typical, although she couldn't stand ever admitting that.

We headed out to her car, and I quickly realized that, instead of parking anywhere else in the big empty driveway, I had to park directly behind her car. We were nervous wrecks, but quickly turned all those feelings into jokes and laughter to help lighten the mood and cope with the news that we might receive at her appointment. She thought it'd be funny to show me just how awesome she was at the fact she could get her car out in one piece without me having to move mine back even just twelve inches, that very well could have gotten us out safely and in a timely manner.

Just picture this, a Jeep Grand Cherokee tightly wedged between the brick exterior wall of her house and the front of my Audi parked closely behind her as she started to finagle her way out. She reversed a few times, put the car in drive, moved forward a few more inches and repeated that about thirty-five times, while she turned the steering wheel left and right in between each gear shift. Not to mention the number of times she stuck her head out of the driver-side window to verify she indeed had plenty of room to prove her point. "Mom, are you sure you don't want me to just move my car?" I asked her.

She laughed and said, "No! Just watch! You'll see!" Not only did I keep watching her, but I also kept watching the clock tick by, knowing that by now, we were definitely going to be late, but this was way too funny not to be recording.

She'd be proud to hear me admit to you that she did, in fact, make it out without plowing into the side of the house or putting even a single scratch on either of our cars. You're welcome, Mom, I told them, and we are all very proud of your insane talent.

At this point, there was not even a minute to spare, so the coffee that I had intended to grab along the way that actually contained caffeine (unlike hers), wasn't going to happen now. I turned down her offer of sharing her coffee, because seriously, who drinks decaf anyway? However, I did take her up on splitting half of her Special-K cereal bar that tasted just as bland and disgusting as I could have imagined her coffee might have tasted.

Forty-five minutes later, we finally made it to Moffitt. She gave me the grand tour from the second we pulled onto the property until the time we hopped out of the car in the valet line at the front entrance.

That was my first time to go there with her, so I was a little shocked to see valet at a place like that. I thought either Mom was totally VIP, or they just knew valet would make everybody's life easier. Most likely, it was that Mom was VIP, but either way, it was pretty cool.

We laughed at each other as we walked the bright white halls, just as the sun was coming up. Carrying on our conversation, I slowly trailed behind her without her realizing she had started talking to herself. When she turned around to look for me, I told her, "OK, Mom, stop there and just stare out that window for a second, so I can get your picture."

She rolled her eyes and said, "Crystal, this is not a photoshoot." She tried convincing me not to take the shot, but it didn't work.

"Mom, hush, just do it and don't look at me." It was then that I snapped one of my favorite photos of her ever. And by the way, despite feeling caught off guard and uncomfortable, she modeled for those pictures like a pro. She did perfect—check it out for yourself, it's on the back of this book!

That was the moment I stopped to stare. While she thought I was still snapping pictures, I looked in awe at how pretty she was. Not only was she there awaiting uncertain results of this clinical trial in which she'd vulnerably taken part, but she's made this morning so special already because to her, life just really isn't that serious. She showed me without realizing it that life doesn't have to be this big ball of negativity that you carry around with you everywhere you go. Even though we were there for reasons we didn't appreciate, it was still another day spent together, regardless of the location, and another opportunity to make memories together that will last a lifetime.

It confirmed the real truth behind her mantra, "Cancer doesn't define me," and she showed me that without realizing it. Damn right it doesn't define her, because with or without cancer, she's still such a joyous, inspirational, and happy person! She drinks disgusting decaf coffee, has mad skills at backing a blocked car out, but she was someone anyone would be incredibly lucky to have in their life.

We were finally taken to the exam room, which seemed more like an interrogation room (not that I've ever been in one, but I have seen all the crime shows ever made). We waited for the doctor, who was going to discuss the results of this trial and how well this drug was working for her. We sat there beside each other in a close-knit corner and continued to laugh, snapping selfies of us together. In the middle of our laughs, as the camera shutter got stuck, we wondered if and when it was even taking pictures, we then realized the doctor had already walked in and sat down.

"Oh, good morning," Mom said, feeling a tad embarrassed.

"Good morning, Mrs. Heath," he replied, laughing. Mom introduced him to me, and he quickly responded, "It's nice to meet you, Crystal." I was quick to judge him, just by his look and demeanor.

"You, too," I said as I stared at him with a hopeful smile and judgmental eyes. I was trying to telepathically relay the message to him that he had "better give us good news or else!"

As the conversation started to unfold, it didn't go anywhere close to what I had expected. I awkwardly felt as if not just *her* fate, but *our* fate was unfairly put into the hands of this man sitting in front of us. It was an uneasy realization.

He suddenly began his report, "Mrs. Heath, unfortunately," (boy, he had no problem getting right to the point) "due to disease progression, it is necessary at this time to pull you from this clinical trial. Your CT results showed more metastasis, and all the lesions that you had have increased significantly."

As he kept talking, his voice faded. I glanced over at Mom while she kept her composure, so I grabbed her hand and held on tight. My heart started pounding erratically and I clenched my jaw, throwing daggers his way from my eyes that screamed, "How dare you!" I officially hated this man! He obviously didn't get the memo of delivering only good news to her. I believed he was incompetent and was reading results from another patient's chart—those weren't the results he was supposed to give her. My mom, you know, the beautiful and hopeful person sitting so close to me that I could now feel her heart pounding, too! She doesn't deserve any of this, yet still sits there like a champ listening to his bullshit.

She sat there hiding her emotions, while I was clearly not hiding mine. I was pissed off as I began to sink back in my chair when the tears started to gather in my eyes, feeling like he had just punched us in the heart. Mom sat there so confident, calm, and positive, because she was already prepared and had planned to receive this type of news. He laid out on the table a few secondary options that he could offer her, like how she could try yet another trial involving a different type of drug along with infusion chemo. That option was a Phase One Trial, which basically meant it was a "guinea pig trial." Right then, Mom spared him his breath and made it clear that she wanted absolutely no part of that. The second option he proposed was to take another specific chemo drug as a single agent, while the third one was to take that same drug along with another medication called Avastin.

I perked up at that option, because I was familiar with Avastin. Working in ophthalmology, it was used daily in our clinic for patients with uncontrolled diabetes and macular degeneration. I felt that since this medication was something I'd been around every day, perhaps that was the best option for her. I could consult with my doctor at work and, along with her oncologist, we could all come up with the perfect cure for the cancer that kept trying to take her from our lives.

It sounded like a good alternative to me, considering it was the only one about which I felt I had any knowledge. When she showed some interest in it, he explained to her, "Taking Avastin along with chemo can increase the benefits by forty percent." We felt hope, since forty percent was good news at this point and I could finally breathe.

That was until he kicked our hope back down to the floor again saying, "However, the drawback to that is bowel perforation!" What an asshole. Of course, I realize now that he was just doing his job, but seriously, that was a jerk move. Nobody is going to jump at such a shitty option, knowing they might perforate their bowels on top of fighting cancer. That's the cause of all this in the first place! I shut down, feeling defeated and hopeless that nobody was helping my mom. After that horrendous discussion I'll never forget, we left feeling extremely bummed. I can only personally speak for myself, but I know Mom, even with all her positive reasoning, felt the same way.

At this point, she now had five lines of treatment, so that disqualified her from any further Phase Two or Phase Three trials and her standard options were narrowing. You hear me? N-A-R-R-

O-W-I-N-G!

You know that feeling that you instantly get when you hear that a loved one of yours has cancer? That horrid thought of "Great, now they're going to die!" That nauseating, gut-wrenching, and inevitable feeling that naturally accompanies the word, "cancer," was ruthlessly resurfacing.

I was left feeling cheated, as if this trial had just robbed us of the happy and amazing morning we had just experienced together. Spending time with her, no matter where we were, was always my favorite thing to do, but I felt gipped of that now. How can God just sit there and watch us together, singing together in the car, laughing together, telling jokes, and goofing around, yet still end our morning this way? What else does He expect from her, someone who has done everything He's ever asked her to do? He still throws these mile-high boulders in her path that she has to try and climb while staying faithful and optimistic, with dwindling strength to even keep up?

As I stared out the passenger window, my head was filling with anger and confusion. When I felt her hand touch my knee, I didn't know what to say or if there was even anything that I could do but pray to God right now. That wasn't very high on my priority list any more, not after today. "It's all going to be okay, honey," she told me in her calm motherly voice.

She asked me to check her text messages while she drove us home. Reading them out loud to her, I realized that everybody was worried about the results she had just received. However, when they learned the news, I was the one to whom they turned. Her family and friends had known I went with her and they wanted to know how I was doing and how I took the news. She wouldn't let me respond with my true feelings, so she told me to set the phone down and she would call them back when we got home. That was probably a good idea, because there's no telling how I would have responded, which would have never helped anybody else cope with such shitty news.

She arrived home with a head full of information, ready to ponder on and research what her next step should be. She reached out for advice, prayers, and uplifting inspiration, while relying heavily on her faith to answer the question of, "Where do I go next?" Before making any definite decisions, she wanted to go back to her original oncologist to discuss her feelings with him in hopes of gaining his personal and professional advice. That was an appointment I was not going to miss, because I wanted to make sure I voiced my not-so-professional-yet-very-emotional-I'm-not-going-to-lose-my-Mom demands.

Mom, Dad, Meagan, and I attended that appointment, because, well, you know it was another one of those days when I just didn't make it into work. We sat in the waiting room, four-deep in the corner, where the three of them carried on a conversation that I couldn't hear, because my hearing was diminishing fast, as I was sitting directly under the speaker of a blaring TV. They got up when her name was called, but I quickly realized I was being left behind. I hadn't heard her name called, since I was suffering from acute hearing loss. I ran to catch up as they piled into the exam room. Mom climbed up on the uninviting patient "lounger," while Dad grabbed a stool and pushed it to the back corner of the room but still at Mom's side. Meagan sat in the only extra chair, so I made myself at home on the tile floor against the wall, Indian style, in front of Mom.

When the doctor came in, he was very happy to see her. To him, she was a patient who always brought light and a breath of fresh air into his hectic and demanding day. She's the type of person that makes you feel at home, even when you're at work. Unless you're me, then you don't want to be at work when you know she's at home. She was just good at making any situation comfortable, but she always stayed very open and honest, yet stubborn most of the time. He knew her and she knew him, so he didn't sugarcoat his professional advice and Mom didn't sugarcoat her opinions, like ever. So together, they made a great team.

We discussed the sad fact that the clinical trial was now over for her, but how she'd left with a few options from the doctor at Moffitt. She explained to him that even with those options, because she had so much trust in him, she wanted to discuss them together before making any final decisions.

He shared his professional opinion on the benefits and very real drawbacks of each option before he dropped this charmer, "Honestly, Pam, I don't feel that there are many options left for you at this point." And here we go again! Mom immediately faced me with a look that she knew I'd know was silently telling me, "Crystal, don't say a word."

I felt myself starting to dislike this doctor, whom I once thought I liked. My focus on the conversation blurred as I blocked the rest out, trying to comprehend what he had just told her. I tried to stay focused on her face and watch how she reacted to all this nonsense. Wouldn't you know it, she stayed very calm again. In fact, she was nodding as if she agreed with these absurd facts. He talked about the "benefits" of stopping all lines of treatment and how in making that decision, it would allow her to enjoy her life as much as she possibly could.

Not only had I just overheard more shocking bad news, but now the doctor she trusts the most just told her that perhaps stopping all treatment was best. I couldn't believe what was happening! Why would he recommend that to her? Then they started discussing her quality of life. Her wishes from the very beginning were to maintain that as long as she possibly could.

I felt like her quality of life was great. I mean, she's still doing her twenty-three hours of "bill paying." She still kicked ass as the best mom on the face of the planet, and she literally hung the moon for all her grandkids. I didn't understand why this was even in the mix of questions about her fate and future life. I thought eventually, I'm just going to wake up to my annoying alarm clock, telling me to get my ass up and get ready for work.

But that didn't happen. Unfortunately, it was a nightmare that was very real. The questions kept coming, but nobody was answering them. It started sounding like everybody believed this journey was over, but it wasn't, not at all. "Maybe I'm just overreacting or interpreting this all wrong," I thought, as my attention went back to their discussion.

"The three options that were presented to you at Moffitt are good options, but to be blatantly honest (great, here we go again), "I think there is too much risk involved with those lines of therapy. At this point, I don't believe that is in your best interest," he told her. It wasn't a dream.

I shook my head back and forth, speechless now. "I agree," she replied. What is going on here? Doesn't anybody care what we think? What about our feelings and input on the fate of our mother's life? Unfortunately, that kind of decision wasn't about the rest of us and our feelings. Yes, all her decisions were based solely around her family, but leaving a decision of that magnitude up to me or my sisters and brother, or even Dad just wasn't our place to make.

I had to sit back and forcefully take it all in, remembering it's my mom who we were talking about. I listened to her discuss her potential fate and if anything else was out there that could possibly help her. I tried doing what Mom taught me and prayed. I prayed to God while I sat on that tile floor, explaining to Him that I believed He was in control and that I just knew He was going to take care of her. I tried convincing myself that those feelings were true, but deep down, I had so much doubt. Have you ever tried to talk yourself into something you believe is completely false? That's how I felt at this moment.

I still hung onto the hope I had, believing that God wasn't done with her. His intentions are to keep her here for many more years, and that this is just another setback that she's going to get through. Mom sat there in agreement, seemingly at ease with this discussion. Dad sat in the corner looking disturbed and questioning, but still had Mom's best interest at heart. Meagan focused intently, listening to all his advice, but she seemed open-minded about this, too. I sat there confused, sad, and miserable. I watched as Mom remained positive, knowing she had every intention of tackling whatever was coming her way.

They talked about the means of life, and he shared tips on living with little to no pain. I looked at Mom, trying to learn something from her behavior and reactions, so I could be supportive and helpful. She kept her cool and even laughed at times. I tried keeping my cool, too, somewhat, but in no way was I laughing.

The doctor continued, "If you don't continue with any treatment, but instead choose to live your life the best possible way that you can … well, I don't like to put a time frame on things, but …"

There's no way he's going there right now, I thought as I began to really get upset.

Side note: one thing I always appreciated about her doctor was the fact that nobody, ever, put a time frame on her disease.

By the looks of it, I think he's about to go there and it's not going to be good. I'd advise you to stop now, Doc!

He didn't stop and Mom looked at me, knowing how this was about to go.

"To give you an idea, I believe"—wait for it—"you have ... LESS THAN A YEAR."

What in the hell just happened? I couldn't believe what I just heard!

"Did he really just say that?" I asked in front of the entire room. It made things awkward and slightly uncomfortable, as I immediately dished out my feelings with no filter.

Although the doctor told her she didn't have long, she just smiled and shook her head. Everybody knows "less than a year" flies by, but all she said was, "Bring it on."

I felt like the plug on my inner emotions had just been pulled. I suddenly didn't feel anything, except ruthless, fuming anger! I became instantly nauseous, and my heart and soul felt so painful it was worthless. The world around me became dark, leaving me feeling like there was no purpose to keep moving forward after what I'd just heard. I was stone cold and my eyebrows dipped down in disbelief towards my nose, as I clenched my hands in fists, grabbed my purse, and stormed out of the room. I couldn't have left any quicker. They came out a few minutes later to find me leaned up against the wall in the hallway staring cold-heartedly at a hand-painted cancer ribbon framed on the wall, knowing I wanted to smash it.

I heard Mom still conversing with the doctor as they both exited. I knew even though there had just been so much bad news that I was trying to process, I couldn't show that in front of her. But I couldn't think at all, much less figure out how to show support during this moment that she'd most likely need me the most. I felt empty and heartbroken—I couldn't handle this any longer.

Mom walked into the restroom, as I looked over at Dad and Meagan. They stood there and stared at me. I could tell they were wondering if they should try to console me or let this ticking time bomb explode, hopefully before Mom walked back out. They saw tears in my eyes, just like in theirs, so nothing was said. Mom walked out of the restroom as I desperately wiped my face and looked around to find signs that would lead me out of this hell hole before she witnessed how devastated I really was.

The clinic was empty and almost everyone had gone home. I was determined to get out of there, so I blindly groped my way through the maze of old ugly waiting room chairs, yellow wooden check-in desks, and overly faded expired magazines. I was lost, yet somehow walked on in a trail of hurt to eventually find my way to the elevators labeled with a steel wall plaque loaded with useless information.

I was mad at the world and at the fact that nobody was there to help me find my way out. What kind of customer service is that? With all the money they're collecting from every cancer patient who walks in these doors full of hope, that just gets ripped to shreds, I must add, that they should at least be able to afford exit signs, damn it! I was angry that the elevator took so long, considering the clinic was almost empty. I even became annoyed at the sound of the elevator bell when it hit the ground floor.

We walked out into the atrium of the clinic, and I suddenly felt the sweetest arms wrap around my shoulders. It was Mom. "You weren't expecting to hear that, were you?" she asked me. I looked at her, hopeless and hurt, but continued to beeline my way to the parking lot. "If you think I'm scared, you got me all wrong," she told me, as I oddly searched for our car in an extremely unpacked parking lot with a total of three cars.

When I broke down, she grabbed my hand and insisted I continue moving forward with her to Dad's Jeep. We stopped as we reached his car, and she engulfed me in the tightest hug of my life. I lost it, crying the tears I had tried so hard to hold in, but I couldn't anymore. I had tried to stay so strong for her all day. Even in my angriest moments, I didn't lash out like I wanted to, but right now I was weak. The sincerity of her hug made me crumble and I couldn't be strong anymore. She was my home.

"Honey, I know you weren't expecting to hear that," she said. "In fact, I wish he wouldn't have said that while you were in the room. Remember, God is the only one in control. Only He knows the plan for me and for any of us. The doctor was just giving me his opinion based on the studies and statistics, but that's his job. I could go before that or I could go well after that, but nobody knows. You just need to remain positive and remember to place your faith and trust in God, just like I do!"

She was right, but at that moment, I didn't feel like I had anything left to lean on. "We are all going to go at some point in our lives and nobody here on Earth can ever predict when that will happen," she continued. "Crystal, I will never give up, but when the time comes, the good Lord is waiting!"

Her words meant everything to me, but I couldn't believe we had gotten to a place in our lives when those words needed to be said. "So how can the doctor tell you such a thing?" I asked her, "I don't agree with him at all. He doesn't know anything, much less, when you won't be here anymore. The fact is, he said he doesn't like to put timeframes on anything, but he still did, which is so wrong!"

"Baby, I know, but you have to keep moving forward like I do, because nobody will ever know," she said, trying to comfort me and put an end to my pitiful parking lot meltdown.

I knew from that day on I'd wake up every damn day, wondering if that was going to be her last day. I knew I'd end up putting a countdown on her life. Every day, I'd be thinking something like, "Now I only have this many days left with her." That's an awful way to live. How dare he tell Mom that! The pain and remorse I felt from attending that appointment is something hard to explain, when on the contrary, what I had wanted to do all along was attend every appointment with her.

She called me that night before I went to bed to check on me. She told me to completely put everything he said out of my head. She said, "Block it out and let it be."

I listened to her advice and held it close. I eventually learned to shrug it off every time the thought of her dwindling life on earth crossed my mind. Somehow, I continued to make it day by day. I was scared but, for her sake, I continued to push on, only because I still had Mom right next to me.

CHAPTER 21

EASTER

*F*or someone trying to keep their composure and hold their life together as it crumbles in their hands, I might not have any great advice on how to do that. However, a tip I can give you right now is what *not* to do. If you're trying to avoid any type of situation or scenario that leaves you feeling overwhelmed and totally outnumbered—well, don't take your kids to the grocery store like I did.

Easter was that weekend when my family gets together for a fun-filled, *eggstatic* Sunday each year it hops back around. I realized by Friday though, that I hadn't been grocery shopping for anything I was supposed to bring to fill my side of the charcuterie board that sprawls across each counter of the kitchen where we gather! I frantically texted my husband, asking him to pick up the kids, so in peace and quiet I could grab the few things I needed on my way home.

Taking my two boys to the grocery store is something that's *never* excited me, and I'll tell you why. If you're a mom, chances are you will understand. However, if you aren't there yet, or if your kids are the epitome of perfection, here's some insight for you.

Each trip I make to our local Publix is either amusing to shoppers around me, or completely annoying and judgmental by some, *who I'm sure never take their children into a grocery store*. It works like clockwork every time. I start out threatening them with their lives, just as I put the car in park, telling them not to touch a single item on any shelf in the entire store. After I get two "Yes, ma'am" responses, we'd walk in holding hands, feeling quite confident that this trip was going to be so much better than the last. "Maybe my threat *this time* will actually seep a tad further into their little brains."

"We got this," I'd think—just as they start arguing over which one of them was going to push the shopping cart. Then I break the news to them that neither one of them is going to do that, since they're *both* getting inside it. Having been in the building for a total of fifty-eight seconds, I'm already re-threatening them, because they've grabbed something off the very first display in our path, exclaiming "Mommy, it's free!" They completely ignored the BUY ONE, GET ONE printed in the display, before that very attractive and capitalized, bold word **FREE**! They grab it, while I pretend to be calm, because we are just walking in. I tell them, "We're only going to be in here a few minutes, so we don't need to buy that right now, boys, because nothing is free!"

Ladies and gentlemen, right here is when the first full-on tantrums of the trip begin *smack in the middle of the bakery.* I always figure that if I just ignore them and walk away, it'll stop, because the attention is only going to make things worse—right? After a few embarrassing seconds of screaming, I bargain with them that they can have a cookie only if they behave and sit quietly until we're finished shopping.

They seem pleased, chowing down on their sprinkled sugar cookies. I now feel like I have this whole parenting thing under control. That is until I zip down the chips aisle and mom-of-the-year over here to my left has given *her child* a snack to keep quiet! *Thanks, Karen, now all of a sudden, my kids are starving to death!* The protein bar and raw almonds in my purse suddenly don't sound the least bit appetizing to them, because *why should any of this work out in my favor in the first place?*

During the beginning of tantrum number two, I remind them to use their inside voice or we will be kicked out. Then the bakery will throw every cookie that they ever made into the trash can on our way out. As if that line doesn't scream, "Yeah, right!" loud enough, they shrug that off and continue on with their own bargaining tactics. I give in, because quite frankly at this point, I'm starting to freak out!

I grab the nearest bag of goldfish and tell them they can open it before we buy it, if they'll just sit there and play the quiet game until we're done. As I rush around, grabbing the few things I came to buy, I scour out the shortest checkout line. Wouldn't you know, this is the perfect time for my kids to say, "We swear we will share this whole container of mints with you and each other, if you'll buy it for us, just this once, Mommy!" Great, now I have to break it to them that I'm not going to do that.

Well, cue the waterworks. Right now I don't care who is watching or how loud they're crying. I finally get to the end of the line and start to pay for my things, while my children remain completely inconsolable. You'd think their world was ending. People are starting to stare again, and now I wish they'd stop judging my parenting skills. In this moment of weakness, I finally decide to throw in that container of mints and justify my reasoning later.

I rush to the car, buckle them into their car seats, and hop into the driver seat, feeling defeated, outnumbered, and totally taken advantage of. Then I call up Mom, explaining to her how the boys misbehaved during what was supposed to be a quick trip, making me look like such a bad mom. She always thought it was funny, but what annoyed me even more was when she would say something like, "Honestly, Crystal, I don't feel bad for you at all. I remember trying to do that with four kids at once, three of whom were the exact same age!" That is why I choose to conquer the grocery store completely and peacefully solo! *Take my advice on this one and try it. You'll thank me later, I swear!*

The next time, I did just that. Thankfully, hubby wasn't in a meeting for once and was actually able to pick them up this time. I ran into a pleasure-filled Publix, grabbed the few things I needed for Easter and made it home in no time. No tantrums, spent a good $100 less, NO MINTS, and I was even able to grab a bottle of Caymus wine on the way out. *Pure Joy!*

Easter at Meagan's that year came fully stocked with deviled eggs, ham, green beans, fruit, carrot cake, about six cases of beer, and probably nine bottles of wine. *Totally normal.*

Garnishing the dishes with their final touches, kids running around the house, TV blaring, dogs barking, and Mom making a cozy spot in the corner of the couch to place Grandma in for the rest of the day, it was completely insane, but it was us. With all the hustle and bustle going on, it was easy to miss things here and there. However, I didn't miss the fact that to me, Mom didn't seem to feel very good. Anytime I noticed her not acting like herself, even if she denied that anything was wrong, I'd get worried and become quiet. I tended to close off conversations and shut down, trying to figure out what was wrong with her.

I tried everything, like asking her if she needed anything or if she wanted me to make her a plate of the homemade banana pudding that she couldn't wait to dig into. I cuddled next to her with my shoes off and feet up to the side as I leaned into her tiny shoulder like I was a small child again. "I haven't been able to eat anything for the last few days, because I can't keep it down," she said.

That was all it took to remind me of the horror behind the doctor's assumption that she only has less than a year to live. I wondered if this was the start of it. Why is this happening to my mom? I couldn't believe that he actually might be right.

I tried to stay calm, but inside I was terribly worried. I didn't like to see her not feeling well or knowing that anything at all was bothering her. She had always looked forward to getting together with her family for all the holidays, but this holiday wasn't the same. She wasn't even able to eat any of the food for dinner and never once tried the banana pudding.

My heart started breaking, knowing there wasn't anything that *anybody* could do to make her feel better. She was miserably hungry, but even more uncomfortable just sitting there, and a mix of both, which made for one bad Easter.

We tried to steer the attention away from the fact that she obviously didn't feel good by rounding up the kids and getting their baskets ready to go outside to hunt eggs. I grabbed Mom's phone to take pictures, so when she got home, she could look through them and relive the laughter and happy moments with the grandchildren. But then she said to Dad, "I need a chair to sit in outside while they hunt for eggs." I knew right then something was terribly off. She was never the type of person to sit and watch the kids—ever! She was always the one who joined them and made it so much more fun and interesting. She was the "coolest Memaw ever!" that, without a doubt, made every grandchild so excited about whatever it was they were doing together. She was silly and always the biggest reason behind all their little giggles.

After we sat her in a chair outside, I began snapping pictures of the kids, but I kept turning my attention back to *her* every few minutes. I couldn't have fun knowing something was wrong with her, and it was hard for the others, too. I tried to fill her footsteps a little by joining in the egg hunt like she would, but it wasn't the same. The only thing that did remain the same was the kids' laughter as they scoured the yard.

Rennie being Rennie showed off his true colors by placing an Easter egg on top of dog poop and betting on which kid would be the one to pick it up. However, Mom quickly picked up on what he did.

"Rennie," she yelled at him from the other side of the yard, "that's disgusting! Move that right now!" She was laughing slightly, but obviously trying to hide it, but nobody listened. We knew it'd be funny placing bets on which kid grabbed that brown egg. It was too bad Katie wasn't hunting for eggs that year, because she most definitely would have been the one to fall for that one!

Shortly after the egg hunt, we crammed back into the house with baskets full of candy. While the kids spread their candy out all through the living room, we continued to snap pictures and memories of another Easter together. We could tell that Mom was trying her hardest to have fun and enjoy herself, but the pain seemed unbearable, especially when she decided to go home not long after that. Thanks to cancer, it put quite the damper on our Easter that year. I know God has a plan, but that was a terrible plan!

CHAPTER 22

ROOM 106

*W*e survived Easter, but the worried feelings were something none of us could shake, especially after getting a text from Meagan the next morning in our ongoing family text group labeled; "Fam Jam," saying, "I just wanted to let you all know that Mom spoke with the doctor this morning. He wants to admit her to the hospital, because she still isn't able to eat anything and keep it down. They are going to run tests on her to try and figure out what is going on," she said.

As soon as I started typing to let her know that I was cancelling all my plans for the day and was about to head that way, she beat me to it. She texted,

> No need to come to the hospital right now, since we haven't even left her house yet. Once we get there and she is settled in her room, I will let you know when you can come and where she will be."

Appreciate it, Sis, but really? "I'm heading there now," I said aloud to myself, as I put the phone down. I couldn't go about my day with my so-called plans, knowing that Mom was being admitted to the hospital and that I was just supposed to wait for permission to go. *Spoiler alert, I didn't wait.*

I parked quickly, not paying much attention to where, since Mom wouldn't be here that long this time. In hindsight, *I could have made my life a lot easier if I didn't have to search the entire premises of the hospital grounds looking for my car later!* Needless to say, I was in a daze—more in denial that something was really wrong, but mostly oblivious to the reality of it all. I tried to talk myself into thinking I was feeling calm and positive, but the second the glass sliding doors whooshed open and the cold hospital air hit my face like a ton of bricks, so did my uneasy emotions of being here once again.

I walked past the small coffee counter, with a very generic and whopping four options on the Starbucks menu that I seemed to live on the last time I was here. I made my way to the sixth floor, where I stood facing a big wooden door. I grabbed the metal L-shaped handle and came to a halt, mumbling a quick, "Lord let this be nothing," and then walked in. Mom was sitting up in the bed already having a conversation with a few visitors. *I'm not quite sure how anybody else beat me there,* but no matter what happened now, I was there to stay.

Not minding Mom's numerous visitors, the nurses came in and out, checking vitals and hooking her up to random IVs while we entertained her company. Once the afternoon concluded and shift change started, our family of six was all that was left.

"We need to all sit down and have a very important discussion, just us as a family," Dad said. I always felt like that was never good, partly because any time we had a "family discussion" before, things were very serious. "Sit down," Dad demanded as he pulled up a chair next to Mom. Rennie and Meagan sat in front of her bed. Katie had just gotten off work at the same hospital so she was still in her scrubs. She plopped herself up on a counter in the room, while I stood there looking around. "Crystal, find a seat," I was told. So I crawled up onto the bed with Mom. Hospital beds aren't very large, usually being sized just big enough to fit yourself and *maybe* two pillows, but *shocking*, I found a way to squeeze in next to her and grabbed her hand.

"I wanted you all here to discuss the options that I have," Mom began. The conversation we had between the six of us that night was a private discussion that I won't share, but what I will tell you is that we concluded Mom was to proceed with a much-needed surgery. It was highly anticipated as successful, but very risky. A tumor was blocking her small intestine, preventing any food or fluids from going down. Considering the cancer metastasis and sudden onset of malnutrition, which was rapidly growing with each minute that passed, saying it was *very necessary* would be quite an understatement. The doctor's intention was to section off a piece of her intestine in hopes of bypassing the tumor, so she'd be able to eat and drink again.

To have an extensive surgery like that, you must have all your ducks in a row before proceeding. However, the next morning her ducks were far from being in a straight line. Her blood platelet level had plummeted to 33, which was entirely too low for any surgery to be done.

Therefore, they delayed the operation, and instead gave her more platelets to replenish what was lost in preparation for the surgery. The next day, not only had her body rejected the new platelets, but her levels were even lower, now down to 15! It was a trying and emotional process, bouncing back and forth day to day trying to flood Mom's body with healthy levels of platelets, enough to have the surgery she needed. It became very discouraging because her body wasn't reacting the way it should have. They gave her two more bags of platelets that day, only to find out that night not only had her levels continued to decline, regardless of all the extras, but now her hemoglobin had gone down with it.

That wasn't at all what was supposed to be happening! I didn't understand how we could be in a hospital with all these doctors of vast expertise and countless means of making *any* patient better than they were when they came in. Sadly, the surgery at this point was cancelled. Not only was she still starving for any type of food, but she was starving for hope, just like the rest of us. Being told to just relax and wait in that situation was not easy by any stretch.

Mom met with a very sweet and young hematologist-oncologist the next morning, who strongly felt that her rapidly decreasing blood levels were caused by all the lines of chemo she had gone through. "There's a good chance, due to the amount of chemotherapy you've had, that your body is just taking longer to recover," she told Mom.

We waited days for good news, but the more we waited, the more her body negatively reacted. Even after being given a medication called "Neupogen," which was to help her bone marrow reproduce at a faster rate, she was given even more units of blood and antibiotics through an IV pump, only to find out that now the risk of infection in her body had greatly increased due to her deficient white blood cell count.

Banning all visitors to her room was a hard decision to make, but we had to do it. Being confined to a hospital room, the visitors seem to be the only thing you could look forward to, because the TV shows get repetitive and boring after being forced to watch them while you suffer from aches and pains, and become stiff after being cocooned in those faded off-white sheets for days.

Unfortunately, we also had to put a stop to all her flower deliveries as well, which piled in more and more as the days went by. What a nice gesture it is to have huge bouquets of roses and daisies brighten your cold and dark hospital room. Just like living the rest of this journey with positivity and happiness seemingly dwindled, so did the joy and brightness from the flowers. It was a low blow to her self-esteem, but we continued to stay by her side. We weren't going anywhere.

The next day, I actually stopped by that fake Starbucks in the lobby and ordered a large coffee with extra espresso, just to be able to spend the whole day at the foot of her bed, watching her doze on and off in the dark. I spent it shopping online and watching reruns of *Family Feud*, trying desperately to avoid responding to all the missed calls and text messages I had gotten for several days that I purposely ignored. I felt like if I didn't respond to them with the way things were going down, then maybe it wasn't really true, because the truth hurts much worse having to physically verbalize it.

It was getting late by now and I knew I needed to go home to my little family. She was lying there sleeping so well and I didn't want to wake her, so I stood there watching her breathe. She looked so beautiful. *Like, nobody looks that beautiful when they sleep—most definitely not me! Usually I'm all over the place, with a big messy bun on top of my head. Sometimes I even wake up with makeup still on my face from the night before.* Mom, though, looked stunning. She lay there peacefully, with a cute scarf smoothly wrapped around her head and face. She was all cuddled up with her pillow that she'd slept with for many years, while she rested under her own teal blanket from home. All while the IV pump next to her did its thing in her right-hand vein.

I thought for the first time, in what seemed like weeks, how extremely blessed I really was. I'll be the first to admit, feeling that way never came easy to me when things weren't going in our favor, but right now, it was easy. I thanked God for her after realizing how special she is to so many people and just how many prayers and thoughts were out there being spent on her! When you read over five hundred notifications and comments on each social media update and see each post being shared at a *minimum* of twenty times, I guess it's hard not to feel so blessed having an inspirational and loved woman in your life that you're lucky enough to call "Mom."

Her doctors were working overtime to come up with a solution that could help her. Many other doctors would stop by her room just to meet her, and some even made calls from the operating room just to check in. It was like she had become quite a celebrity around the hospital, one that three different pastors came just to be able to pray over her from outside the door.

Those feelings of gratefulness and inspiration only lasted for a short while because, unfortunately, the anger that I felt at this time seemed much worse. I didn't understand why God placed this woman who was loved by so many in that hospital bed to suffer. It was so wrong. It was a rollercoaster of trying faith and relentless emotions, *and I hate rollercoasters!* I felt so lucky, yet shattered. Lucky knowing that God gave her to me, that beautiful soul in room 106, but shattered knowing there's a disease trying very hard to take her away.

As I grabbed my things to leave that night, I snuck in a goodnight kiss on her forehead, thinking she was still asleep, but she wasn't. She flashed me a smile when I started to walk away. "I'm heading home now, Mom, but I'll be back tomorrow," I whispered, trying to wipe away the tear that fell down my cheek.

"OK, sweetheart," she said with another tired smile.

As I turned to reach for the door, I told her, "I love you so much."

"Crystal?" she whispered. When I looked back at her, she said, "Honey, don't cry. If I wanted to give up, I would have done that a long time ago."

"I know," I said with a faint smile, as I walked away.

When I looked back for one more glimpse of her, she said, "I love you the most," and she winked, as the door closed behind me.

It didn't matter what caused her struggle or endless days in the hospital or even what the root of our devastating journey had been. All that mattered was Mom and her will to fight. She didn't look at it as if she was the one fighting a disease known for killing. What mattered more to her was having the strength and courage to get through it, so she could continue being the mentor and mother she was meant to be all along. She taught many of us lessons of perseverance, even when she had no intentions of doing that—*she was just that good*. Part of her job clearly was to lift others up, even in the traumatic times surrounding her, and she'd always been fine with that.

No matter the hurdle, she taught you to jump, instead of fretting over how big the hurdle. It's a life lesson worth carrying with you in everything you do.

CHAPTER 23

FATE IN SURGICAL GLOVES

*F*or the next several days, we waited for Mom's numbers to raise enough to continue with the bypass surgery. Still on this emotional rollercoaster, some days were more positive than others, although uneventful. However, this meant nothing was changing, which wasn't good when we were depending heavily on the inflation of her blood levels, just so she could feel better again. Mom was hungry and the nutritional IV wasn't providing any more than the very bare minimum.

At times, even she felt discouraged and irritated having to sit in the same bed, in the same scenario of the same hospital. Normally, she was never one to show any type of depressed feelings, but after several days of confinement, it was taking a toll on her. She was tired of sleeping too much, bored out of her mind, and her body had now become sore from lying there for days.

Enduring struggles and hard times like this turns any variation of good news into something that most people wouldn't even think twice about. We zeroed in on Mom's numbers and focused solely on her anticipated progress. Hearing that her levels had come up, *even just a point or two*, we cheered and were truly elated! That seems so small to the outside world, but when you watch your mother beam with happiness after hearing that her body is finally doing what it was supposed to be doing all along, you feel grateful for many more aspects in your life. Things are more complex, causing you to dig deeper to find what is truly worthwhile and what really matters.

Meagan was very good at updating Mom's followers across all her social media accounts, because they, too, were anxiously awaiting any type of good news, just like the rest of us. She had such a wide range of fan club members, with so many checking her timeline even before stepping out of their beds each morning. They supported her, choosing to be in it for the long haul of her inspirational and heart-wrenching journey, right alongside her.

She was cheered on and celebrated when her levels rose, and she was offered more and more prayers when her levels went down the wrong way. We are forever grateful for every one of them! Now, it seemed that the whole community was on that same rollercoaster that nobody signed up for in the first place. It was heartbreaking and inspirational, but the tenacity of her will to fight was astonishing to everyone following along.

When the doctors witnessed her tired smile narrowing as she became less social, they also knew something had to give. She was given a few blood transfusions with intentions of boosting her hemoglobin enough to at least provide her some energy to socialize. Then they hooked her up to IV nutrition, trying to fill the absence of food that her body hadn't had in quite some time. The doctors stayed optimistic, trying to keep us uplifted during this excruciating waiting game, but we all felt like somehow our fate was in their hands. I specifically depended on their knowledge and expertise, hoping that the decisions they were making, were going to keep my mother alive.

As I watched my hero resting hopefully but helplessly in a hospital bed for weeks, it ripped me to shreds. I struggled at the sight of her shifting emotional state, crying more and more, fighting off the many voices in my head saying that everything is going to be okay, while others yelled, this isn't going to end well. Our family dynamic grew stronger, but at the same time changed into six very different ways of coping. We felt lost and helpless because the reality behind it was terrifying.

The next day though, well, that was a big day! She sat up in a chair for most of the day, striving for any type of new comfort, but finally she was smiling *and* laughing! That was huge, because little to none of that occurred during the last two weeks—a tiny triumph during a time of so much loss.

I think being given antibiotics and another Neupogen injection to stimulate her bone marrow reproduction gave her the boost she needed and deserved and we all enjoyed it. Even though we still weren't allowing any visitors except for a handful of immediate family members, this was the day that Rennie and his girlfriend, Maddie, came to hang out with her. I'm pretty sure you feel like you're good friends with Rennie by now, so I'm sure it'll come as no surprise to you when you hear his awkward tactics for that day. He's a genius at making any situation, big or small, extremely weird. He always shows pure enjoyment in the reactions he gets from the people in his vicinity when it all goes down.

When the three of us finished lunch downstairs and headed back up to Moms' room, I immediately saw that mischievous look that he gets on his face when he's planning something and it's usually never good. Anytime I've seen it in the past, something awfully inappropriate is about to happen. Just as we stepped out of the elevator and walked towards her room, he speeds up in a very smooth way. Naturally as his lifelong sidekick, I sped up, too. That left Maddie, totally oblivious, trailing behind us, not knowing what was happening.

When we entered Mom's room, he quickly turned back to shut the door before Maddie came in. "Rennie, what are you doing now?" Mom asked, knowing too that he had something up his sleeve. I couldn't help but stand there with him, helping to keep the door closed as Maddie tried desperately to open it, yet knocking quietly in respect for the rest of the oncology floor. She tried to stay calm from outside the door, but she was super-confused, as were Mom and I.

"Real quick, Mom, I bought Maddie a ring and I wanted to tell you that I'm going to ask her to marry me!" He dropped that one on us with zero care in the world, even though he'd just made everything uncomfortable—exciting nonetheless—but weird, since we were still tag-teaming to keep the door closed.

"I'm *so* happy for you, buddy!" Mom told him with the biggest smile on her face.

"Rennie," I exclaimed, "are you really doing this right now? I mean, oh my gosh, yayyyy! I am so happy for you!"

"I think that's really great, Rennie," Mom told him, giving him the permission he so slyly was seeking.

"Yeah, you know, I'm really … "

Then I interrupted him, "but can you, like, just … open the door?"

"Nope, not yet!" he said, "I'm really excited, Mom, and I wanted to tell *you* before anybody, because I knew you'd be so happy," he told her smiling from little ear to little ear.

I couldn't stop laughing, because at this point, Maddie was knocking even harder, demanding from the hallway, "Rennie, this isn't funny, open the ... "

He swung the door open before she could finish, and now things were much more awkward. "Oh, hey, Maddie! Where were you?" I asked her.

"That's not funny," she said, "I was ... " but Rennie chimed in before she could finish talking again.

"Yeah, sorry. The door closed before you got here and I tried to open it, but I ... umm ... I think it must have been jammed!" he told her. "My bad!" She laughed, slightly embarrassed, but very nonchalantly like she'd *totally* seen this movie before.

We had to quickly start up some sort of conversation with not only Maddie, but now a huge elephant in the room, too, trying to avoid giving away the smooth permission that he had just snuck out of Mom! We wanted to be happy and celebrate such great news, but considering she had absolutely no clue what had taken place, it was a surprise that we had to keep quiet.

Instead, I tried steering away the attention. "Mom, when was the last time the doctor was here?" I asked her. She didn't have a chance to answer though before Rennie pulled his phone out and held it in Mom's face.

"Isn't that a really pretty dog, Mom?" he asked.

For a split second, she looked confused, but quickly caught on! "Oh my! Yes, that's such a pretty dog, Rennie! I think that'd be a great ... umm ... fit for the both of you," she remarked, carrying on with the secret.

He moved the phone, now right up in my face, and I stepped back to see it. That's when I realized that it was no dog, but a picture of a gorgeous diamond engagement ring. I thought, *Don't ruin it now, Crystal, but he's forcing you to play along.* "Wow! I really like that dog! That's definitely a keeper, great choice!" I told him, as he abruptly stuck the phone back in his pocket before Maddie could catch on.

To this day, I'm thinking that they must have been talking about getting a dog at the time, because otherwise, I'm not sure why Maddie acted so *not thrilled* at his awkward antics for approval, but it worked. He knew what he was doing by sharing that news with Mom. It also allowed us to steer our attention and heartache far away from cancer and the hospital for a little bit. I'd also say it was an unforgettable way of doing that. You know the saying, "There's a method in his madness." While I'm not entirely convinced that that's completely accurate in his case, as most of the time his madness probably doesn't have a method, this time, it definitely did and it's a memory we will quite possibly *never* forget.

The next morning, they woke up Mom for bloodwork around 3 a.m. to be sure that the results would be back in time for the doctor when he made his rounds at 6 a.m. We were still playing the waiting game, which by now felt like an episode of *Deal or No Deal*, except eventually someone takes a deal for the win … but we weren't quite there yet. Apparently, the doctors weren't even remotely satisfied with her numbers, because the surgery had yet to be rescheduled.

Amid her very eventful days (I'm joking–they were extremely boring), Mom received a call informing her that her brother, Bubba, was in the emergency room. Suddenly she became frantic and I heard her yell, "What do you mean, he's in the ER?"

She found out that Bubba was admitted to the hospital mainly for stress and dehydration. He only has one speed, but regardless of being told to slow down and take care of himself, working hard and taking care of everybody else always came first. *Sounds familiar, right?* Once he got settled into his own room, they were able to talk to each other. However, he was terribly worried about Mom and not being able to be there with her. She was also worried about him, so she felt the same way. She sat with us quietly for the rest of the afternoon, clearly pondering ways that she could make it all better for him without physically being by his side.

Before she went to bed that night, she called to check on Bubba one more time, knowing pretty soon they were going to load her IV pump up with Benadryl and she'd be out like a light. "How is he?" she asked. "Is he awake? Let me speak to him, please," Mom asked Aunt Laura.

She responded, "He's awake, but ... he's throwing up," she said. Mom felt, in a sense, that she had let him down, because she wasn't able to be there with him. Nobody else saw it that way, but that's who she was, always striving to care for the ones she loves and putting her own problems aside. Aunt Laura explained that she believed it was purely nerves getting the best of him.

Mom and Bubba were very close, having an extremely special connection. She knew that most likely he was having a breakdown about her being in the hospital without any answers or solutions to getting her out. He looked up to her for guidance and advice, but his not being able to fix her did indeed break him down. It didn't help that at the same time both of them were in two separate hospitals, an hour away from each other.

The nurses came in to load her IV pump up with medications, but before she went to sleep, she texted him,

> Just letting you know they are about to give me a large dose of pain meds, along with Benadryl, to start another round of platelets, so I am going to be knocked out for the night. Keep sending the texts, so when I wake up, I can see how you're doing! Pray hard, you're going to be OK! Love you!

> Laura? Please kiss him for me!

She waited for confirmation that her text went through before she set her phone down and went to bed.

My mom, as selfless as can be, was fighting such a horrific battle, but never failed even once with her duties as a big sister. She tried hard to take care of him, all while being hooked up to her own IV. It's not every day that you find people as strong as she was. She would most likely tell you that it's because she had nothing better to do with her time in the hospital except call and text people. While that may be true, that's not what I'd call it.

A few weeks after she was admitted, the doctors were still closely monitoring every decision her body was making. Her white blood cell count was at 0.3, her hemoglobin at 10.9, and with her platelets at an all-time low of 4, numbers that were crucially and deathly low. It was cruel what her body was doing, and it started taking a toll on all of us, but especially on Mom. Our emotions went up and down right along with her blood numbers, so it was becoming way too hard to hold on to positivity and faith, the two things that we needed the most.

That saying, "When it rains, it pours," was one I always liked. It just reminds me of one of my favorite songs. However, when you actually start living with that statement, you'll hate it! I'm assuming my life figured it wasn't as eventful as it thought it should be, so it threw another curveball, while I hadn't even stepped up to the plate yet! Besides my husband and children back at home, the other little beating heart that brought so much joy into my life was my mini goldendoodle, Finley. So sweet, nearly eight months old, we are attached at the hip.

He woke up one morning acting very strange while I was getting ready to head to the hospital. This specific morning wasn't like all the other mornings, when he tried to play sad and pull on my heart strings. He knew I was going somewhere, and he unfortunately couldn't come along. I sat down beside him, trying to get him to play with his little red monkey, but he didn't budge. Not even able to lift his head, he lay there almost lifeless, clearly in pain.

I freaked out and immediately dialed up Mom, because you know, she didn't already have enough on her plate. "He isn't acting normal, Mom! He won't eat or drink anything and he won't play. All he's doing is laying there with the saddest puppy-dog eyes I've ever seen," I told her.

Yes, I'm a mom to actual little humans, with a motherly intuition, but I'm also a mom to this little angel laying in my lap. I knew right away that something was *terribly* wrong! She demanded that I hang up the phone with her and call the vet right away.

"Is he vomiting?" the nurse asked me.

"Yes," I replied.

"Is he eating or drinking?" she asked again.

"No," I told her.

"Is he going to the bathroom?"

"No," I said, now starting to cry. I rushed him to the vet and immediately carried his almost lifeless body through the lobby straight to an exam room to see that the doctor was already in the room waiting for him—total VIP status.

"He usually prances in here with his cute little bowtie, but he's definitely not like that today," the doctor said.

I'm well aware, I thought. They had to pry him out of my hands to take him for tests in the back room, completely out of my sight. I sat down and cried, feeling defeated. With everything we were going through, this is happening now? Playing that awful waiting game yet again, I tried so hard to keep it together by calling Mom. I knew she could help in a way that only moms know how to do.

"Honey, don't get yourself worked up yet. You did the right thing by taking him in right away. Until you have a reason to worry, don't! It won't change anything, and quite honestly, I'll be mad at you if I have to figure out a way to break myself out of this hospital just to come pick you up off the floor of the veterinarian's office!"

She was right. I hung up the phone and sat there, waiting for my baby to come back, staring at the big metal examination table next to the counter flooded with heartworm prevention pamphlets and a jar of peanut butter was *not* helping! The doctor came back in swiftly, chasing Finley who had just ran straight to my arms. He was shaking and glaring at me with a look that screamed, "I'm with my mom. Don't touch me anymore!"

They had found on the x-ray what looked like a sock that was lodged in his intestine, blocking any food and water from going down. "Are you kidding me?" I remarked. *Does anybody else want to have something grow or lodge itself in their intestines, too? Then we can all have one big, giant, life-threatening party that everybody seems to be a part of these days.*

I held my head in my hands, crying, trying to grasp the fact that I was just told he needs to have emergency surgery, right now, to help save his life. I needed to hand over $2,000 to them, like yesterday! *No big deal, lady, let me just pull that out of my back pocket! Now what am I supposed to do?* I thought. *Oh, that's right, do what I always do—call Mom!* Thankfully she came to the rescue once again, giving me her Care Credit card number over the phone. Gosh, they use those for everything these days. Fortunately, they were able to start his surgery immediately, so he didn't die right there in my lap that day.

For the next several days, I ran the mileage up in my car going to and from both hospitals. I spent the days waiting around with

Mom and ended them lying with Finley in his cold kennel tucked under his dark blue-and-white-striped blanket. Every five minutes, I adjusted that awful plastic cone wrapped around his head, just so he'd lay there comfortably and stop trying to chew off the IV in his paw. It was exhausting, but apparently that was my life for the time being.

Finley finally went home with a bag of medicine in tow, still wearing the cone, but he was getting better and that's all that mattered. Remember that rollercoaster? Well, I liked it right now, because things were starting to look up, including Mom's blood numbers. We got news that they'd gone from 4 up to 68! I was happy, assuming God had felt bad for me and decided to give me a break. Although I'm quite positive my assumption was just that, it *was* something I used to try making sense of all this. Mom's body had now started producing platelets all on its own, which was exactly what it was supposed to do this whole time.

We cheered, gloating that her numbers were improving so well. A few days later, it hit a whopping 134, so she was finally cleared for surgery! Along with two Bible verses that she claimed to have held tightly to this whole time, Mom posted on social media for herself:

> I am holding my own for now, with Gods sweet mercy. Heal me, LORD and I will be healed; save me and I will be saved, for you are the one I praise.
> I will restore you to health and heal your wounds.

Now that surgery was scheduled for the next morning, I tried getting some sleep, but I didn't. I tossed and turned, googling "surgeries to bypass a tumor." I read through almost all six hundred comments that flooded Mom's update that she had just posted an hour ago. Just as the sun began to rise, I headed out the door for the hospital, pulling into the parking lot on two wheels. I ran down the stairs, up the elevator, and into room B-667, to find the nurses unlocking her bed to wheel her to pre-op. Dad, Meagan, Katie, and I all took turns holding her hand and praying, leaving her with so many kisses and a "We got this!" as they rolled her out of our sight.

"Well, here we go. This is what we've all been waiting for," Dad said nervously. Rennie hadn't made it there yet and I knew he and Mom would both be so upset. I felt sad knowing this, because worrying and feeling for others has always come naturally to me, even in times when I don't want that trait. Fortunately for them, there are so many steps involved in the pre-op process of a major surgery that Rennie was able to see her before she went into the operating room. He reminded her of how much he loved her and told her that we'd be right there waiting for her when she came out.

In the same waiting room where we had sat once before, nobody said much this time. We were ambushed with multiple emotions after making some serious life decisions in a discussion we had with Mom and her doctor a few days prior. We knew this surgery was extremely necessary and we trusted our faith and leaned on prayer that it'd be successful. We were told that if the bypass was unsuccessful, she would have no choice but to be hooked up to a nutritional IV for the rest of her life. If that was the case, the statistics showed that potentially her quality of life, health, and wellbeing would swiftly deteriorate, and the duration of her life would vastly plummet.

"Kneeling prayers, she was just taken back," Meagan's Facebook post read just as Mom's Patient ID Number switched to "SURGERY START." I was perched in the same corner chair that I waited in the last time we were there, wrapped in an oversized hoodie with my coffee sitting completely untouched on the table next to me.

For a few minutes, nobody spoke a word, basking in our own versions of this life and where it's taken us. I fell into a memory coma, replaying scenes from my childhood in my head, as the noise from the hospital in the background began to fade. I saw three little kids in the sunshine as Mom pushed us on the swings. I heard little giggles and birds chirping with the summer wind blowing through her hair, while she beamed with joy and flashed the prettiest smile you've ever seen.

That memory felt just as perfect as I remember, back when I lived it. It was a very real flashback, yet very quick to fade away. The summer sun got darker and suddenly I couldn't see my siblings anymore and Mom had disappeared. I began focusing more on the heavy pain in my chest and faintly, coming in clearer each second, I heard, "Crystal? Crystal! Are you OK?"

I wished they had just left me alone. We were jumping from the swings, running through the backyard, and we had almost made it home.

When you realize that your future is being held in surgical gloves, you can't help but feel all sides of reality. I felt as if I had left my body, watching front and center the horror my family was facing. I watched from above, as my mother was lying on the operating table, while the surgeon sat next to her reaching for another stainless steel instrument to use inside her body. It was terrifying each time we snapped back into those raw moments.

Every time the phone rang at the nurse's desk, we sat hopeful, holding our breath and hoping that just maybe it was our turn to receive good news about Mom. A few phone calls later, it *was* our turn! "Mr. Heath?" said the young girl standing up from behind the desk. Dad ran over to grab the phone, while the rest of us narrowed in, dissecting every hand gesture and facial expression he was making, trying to pry the news from him before he could even hang up to tell us.

"He successfully did the bypass!" he told us with pure giddiness and pride. The whole room stood up enthralled in her success, celebrating, whistling, clapping, and loudly cheering for our sweet and deserving MOTHER!

CHAPTER 24

WHERE'S OUR MOM?

*W*e waited to be told that it was okay to go in and see Mom, but sitting too long causes overthinking. Then the emotions you try your hardest to dodge seem to bombard you. You hear the nurses talking about their personal lives and how the only problems they seem to have are with their toddlers, doing things like taking her diaper off in the classroom at preschool.

You pretend to be interested in the hand-painted butterflies on the wall as you pace by them over and over, because it's supposed to bring you some sort of joy while the rest of your life crashes down. You walk around feeling like your sadness is invisible because nobody else can seem to make it go away. It hurts, but you chug along because you have no other choice.

A few hours after her surgery, the five of us finally were able to go in and see her and make her aware that the doctor was able to do the bypass successfully. Although she was still groggy from all the pain meds and anesthesia, she still had enough in her to at least mutter a small groan our way, letting us know that she heard and was thrilled.

We were back in the waiting game for the next couple of days to see if the bypass was going to work as intended. She slept a lot but, regardless, we were there the entire time. With each passing day, she'd mumble a few more words, slowly coming out of a comatose state that was left over from surgery. Occasionally, she'd chuckle at Dad or Rennie's jokes, and eventually she became more independent, even sitting up in bed. The nurses came in and out of her room, verifying that her vitals were stabilizing. Just a few days later; they had her up and ready to walk. She was finally given real food and I watched as she struggled to walk from the bed to the bathroom. However, in my mind, eating and walking meant that cancer was losing.

Watching her struggle to take a mere three steps across the room made me so proud. It showed me that her strength wasn't taken away and that she still had some fight left in her. Much like life, a few steps forward can drastically change your entire world. It reminded me of my own struggling faith, which wasn't in the best place at this time. I went back and forth with God, as there were times I was on His side and plenty of times I wasn't.

I knew all along that being on His side is the only way to go, but I struggled with that as I witnessed Mom battle this disease that He very well could have spared her. When I watched her hold tightly to the IV cart and the nurse's arm as she moved one foot in front of the other, I felt angry with myself. I couldn't believe I had wallowed in my own self-pity, liking God some days and disliking Him on most, yet Mom's faith never seized.

She always put forth the effort of loving and leaning on Him first, before anybody or anything. If the roles were reversed and I was the one being forced to walk just two days after a surgery like she was, it's safe to say it would not have gone as gracefully as it did with her. Although that's entirely too easy to admit, since I wasn't the one in that position, but unfortunately, it was her. She had no idea the lessons she was teaching us as we watched her take those few short and courageous steps across the room that day.

She was continuing to recover, and more progress was being made. She was feeling better—a little more alert, still in pain, but managing it. The doctor told us this would be a very critical and crucial period in her recovery. We were also told that those platelets for which we had all been praying came up to 286, completely homemade. *(Cue the music: Puff Daddy "Can't nobody holdddddd her down".)*

She was slowly gaining back her strength and, most importantly, her smile. We knew she felt the best when she finally asked—I mean, demanded—us to bring the grandbabies up to see her. She missed them, never had she gone this long without them, and they were the first things on her To Do list.

We had kept them in the dark during most of this time because, knowing how little kids' brains work, they most likely would have been terrified to say the least, and that's not at all what we strived to do. As parents, you don't get a handbook at childbirth, and you most definitely can't find any type of accurate parenting tutorial on YouTube. You aren't exactly sure what to do when situations like this arise, *especially about Memaw,* so … you just kind of wing it. All they knew was that Memaw was in the hospital because of her cancer, but the doctor is trying to take all of that away.

I knew my life had drastically changed over that last month, but I didn't realize at the time that theirs had, too. While they continued playing their baseball games and attending school, they still recognized that Mommy had been very absent for a while. It broke my heart when I thought how they must have felt not having Mommy around. They were temporarily living in my worst fear. I couldn't imagine what life could be like without a mom, but those resilient little humans proved that it is possible, somehow.

I relied on my husband to pick up the slack and, for several weeks, he became a single parent. Truly the dad of all dads, he never questioned me in passing as I ran in and out of the house, only stopping there to sleep before I left again the next morning.

They struggled too, in their own small ways. I had received a few emails from their teachers with concerns that they were not paying attention in class and acting out unusually. I had to explain what was going down behind the scenes, which backed up their actions, proving the lack of attention and knowledge, we as their parents weren't giving them. They knew Memaw was sick with something called cancer, and their mommies were gone a lot lately, leaving them to muster up their own opinions in a very limited, kid-friendly way about Memaw and something being wrong.

Meagan took her daughters, Maddie and Chloe, up to see Memaw first. It was their little laughs that did it for me. Maddie sat in her lap laughing and shared school stories with her. Chloe, with her bag of Cheerios in tow, assisted Memaw in a walk around the nurses' station, helping her push the IV cart along with them. They laughed and danced around the room, twirling in their dresses, flooding Mom with all the joy she'd missed out on. Their little hearts were full again and Mom's was filling back up quickly, especially watching tiny two-year-old Kinsley, Katie's daughter, sing and draw on the hospital windowsill with all kinds of crayons. To her, she was simply "making Memaw's room colorful." We couldn't disagree.

I went to bed that night with much more strength, which was fueled by the day we'd had with Mom, because for the first time in nineteen days ... I saw my mom SMILE! Not only did she glow, watching her granddaughters be total girly girls, but she laughed uncontrollably when we shared the text messages we had been getting from Dad. He was so proud of himself, sharing with us what felt like nineteen different times. He was cooking meals for himself and bragging that it wasn't even takeout!

It didn't matter that it was mostly rotisserie chicken and Bud Light, but hey, it wasn't from a restaurant! He was even surprised to find out that he, indeed, did know how to fold his own laundry. *Who would have known?* You knew Mom was extremely proud when she told him, "Good! Now you can do that all the time!" I'm pretty sure once she came home, he conveniently forgot how to do it, but either way, he learned to fend for himself! *Men ... I swear.*

We became much happier as a family, knowing that each day she smiled and laughed was another day closer to her coming home. I overheard her mumble during one of the girls' ballerina spins in their sparkly tutus that, "God is good."

At that point, I believed so, too. I was back on that train with Him now, because things were going in the right direction, although she never left that train. She remained faithful and courageous, struggling to get through what was harder than most people will ever have to tackle. She did it with grace, knowing she had no other option but to continue fighting, using God as her pillar to lean on. Even losing her dad while having this battle made it that much harder, but she stayed thankful knowing how blessed she was to have him for so many years. She knew how blessed she still is, knowing that He'll be right there waiting for her one day.

I told her, "God only gives his hardest battles to his strongest soldiers," as I left for the night. "Yes, he does!" she replied, leaving me flooded with grace and relief. I walked to the parking garage, past the nurses' station, and even smiled at them as I walked away, thanking Jesus for today. We had learned that those days were very unpredictable, but today ... well, this was a good day!

Now that she was showing so much improvement, I didn't rush back to the hospital the next morning. Instead, I tried spending the time I had missed over those last couple of weeks with my boys. Jaxon and Tanner are usually found on Facetime with Maddie and Chloe, close cousins to say the least! I'm almost positive Maddie told them she'd seen Memaw yesterday. It was most likely in a roundabout way, because Meagan told her to keep it a secret until *they* were allowed to go see her, too.

Tanner had a T-Ball game that morning and, ironically, he didn't feel good. "I don't want to go," he told me as I tucked in the oversized uniform shirt into his overly baggy baseball pants. I took his temperature only to prove to him that thermometers don't lie. "See, you're not sick, so you have to play your game today."

"But I can't, I'm sick," he tried debating again.

That was until I dropped this one, "If you're sick, then you can't play and if you don't play, well, then you can't go see Memaw after the game!"

Their eyes lit up like the Fourth of July! They screamed (an ecstatic understatement) and they were acting as if I had just told them, "We're going to the most expensive toy store and you can buy anything you want." This was *way* better than that. They hadn't seen Memaw in nearly three weeks, and never before had they gone three whole days without her, so this was beyond worth it having to play a baseball game first, just to be able to see her. It was an even bigger post-baseball game reward than they could have ever hoped to have.

Tanner is the kind of kid who you'll find weaved into the definition of a "clown," much like his Uncle Rennie, but to them, he's "Bubba." Tanner is such a neat little boy, but has no care in the world about when it's time to be serious, like in the middle of a baseball game, although I do love that about him.

His game that morning was far from boring. In fact, I don't even think the word "boring" has ever been involved in any part of Tanner's life, if we're being honest. It was quite an eventful game and I had truly missed that so much. He's never been one to just run out on the field to play and then run off when he was done. It's a total show to him, comical always!

He may or may not have stood in centerfield picking flowers for Memaw, playing catch with himself and an invisible baseball, and yelling to the crowd, "Will somebody just get me a cheeseburger?" He doesn't grasp the concept of positions, nor does he have a care in the world about the meaning behind those positions. If the ball is in play, it's going to be his. It didn't matter if the ball is rolling to home plate, he's after it! He finds the laughs from the bleachers amusing, and it's even better to see how many of his "fan club" watch him when he's up to bat. He doesn't understand why each time he'd step into the box, the umpire would have to tell him to watch the ball and not the crowd. If people are watching, he's going to put on a show. He's going to play his hardest knowing that *Memaw* will be waiting for him after the game.

We couldn't wait any longer after his game. We went straight to the hospital, even skipping the team huddle because "Coach, we have to go. My memaw is waiting for me!" he said, running away with his too-big-for-his-body bat bag in tow right behind him.

As soon as I opened the door to her room, they all ran in like it was Christmas morning and they had just spotted their most anticipated Santa present waiting for them right there. "Memaw!" they yelled, bombarding her with hugs. We tried telling them that they had to be quiet and not to run in the hospital, but it was entirely too late. They were already getting caught up in her IV cords and knocking over her Styrofoam cup of ice water.

Jaxon asked her what she had taped on the top of her hand, and Tanner was over there attempting to push *every* button on that funny beeping IV cart next to her. *The Bell boys are in the house!* It was total chaos to put it mildly but this was most likely why she always swore she was so partial to boys—she loved that they didn't ever hold anything back. They lived with endless energy, questions, wonder, and sometimes not very good decisions, but their hearts held more love for Memaw than it did for anybody else, ever.

The only way she could have hugged them any tighter than she was attempting to do was if she had gained all her strength back. However, she wasn't there yet, and I could see the struggle. To them, they were finally "home."

Their world was back, right in front of them, sitting in that chair and laughing at the stories they were telling her—stories about the fake homerun that Tanner had supposedly hit just for her at his game, and the proud accomplishments (which were actually true) that Jaxon had been making in school. He told her about all the wins of his baseball games, and Tanner continued butting in and openly sharing all the not-so-good decisions that he had been making in school. He told her that he didn't understand why all his teachers kept putting him in "time out," because "I don't do anything wrong, Memaw!"

It was like a box filled to the rim containing everything that had gone on for the last three weeks. They were anxious and quickly unloading it right there in her lap. She listened so intently to the reason behind the medal Jaxon wore around his neck from his baseball games, and praised him for all his good grades and awards that he received at school.

"I would have loved to be there to see you, Doodlebug," Mom said to Jaxon, "I know you would, Memaw, but it's OK, there will be more!" he told her so innocently. She was prouder of him than anybody ever was. Because he knew that, he wore his medal to the hospital that day.

"Memaw's going to be so happy!" he exclaimed. Mom tried to get Tanner to stand still and pose for a picture with her in his three-times-too-big uniform shirt, halfway untucked, stained with orange clay, and his baggy gray baseball pants with one leg pulled up so high you could see his mismatched light blue baseball socks, and the other pant leg pulled down to his dirty untied cleats. She tried fixing his sideways hat, but eventually just gave up and smiled for the camera. Those moments that were captured are very special photos today. You can see the love and happiness beam from all three of their faces, because the light in the world now was shining *so* much brighter!

Life seemed better now, watching her interact with her grandbabies. Seeing her recover so quickly made it easy to appreciate. I sang along with the boys in the car on the way to school drop-off the next morning, laughing about yesterday and cheering at the fact that "Memaw is coming home soon!" I personally felt happier and relieved that what seemed like the hardest part was over.

I arrived at the hospital, grabbing my coffee on the way up, only to realize when I got there that something was strangely different. "Morning, Mom!" I said, as I walked into her dark room all bright-eyed and bushy-tailed. Dad was already there, but by the look on his face, something wasn't right.

"Good morning," Mom mumbled back to me. Feeling confused all of a sudden, my heart dropped. Something was off, way off!

"What's wrong with her?" I whispered to Dad but, all he could do was shrug his shoulders—he didn't know. The day before was such a great day, but this day was completely different. She didn't act the same, sitting up in bed in the dark, just staring at me. Even her staring was eerie, as if she were looking through me, not at me. There wasn't a lot of talk that entire day. Instead, she slept much more and rarely muttered any words to us that whole time. *Maybe she's just tired*, I tried reasoning with myself. *She has been put through a lot and yesterday was eventful with all the kids.* Deep down, though, I knew in my gut that this was something more serious.

The next afternoon, she was discharged and Dad took her home. Hopeful that she was still just really tired from it all, we stayed excited, knowing that she was finally able to rest in her own home, with her own things, in her own bed. Her not acting right was something nobody wanted to talk about, but I think we all knew it meant something much bigger. "Now that she's home, I think it'll be easier for her to catch up on rest and I'm sure she'll recover in no time," I told Dad, trying to stay optimistic and cheer him up because he had been looking very worried.

We spent those next few weeks with her at home, watching reruns of *Ellen* or laughing at *Ryan and Kelly,* but all she did was sleep and sit there staring at nothing. We knew, as a family, that we could be the best caretakers for her, so naturally we did everything for her every chance we got. We craved our old normal life back, and somehow we felt like we could play a part in that happening.

We placed the rest of our lives on hold for that last month. None of us had intentions of doing anything differently now that she was home. We became consumed in her recovery, not wanting her to spend even a minute alone. Even though she wasn't talking much with anybody, the words, "Go home and spend some time with your family," still made its way out.

"I'm fine. I'll still be sitting here tomorrow," she'd say. Although she was right about still sitting in that same chair, "fine" is not what we'd call it.

My sisters and I spent every other day helping her shower and sitting on the bathroom counter spending time together, laughing with her like best friends do. Those days I still cherish. We enjoyed being her personal fashion assistants and picking out her clothes that she'd spend the day in. We'd even argue about which pair of comfy socks was the cutest for her feet, considering the mint green grip socks that they give you as a parting gift from the hospital are not cute. The showers she took were the only "outings" she had during those days. Once cleaned and freshened up, she went right back to that same black leather chair.

The days back home passed very quickly considering how uneventful they were, but just as quickly became very worrisome, especially when she started talking less and less to us. She sat there most of the time, blankly staring with glassy eyes, but now her beautiful smile became so much harder to see. She didn't seem to have any interest in anything anymore and her mental status was quite obviously declining.

Along with that, her physical status began to change as well, with no appetite, loss of all energy, and even her ability to write started failing her. We watched as her weight dropped like liposuction gone wrong, and her right foot began oddly dragging behind her body, as she attempted walking to and from the bathroom. That's when we started to freak out. "Mom what's wrong?"

I think each one of us asked that question numerous times throughout those days, but a mumbled, "Nothing," by her was the only answer we ever got. Watching my mother stare at me, like I seemingly wasn't even there, is what broke my heart. We wanted her to know that we *were* there, we had been there the whole time, and we weren't going anywhere. She wasn't alone in any of this! I wanted to continue asking her random questions throughout the day, hoping that it would keep her mind as sharp as possible, but at the same time, I was afraid to do so. I didn't want her to know that we all sensed something was seriously wrong. In turn, it would bring on doubt and unpleasant feelings for her.

The end of May, her fifty-eighth birthday rolled around, as we attempted to keep everything as normal as possible. This meant all our families were there and kids were running through the house and getting in trouble for doing so–usually by Papa. Jokes were told so that laughter became louder than the blaring football game on TV. That was normal. But even when demanding that the dogs stop barking when someone walked down the boulevard outside her house, she didn't budge. She just sat there, mostly emotionless the whole time. Occasionally, a quick smirk or two occurred when Rennie and Dad chimed in about something inappropriate, but even those cute smirks became few and far between. She didn't seem to be there with us.

Since it was her birthday and chaos was completely at its max, cake right now sounded like the best idea. I was sitting on the footstool of her chair, just listening to the whispers coming from the kitchen, while Meagan and Katie tried desperately to shush the kids enough to keep it a secret from Memaw. "I'm putting the candles on the cake!" I heard from a little boy's voice.

"No, I am!" followed right after, this time, from a little girl. I laughed, mainly because I wasn't the one in the kitchen this time with all the kids.

"Shhh, OK let's take it to her," Meagan whispered, just as Katie joined in. "Ready? 1-2-3 … ". They were coming in hot around that corner to her chair, flailing their little arms so we would all chime in singing, "Happy Birthday," too. She turned to find a big chocolate cake coming her way. The candle glow on her face made the perfect lighting for pictures and, boy, are they the best pictures you've ever seen!

"Make a wish, Memaw!" Jaxon shouted.

"OK, baby," Mom replied. We sat there impatiently waiting because, at this point, the candles were about to melt onto the actual cake when she finally made her wish and blew them out.

"Memaw gets the first piece!" Maddie yelled, starting a line of all the grandchildren to get their piece next.

"Not right now, honey," Mom said. What? We were confused, because it was chocolate cake. Mom never turns down anything chocolate, much less cake! Katie told her, "Mom, you have to at least take the first bite, because it's all for you." She agreed to take a small nibble, but nothing more.

We sat there feeling helpless and greatly confused by her turning down her own birthday cake—that wasn't like her at all. What happened in the hospital from the day we visited *"our mom"* to the very next day when it was most definitely was not "our mom?" We were all deeply saddened to see these results from a surgery that was supposed to make it all better.

Another month went by with no changes. She was still quiet and emotionless, sitting in the same chair from morning to night. She didn't speak much and when she did, it was mumbles that only her family could make out. Many friends and family wanted to come visit her now that she had been home and settled in, but even they became few. It's hard to visit with someone in a state like she was in, but it's even harder to keep your composure when you see it right in front of you.

A few friends though, it didn't bother. They'd come just to sit and watch *Ellen* while Mom slept, because to those closest to her, just being in the same room was plenty good enough. She gave off a sense of brightness and much comfort that let you surround yourself with her. It was such a gift that she never really realized that she had all along.

Those days felt like they were dwindling for me, specifically. It didn't matter if I could just sit on the couch across from her, watch her breathe and let the dogs out on commercial breaks. I didn't mind constantly changing the volume on the TV according to her sleep schedule. Her comfort was always our priority. I answered a few text messages but ignored most. She didn't take interest in anything now, but even knowing that, I still felt like as her daughter it was my duty to offer comfort to her. We had all the tomato soup, banana pudding, and fried bologna sandwiches that she could ever need, but most of the time, she wasn't up for even that.

It's heartbreaking when you come to the raw realization that your days have now turned into intense caretaking but, when it's your mother, you never really see it that way. It was our job and, quite honestly, it was probably the first job I ever had that I never really minded doing. (Slightly kidding.) When you become enthralled in breathing patterns and the feeling of her pulse against the palm of your hand, it takes over every emotion that you could ever possibly experience. At times, I'd make myself walk outside for a few minutes of fresh air, but as the days passed by, even that lessened tremendously. Nobody wanted to leave her side, living in the fear of life's worst possible ending.

We knew that the mountain house in North Carolina was one of her favorite places to visit, but on the flip side, so was our beach house. She often took two weeks for herself there each summer because, to her, it was relaxation at its finest. It was a place she put so much time and effort into making it perfect, truly a home away from home. It was cozy, decorated in driftwood, bright beachy colors, and a handmade flip-flop front door wreath. Homemade meals and cold glasses of white wine were always on the menu. It was the place that made you kick and scream when you realized that vacay was over.

In this quaint but growing historic little beach town, the fireworks for the holidays were something you didn't want to miss. Hometown fireworks didn't stand a chance to the fireworks that went off on the beach as you sat there on sandy towels, watching miles and miles of them down the eastern coastline. Now that Mom had been home for over a month, the weekend of the 4th of July seemed like the perfect reason to sweep her away to the beach for a change of scenery and an overabundance of fresh salty air. It didn't take much for her to be happy there. Whether she was lounging in a chair on the beach, sipping jalapeno margaritas at the Mexican restaurant downtown, singing to Jimmy Buffet on the boat, or sitting with her toes in the water on Disappearing Island, for her it couldn't get much better than that.

She wasn't herself back home, like we thought she'd be after spending a month in the hospital. Taking her to the beach felt like we still had hope of bringing her old self back to life and that was the surest way to do it. Unfortunately, just like how the rest of life seems to go when you're hoping for a change, you can't expect things to always stay the same because sadly, they just don't. It's a rude awakening when you're trying so hard to find that comfort in a life that you once lived.

During this getaway, we realized that our wants just weren't in the plans that were made for her. She was sick the entire time, never truly able to even leave the front door of the beach house. The grandbabies spent hours swimming in the pool and building sandcastles on the beach, Usually, Mom would be there to load them up with sunscreen and lug all the buckets and shovels for them down to the beach, but this weekend, she didn't. She was physically there in the vicinity, but she was very much absent. Never once in her entire life had she spent those days at the beach always in the house and lying on the couch sleeping, especially if the kids were there with her.

This time was different, and it hurt. She was spending those days the exact same way she had been spending them at home, uninterested, fatigued, and silent. It was rare, but a few times she would crack a smile, stringing us along, knowing for a fact that she was in there somewhere. However, it was pulling her out to stay that wasn't exactly working out very well.

Leaving that weekend to come back home, she mentioned to Dad in a seemingly defeated and tired voice, as they pulled out of the front gates, "Well ... that was a nice visit," which left him in secret tears. His heart sank because he knew right then and there that this would most likely be the last time she'd ever spend in New Smyrna Beach.

From childhood to adulthood, I think we're mostly taught that life is all about making memories and cherishing everything you have. Naturally it's hard to realize that and remember it when times are difficult. Some days seem good and it's easier to take the pictures and write down those funny things that someone said or did. But on those trying and tough days, it's always much harder to keep that appreciation at the top. Our minds allow us to wallow in that sadness and our brains block out the moments that could very well still be good. That beach trip was supposed to bring our mom back. It was meant to be fun and memorable, living in unforgettable times with her, but sadness was the only thing felt when driving home.

We are human and we're greedy, wanting things to turn out our way. However, the truth is that they never really do. God's truest tests happen in those troubled times. The only way to pass that test is how we decide to deal with it and which parts we choose to store away as worthy.

CHAPTER 25

A JOB WELL DONE

*U*p to this part of my life, I thought I had seen it all. I never imagined having to witness my mother, of all people, battling cancer. Always such a healthy and happy person, I thought that there was no way she would be the one given something like that to have to fight for her life, but I was wrong.

I watched her force feed herself, almost choking on the medication, and I heard her ask for help just to walk to the bathroom. I watched as she sat in the shower with not enough energy to even wash her own face. There were many days I helped dress and bathe her and brush her teeth.

The worst though, out of all of those days, were the days I saw her cry. Although extremely rare, when it did happen, it rocked my world. Mom was a warrior tougher than nails, but at the same time, she was human. I thought the sight of her tears was the worst thing that I could possibly witness with my own eyes, but once again, I was wrong. *That wasn't the worst!*

As the days went on, my heart knew way more than my head ever wanted to admit. I watched her spend more and more time in that chair with her eyes closed. She ate less and less and became more dehydrated by the minute. Whether I ever verbally and physically admitted it or not, she was showing all signs of going downhill, fast. The day came when she stopped conversing with all her visitors and never once picked up her phone anymore.

"Mom how are you feeling?" we'd ask her. "Do you want me to get you something to eat or drink?" but after a while, we stopped getting back any responses. Even then, we'd still make her lunch and refill her water, trying desperately to trick ourselves into feeling like she still needed us.

Unfortunately, she wouldn't eat anything anymore and we'd have to force her just to sip her water. She taught us as a child how to force someone to drink something when they weren't feeling good.

She did that to us with Gatorade when we played sick just to stay home from school as kids. So we were good at that one, although water was the only thing we were able to make her sip, which sadly only happened about three times a day. It wasn't nearly enough to keep her hydrated, as a mere gulp in total wasn't going to do much anymore.

I'd spend hours during those days, cuddled up with her and holding her hand. Each time I'd sit with her, I closed my eyes pretending that none of this was really happening. It was unfamiliar and honestly very scary that our once fun and eventful life had suddenly come down to these days. Resting my head on the same pillow she was, I sat there consumed in not only her, but the essence she gave off. I thought everything that I needed in the world was right there, sharing the same chair as me. I couldn't help but thank God during those moments that I'd be so close to her that I could feel the warmth of her frail body against mine.

Dad tried keeping up with work as much as he could those days, but it was hard on him—very hard. He felt like the rest of us did— scared and fearful when we were with her, and completely absent minded when we weren't.

He came home early one night, most likely due to our home life consuming his entire thought process, feeling uninterested and worthless on the job. He walked in with a worried but let's-get-down-to-business look on his face. "I need to sit down and have a talk with all of you" he said, "It's important because I think it's time that we consider Hospice care."

My heart sank hearing that, because anytime I had heard the word *Hospice* in the past, it always preceded the death of somebody.

"No way," I remarked, "we're not doing that, Dad." *Mom didn't need Hospice,* because she wasn't dying! "That's literally the dumbest idea!" I told them, but they each seemed to disagree with me on this one. She was fighting and doing her best, so we didn't need anybody else coming into our home just to take care of her. We were taking care of her just fine.

It's hard being in a big family, because it was usually always "majority rules" when it came to family decisions. This time, it was no different. My opinion was outvoted when it came to the final decision on what was best for our mother.

I could tell that she didn't want it either. We tried staying quiet as we debated this topic, in hopes that she wouldn't hear the horrible idea we were debating. However, we failed at doing that when the word "Hospice" was said too loudly.

"I don't need that," Mom mumbled from her chair in the other room.

"See! I told you!" I exclaimed.

"Crystal, you have to be open-minded about Hospice—they aren't bad people," Dad said, as he tried reasoning with me. "What they do is a blessing and they only come in to help when the help is needed," he said.

I sat down in tears, shaking my head in disagreement, demanding that they didn't contact them. She didn't need help! I was convinced in my mind that calling them in only meant that she was done. I was hurting and becoming selfish, but regardless of my feelings, they called Hospice.

I was told that one of their nurses would come to meet with us and that I needed to be there. Even without knowing them, I didn't like them, nor did I have any desire to meet them. I did it only because I knew if I disagreed, it would upset Mom at not seeing me there with everybody else. Also, quite frankly, she didn't have the strength or energy anymore to come find me and physically force me to walk with her back into her room. I knew she wouldn't be thrilled with the idea of Hospice either.

However, before I agreed to meet them, I asked Dad, "Did you even ask Mom?" I knew I had asked her, but I wanted to know if he did.

"Of course, I did! She told me she doesn't think she needs them either."

I butted in before he could even finish his statement. "See, I told you, and I don't blame her!" I felt like I was finally pleading my case this time! *Mom and I always made a great team when it came to legit topics like this one and I knew she'd have my back this time, too!*

He heard me out and then continued with his statement that I so rudely interrupted. "But after explaining to her what Hospice meant, she did agree to give them a try, so now you have to accept this."

Ughhhhh! I felt like a little kid wanting to have a tantrum, screaming, "but I don't wanna!" There again he explained to me in detail of all the services they provide, the support and care they offer, and how by depending on them to be there for those medical necessities, it would allow us to be a family and spend time with her, instead of having to cater to her every need.

Quite obviously, I still hated the idea, but I had to go along with it for my family's sake. I didn't mind catering to her, but as they continued trying to change my mind about accepting Hospice into her home, I began to feel guilty. I wondered what would happen if Hospice didn't come and I was the only one left counting her pills. In my current mental state, I might accidentally overdose her or not give her enough pills. Eventually, I might become the reason she kicked the bucket! I stopped trying to persuade myself and my family and just gave in. Fighting to keep Hospice out wasn't worth arguing anymore, because choosing what was best for Mom in the long run was the answer.

Hospice was on the way to Mom and Dad's house, while the four of us kids sat around Mom in the living room, waiting for them to arrive. I didn't know what to expect—in fact, I knew nothing about them. All I'd heard was about someone else's life ending when Hospice was called, so as you can imagine, I wasn't thrilled by any means. I had been so against this decision in the first place, not knowing anything about them, I had already decided that I wasn't going to agree. I thought, *Maybe when they come, if I just shut them out immediately, they'll feel so uncomfortable that they'll decide they don't want to do this either. Then we'll all be happy, and Mom will still be alive!* It was a nice try on my part, although that's not really how it went down.

When you decide to bring them in, just for the record, a nurse waltzes into your home, dressed in white god-awful looking clogs, usually with a clipboard in hand, and outdated bifocals latched onto some overly bejeweled chain around her neck. She'll be quick to hand you all the info that you didn't want in the first place, and she'll even sound nice—like really nice. Our nurse, specifically, came too put-together for anyone's taste.

Ew, she should at least untuck her shirt, I thought. "I'm not going to like her," I mumbled to Rennie, just as Katie nudged me, silently telling me to grow up. After being introduced to Mom, who seemed completely uninterested by the way, the nurse quickly got down to business. Explaining the services and the purpose of Hospice care and everything they provide each patient, I sat there thinking how annoying she sounds, but overly sweet at the same time. I wanted to like her—well, that's probably pushing the truth just a little bit, if I'm being honest—but, I knew for Mom's sake and my family's that I needed to somehow figure out a way to accept it.

This lady went into great detail on all the topics in her patient booklet, entitled *When the Time Comes*. It was miserable and excruciating to hear, unnecessary at this time in our lives, and seriously, way too much information at one time.

After that discussion, I did gain a tad more knowledge of Hospice and their mantra for dying people. Well, I'm quite certain that someone who was dying and needed them, they would truly benefit from their service. It's just that we didn't need them at all. I couldn't believe that they were actually in Mom's house. It felt so wrong—almost like we were betraying her. I didn't want her to feel like we believed she couldn't handle it anymore or that we couldn't either. *Mom's fine, we're fine, it's all fine!*

Until it wasn't.

Her care swiftly shifted from care to comfort in an unrealistic amount of time. At that point, I had no choice, but to lean on Hospice. When you witness that transition, finding out that there's simply nothing more you can do to rid her body of the Grim Reaper of all diseases, you become vulnerable, taking whatever it is you can get.

When the nurse left that day, Dad sat in front of Mom hoping to start a discussion on what they said and how she specifically felt about all of this. "I don't need that," she said, calm in a way that I never really knew how to do. We were on the same page once again—that's my girl! I'm telling you, I can't make this stuff up.

He grabbed her hand and expressed how her wellbeing is the only thing he's working to maintain. He told her he only wants the best for *her* and will never make her do anything to make her uncomfortable. Let's be real he is such a sweet husband. "They come to help keep you out of pain and manage your symptoms, Pam," he told her. "They will not speed things up and they will only be here when we need them to be, so we can be a family, truly enjoying all of the valuable time that we can spend with you instead."

He had a point. *If that's all they do, then I think I can probably agree to this, but can we just call them, "nurses," and not, "Hospice?"* That word sounds so comforting and cozy, but I can assure you when they enter your life, comforting and cozy aren't exactly inside those life boundaries anymore.

Either Mom was just tired of hearing it, which most likely was the case, or she figured, "Fine! What the hell?" She finally agreed to it and now, I knew I had to do that, too. I couldn't be that selfish to just sit there in denial, watching my mother wither away, knowing in the back of my head that there is indeed something else out there that could possibly help her in a way that we just couldn't.

Finally accepting that Hospice was coming, whether I wanted them to or not, we all felt naively hopeful that maybe they could extend Mom's life way beyond the doctor's assumption, because his assumption sucked, and I wasn't ever going to accept that one.

That was until I had to accept it.

Her physical and emotional state wasn't one that any of us were familiar with anymore. It was truly too painful to even comprehend. "Now that we have Hospice, maybe they can keep her around a lot longer, so we can swap life lessons and she can even share with us her bean dip and lasagna recipes while we soak up all her love right here in this house," I said to my family over a glass of wine in the kitchen one night.

"Crystal, they aren't going to make her go away any faster and unfortunately, there isn't anything they can do either to keep her in that chair watching *Ellen* re-runs forever." That was the truth they came back with, the truth that I really didn't want to hear. I was clearly in denial.

"OK, well, then, she doesn't have to watch *Ellen*. We can change it to something else that will keep her mind occupied, like ... *Tammy!* She loves the movie, *Tammy*, and anything with Melissa McCarthy in it is sure to keep her around." Yeah, no, I guess it doesn't really work that way, which is stupid, but I mean ... at least, I tried.

Hospice was foreign to us, which made it hard. The unknown is super uncomfortable and this type of foreign uncertainty is not fun!

We watched over them like hawks, making sure we knew ahead of time every medication they were giving her and for what exactly. Looking back now, I'd say we were quite annoying. I even jotted down all her vitals in the *Notes* app on my phone. I didn't know if I'd ever need those again, but if I did, I had them.

The nurses were coming once or twice a week, which regretfully proved not to be enough. As she grew uncontrollably weaker, they showed up more frequently—and by this, I mean **every single day**! They brought in all the painful reminders coinciding with this shitty part of life, things like those crazy weird-looking breathing exercise machines, blood pressure cuffs, stethoscopes, laptops, and a huge collection of medicine bottles that now seemed useless. Nothing helped her get better, so it was all about her comfort now, and even that wasn't being achieved. She wasn't comfortable and sadly, she wasn't herself anymore either.

Now I'm sure Hospice has quite the protocol to follow when they're up against somebody's ticking life timer, but then they brought in the awful and severely dreaded hospital bed. It felt like an episode of *Doomsday*. It wasn't my choosing (shocking)—though, at this point, she was never comfortable. The chair wasn't cutting it, the amount of pillows and blankets we smothered her in weren't doing the trick, so—well, maybe this horrid bed would do the job? It was already difficult enough having to accept reality, but the reality of that bed just plain sucked! It all just came flooding in, day after day, and soon her house was chock full of every hospital essential that you could ever imagine.

"Yeah, that's probably not going to work," I said to the nurse, standing over her shoulder as she locked the wheels of Mom's bed. I even got down on my knees to watch her lock the bed wheels, making sure even *that* was done correctly. That's no joke. Insane, yes, but a joke? Nope, that was totally true. I was very annoying. I wanted something or somebody else to blame every bit of this on—anything besides fate would work.

I had no recollection of any type of life going on outside the walls of Mom's house. I trusted that my children were being taken care of and any other duty and responsibility that I had in my life, I was not fulfilling at this time. I would admit to you that my employer probably tried to call me endlessly, but I don't even know if that happened, because I purposely left my phone dead and uncharged—ignoring the fact that I technically still had a job.

The sound of the TV in her living room became so normal that I stopped hearing it all together. I'm pretty sure I never heard another screeching tire outside the front door of her house anymore either. My appetite and sleep schedule? Oh, that was gone! The only thing I focused on as she remained in that bed were her breathing patterns and the rhythm of her chest moving up and down. I lived off the feeling of her wrist pulse and I memorized every vein pathway on top of her hands. I found myself obsessively counting every freckle and pigmented spot on her skin. I'm almost positive I even went so far as counting every speck of glitter intertwined into the polish that was painted on her nails.

After I had counted what seemed like all her bodily décor, I stayed there with my head on her shoulder, spinning her wedding bands around her finger, because in those new and trying days that was the only comfort I could get. Nothing else in the world ever mattered to me during that time. If my kids weren't homeless on the streets, starving, and waving a "We need food, God is good" sign, then nothing else mattered. We were everywhere we wanted to be and everywhere we needed to be.

"Ma'am?" I asked the nurse. "Wh … why are her feet so swollen?" It worried me, because she had let her feet dangle off the side of that bed many times before this. I didn't understand why *now* they started swelling so much and looked like they were about to pop. "That has to hurt her," I exclaimed.

"Well, the tumor in her perineum is likely blocking the circulation in the pathways, causing no return flow in her lymph system," the nurse threw down.

I thought, *Whoa – slow down lady. First of all, please talk English and second, that was entirely too much information for me to process all at once. The words "tumor" and "blocking" are not the ones that I wanted you to say!*

That response pushed me back into the couch cushions, desperately pulling out my phone to search for some sort of solution that would stop her limbs from swelling and anything that might magically pop up claiming to cure cancer. Her pulse at this point did become regulated and I thought, *Great, something finally seems to be going our way!* However, her blood pressure began to significantly plummet. She was taken off the aspirin and daily multivitamins, because according to the Hospice nurse, "It isn't doing her any good just sitting in an empty stomach."

"Mom, you have to eat something!" we practically demanded at this point, but she didn't. We couldn't make her do anything anymore.

The nurse, I'm assuming felt that at this time it would be a very, umm … appropriate time to enlighten us with this sweet, loving statement: "You can expect the end to be near when your mom is unable to get out of bed anymore."

Well, nobody asked for her professional and very unwanted opinion, but great! Now that you've said it, what in the hell do you mean, "the end"? The end of the day? The end of her pain until the meds start to kick in? The end of your shift?

Deep down, not really wanting to go there, I knew what "end" she was talking about, but I wasn't in any shape and I was lacking the mental capacity to accept that charming morsel of truth she has so willingly just given me! Allowing the acceptance of her opinions possibly becoming reality wasn't in my plans because after all, she's not God, so she doesn't truly know, but I hope to God that she's completely wrong.

After I threw that statement into the pile of shit that I labeled "lies," I sat there watching her continue to fight for her dwindling life. In a few sacred moments with Mom, we told her things that we thought she needed to know and shared with her our many vulnerable worries and concerns for the life that was quickly coming our way. I thanked her for the lessons that she'd always taught me and for the memories I will never let go.

She would mumble a few unrecognizable words, shrug her shoulders, or gently squeeze my hand just to let me know that she was still listening. It was so painful. Those moments were just as good as anybody else's conversations with somebody who could verbally reply with words. We took turns, going through the family, holding tight to those special moments alone with her. I'd walk outside for a short break only to find myself googling once again, this time "end of life symptoms."

Even though I knew where that had taken me the last time I googled Mom's current situation. I still knew my heart needed to know. And, yes, I asked for it, but it still sucked having Google give me fake, rarely true, mostly fabricated, utter and complete lies as the answer to my desperate questions about life ending that I obviously had no self-control over not asking in the first place.

I didn't believe the internet results or the nurses and doctors, and I most definitely didn't believe that God was good anymore. Everything I was taught as a child growing up in a Lutheran school and church, this wasn't the God *I* remember learning to know! Nobody tells you what it's going to be like when He makes your mother suffer right in front of your eyes. Nobody warns you about this side of God's plan. It's left out on purpose, because the reality of death isn't something anybody ever wants to accept, much less talk about.

I returned to Mom's side about ten minutes later, feeling deeply saddened and worthless. I wanted so badly to believe that she'd be the miracle that would prove Google wrong. I could see the headlines and breaking news now: "Central Florida Woman Beats Googles Odds of When Her Cancer Death Will Occur!" I was relentless and very angry watching my life fall apart while I was trying to desperately grab hold of it. Feeling like it was slipping from my hands, regardless of my death grip (no pun intended), it made the situation worse, leaving negativity as the only thing existing in my whole being. It became like a movie scene, leaving you sobbing into a tissue as you watch the actor tell her dying mother that, "It's OK to let go."

The sight of Mom in pain, the crackling of her breath, and the feeling of her body turning cold in my hands was as painful as it gets. The whispers with her were beyond heart-crushing. It was a pain that I never want to feel again, nor words that I ever want to repeat to anybody for the rest of my life. Telling her, "It's OK to let go," is a permission statement you never want to give.

I didn't mean it. It wasn't OK! I didn't want to say it, but it just came out and, in a way, my heart knew I needed to say it, for her sake. I didn't want to accept what was happening and I never wanted to accept the raw fact that I really might be losing my mom right now. I didn't want her to go. I've never felt pain like that in my entire life. It didn't even feel real at times, because it's not something that I believe I could ever possibly put into words trying to describe even a mere inch of what it's really truly like.

Clueless and utterly confused, I had no idea what to do anymore. I was heartbroken, knowing she might actually believe that permission statement I felt compelled to give. *I'm sure she knows I don't mean it and that I'm definitely not in the right state now to be saying this.* I thought and hoped! All I could do right then was kneel and pray. The life I always knew was broken and shattering so fast in that bed on which I was lying my folded hands. She was still alive, but … *She* was gone.

We knew there most likely wouldn't be a better time than now to surround Mom with all her immediate family members, so we called them all in. She continued holding tight to life, fighting with every part she still had left in her. She couldn't speak to us anymore and even struggled to breathe.

Witnessing the life being sucked out of our mother is more painful than any explanation would ever be worth. I didn't want her to leave me or us, but I couldn't stand the sight of her in pain. I wanted so badly to take her place. I didn't want to lose her, but I wanted this horrid misery that was trapping our family to be over. I wanted my mom's suffering to stop—she'd had way more than enough! I hated the cancer and everything it had done to her. It was stealing her away and leaving us with no remorse or even a second chance at changing its outcome in ways that we weren't sure of yet, but I know could have figured out.

We knew that she had always expressed the fact that any time her quality of life was gone, she would want to go. Naturally, it didn't seem like the quality of anything was left, except the shell of her body that continued to breathe. We wondered what she could possibly be waiting for.

"Wait!" Katie shouted, looking like a light bulb had just lit up in her head, "She's probably waiting on John and Vicki to get here!"

"Maybe she's right!" I said, hoping that was true, because it was giving us more time with her. They had been on standby in the mountains of North Carolina, knowing that the plan was to call them when we felt that the time was approaching. Sadly, it felt like it was time. Dad made the call and they wasted no time getting back to her. It usually takes a good ten to eleven hours to drive from their mountain house, but when you're speeding at a rate of 90 mph, through four states and knowing that you only have limited time left with your very best friend–you get back in an unrealistic amount of time.

This didn't come as a surprise to anybody, considering the close friendship that Mom and Vicki had all this time. Dad met them out in the driveway and together they sprinted through the front door and to her bedside. She immediately knew they were there, lighting up more at that moment than she had in what seemed like several days. Vicki and John were consumed with many emotional tears, worry, sadness, and shock that filled not only them, but the entire roomful of people, who were witnessing that heartbroken friendship circle. She now had her close family and very best friends filling her house and her bedside, giving her all the love and support that we knew how to offer at this time.

You know the stories that people tell when they're feeling worried or scared? Those stories don't seem to have much meaning, but instead are simply just a time-filler. Those were the stories echoing in the living room that day as we filled her couches and chairs. Inappropriate for any other time in life, but right now, they were appropriate and very necessary during these moments. We laughed at them, *partly fake and partly real*, because eventually remembering the whole reason behind that living room gathering that brought us together in the first place, took all the joy and silliness away from those stories that we had forgotten all about until now.

Each person in the room looked at her the whole time, taking turns venturing to the kitchen to reup on the wine or reheat the leftovers that consumed all her counter space. For a few minutes, I noticed she was lying there alone in bed, sleeping through this madhouse of conversations among family and friends, but I couldn't stand seeing her looking so lonely. I didn't know what she was thinking, or if she was even thinking of anything at all. However, I knew she could still hear us and I didn't want her for a second to think nobody cared to be close to her while all this went down.

I crawled up in bed with her and snuggled up between the wall and the side of her body, covering myself with her blanket and lodged my face up against hers. I listened to her breathe and felt the pulse of her neck against my cheek, beating very inconsistently and slowly. I stayed that way for a few minutes, but convinced myself to move my head, because I didn't want to be the one who felt her pulse give up on her.

It was a comforting sight to see our pastor and his wife walk through the back door and into the living room a few moments later. They were good friends of Mom and Dad, the ones you love to have sitting in a group with you, listening to all the non-kid-friendly adult stories that they would tell from way back in their not-so-innocent high school days–you know, the days they learned from living. You see, it wasn't just our "pastor and his wife." They are truly the human beings who anybody would be honored to be around—at all times, not just times like these.

At some point during our family frenzy, somebody asked Pastor Ed, "What do you think she could be waiting for?" That was a hard one to answer because, after all, he's not Houdini. He's just a pastor, but I think we all felt like somehow, he had more answers than any of us did. He did go to school to be a pastor and I think God probably does give him more than any of us since he's the one who put all the time and effort into learning how to mentor people in these awkward and uncomfortable situations that nobody ever wants to be in. *Sort of kidding* ...

Knowing Mom, you know—our entire lives—we knew there was still something else for which she was holding on—something with a legitimate reason. Even though we were all there beside her, in the bed with her, talking to her, and kissing her, all of it—she just didn't seem to be ready yet and we didn't understand why. Nonetheless (and I can honestly speak for every person in the room at this time), we were OK with her not going anywhere, because nobody wanted to lose her—ever, but we knew there was some sort of method behind it.

After a while of really nothing going on, everybody took turns with her, hoping that she could hear us and wondering if her next breath would be her last. It was getting late, so by this time it was dark outside. Pastor Ed and Nancy decided to go home, but reiterated to us not to hesitate to call them if and when something changed, no matter what the change was. As they stood up from their chairs, Pastor Ed said to the room, "Before I leave, I would like us all to grab hands and say a prayer over Pam while everybody is still here."

What an iconic moment that turned out to be! My father, sisters and brother, our spouses, my uncle and aunt, her best friends, and my two grandmothers all stood up, making their way to her bedside engulfing our mother. (Well, almost everybody stood up. But we didn't trust Grace to stand anywhere for absolutely anything. Instead, we wheeled her up on her walker to the side of Mom's bed. We were taking zero chances with that one.) I was still in bed with Mom, wedged closely to her side, since I was physically unable to crawl into her skin. However, I did generously move a few inches closer to allow all the others to get right up next to her as well. It was only fair that I did share a little. I put her hand that I had been holding up against my cheek as I bowed my head against hers, just as Pastor Ed began to pray.

"Amen!" he said, concluding the most moving, miraculous, calming, truthful prayer that I'd ever heard—way beyond perfect for our current situation. We all joined in shouting "Amen," feeling hopeful that just maybe that prayer did something. Maybe there is a miracle that would be here soon. Everyone took their hands off Mom at the closing of Pastor's prayer and started to step back, giving her some space. I mean, not everybody moved their hands, but you get the idea.

We exchanged hugs and yelled, "Thank you" as he left us. He reminded us, "Call me if things start to go downhill and we will be right back here." Unfortunately, they didn't even have time to set down their "to-go" Chinese food on the counter in the house before we called them back. Just as they pulled into their own driveway a mere five-minutes across town, we called to say that we needed them now the most.

There we were, gathered beside her and huddled together as our loving family of six, witnessing our most traumatic fear happening right before our eyes. The others gathered in the kitchen, stood there in despair; speechless and heartbroken. It was our moment. Our moment with our mother and our dad's wife—it was just us, the only "us" that we've ever known. With Rennie at the foot of her bed, Katie and Meagan at her sides, Dad and I leaned over her face together, trying desperately to get her attention. We called out to her in horror, demanding that this life give us just one last chance to hear her voice again. We begged and begged, but we got nothing— nothing except that terrifying rattle of her breathing as she gasped for air just to stay alive. We tried helplessly to get her to open her eyes or squeeze our hands, just to let us know that she was still there with us, but it didn't quite go that way. The faint mumbles and sniffles from the crowd in the background of our family huddle completely went away.

Everything was totally silent, when the only world that we had ever known—just stopped.

While husband and children screamed out to her, severely defeated, watching our worst fear come to life, the clock ticked over to 8:40 p.m. and we lost her.

Our world crashed, completely wrecked, demolishing every ounce of hope that we had tried to hold onto for those last four years. Done. Gone right there, shattered into a billion pieces that will *never* be put back together again. *It was over.*

I'm almost positive that my heart stopped, too. I had nothing left except gut wrenching pain, excruciating sadness, and devastating heartbreak. I couldn't breathe, grasping my hand over my heart, because the pain felt unbearable. I screamed out to her, "Mom, please wake up," but she didn't. "Please don't go. I'm scared, Mom. I don't want to be alone!" But there she was—*lifeless.*

I collapsed immediately onto the floor next to her bed, my head hitting first and the rest of my useless body tumbling down next. I wasn't sure if I was having a heart attack or my body simply stopped working from witnessing what I had just seen. I thought maybe it was shutting down like hers just did and, truthfully, in that moment, I hoped that it did. I collapsed there in pieces, sobbing uncontrollably and screaming, "Oh, my God!" My whole life was gone, yet I was still alive in this new, very scary, and dark life, but completely lost. I was lifeless and alone as the memories of my perfect past began to flash back to me. I could see so vividly all our very best times and I heard Mom's voice again.

"I'm having triplets!"

"Mommy, watch me!"

"Can we come out now, Mommy? We want to see what Santa brought us!"

"Mommy, will you brush my hair?"

"I can't believe my triplet babies are graduating high-school."

"I welcomed my first grandchild into this world today, Sean Jaxon Bell! Memaw loves you to the moon and back!"

"Crystal, I am so proud of you!"

"Can we spend the night with Memaw and go on Papa's boat?"

"Memaw, can you spray whipped cream in my mouth like you always do?"

"I love you so much, Memaw!"

"Crystal, why are you at Target again? Go to work!"

"Memaw loves you so much, Doodlebug. I will always be so proud of you!"

"As long as Dad knows you are all okay, he will be just fine."

"Crystal, I will always be with you, no matter what!"

I was gone from reality, basking in the perfect world that Mom was in, reliving my life right there, as the memories just kept coming.

"Memaw loves you so much, May-Tay!"

"Never forget who you are! You will always be the other half of my heart."

"The day you married Sean was the day I knew that you'd be taken care of forever."

"Memaw loves her sweet T so much!"

"My goal for you is to strengthen your relationship with God."
"Chlo Chlo, Memaw loves you!"
"Rennie, will you pick up a bean burrito from Taco Bell on your way home?"
"Memaw loves her Kins Kins!"
"I have four kids out in that waiting room that need me!"
"Honey, you don't need me to survive. You will be okay, I promise."
"Crystal, I will always love you more!"
"I love you to the moon and back, back to the moon, around the stars forever and always!"
"When that day comes, I will not be scared. I'll be at peace knowing exactly where I am going, and I will see you all there!"

I wanted to stay there forever. It was familiar, calming, and perfect. But instead, I was there flat on the wood floor in a ball of pure shock when I felt a gentle hand on my shoulder. I looked up through a veil of heartbroken tears to see it was my husband standing there wiping away his own tears as he helped me up off the floor.

I didn't want to be helped up. I wanted to lay there and go back to my old life, even if it was only in my head, but I guess that's not how it works in this new life. I am blessed to still have my husband, the one helping me to stand up and put one foot in front of the other to show me that he will always be right beside me.

I felt alone, but I *wasn't* alone. He wrapped his big arms around me, swallowing my entire body, but I didn't hug back. I had never felt so cold in my life and nothing more than completely worthless. I had no energy to hug back, and I had no emotions towards anything but the devastation I felt watching my world just leave us behind. What I didn't realize then was that my world was still there, hugging me with the deepest love there is. My mom had always been my *home*, but now my *home* is him.

I heard the most agonizing cries from my father and siblings. I heard horrid heartbroken sniffles come from my sweet grandmother, who was still slumped over on her walker next to Mom's head, trying to comprehend what had just happened as she watched her only daughter take her last breath. I saw Vicki, Mom's very best friend, dig her head into John's chest, gasping for air as she cried endlessly. She, too, felt alone now. I saw the confusion and heartache on a deeply saddened mother-in-law, and the look of shock and horror on my uncle's face as his eyes poured out tears in rivers. I looked around the room seeing the lives she touched that were left behind. It was then that I heard the horrifying screams of pure terror in my dad's voice when he yelled, "Oh, my God, I just lost my best friend!"

Nobody knew what to say and nobody knew what to do. We'd never been in this position before and we still had her sweet, tiny, cold, lifeless shell of a body lying there in the middle of us all. "What do we do now with her body?" someone asked.

No one knew what to do, so I covered her, because I felt like somehow, I was stopping something bad from happening, yet, the worst had just happened. In a state of immense shock, I untangled myself from Sean and collapsed onto the couch next to Mom's bed. I curled up into a small and scared ball, trying so hard to vanish from the trauma.

Several minutes later, when the coroner walked through the front door to take her away, all I wanted to do was disappear. I may have only been able to disappear halfway into the couch cushions, but I certainly tried my hardest. I pulled the blanket over my head and closed my eyes, so I wouldn't have to witness the sight of my mom being taken away from her own home, from her loving family, and from her sweet grandbabies, who at this time didn't even know she was gone.

In hindsight, looking back today, I didn't realize then that my *actual Mom* wasn't being taken away, but only the mere shell of the body that just gave up on her. It took me a long time to come to that realization, because while I was lying under her blanket in a terrorized body puddle of doom, it wasn't quite the time or place to attempt any kind of logical reasoning.

I closed my eyes, allowing myself to loathe the darkness that I had just entered. As the coroner walked in, I heard the creaking sound of yet another bed being brought into her home. This time though, this was the bed that I never in my entire lifetime thought I would see—the one that was going to escort our mom away from us forever.

That's what did it for me, making me realize that this horrible situation was very much real. But *real* wasn't what I wanted right now. What I wanted was my mom–the one they were currently transferring from one traumatizing bed to the other.

I refused to watch or listen to any of the commotion going on outside my blanket fort of sadness. I put my fingers into my ears to block out all the noise and I sat on the couch draped like a ghost on Halloween, trying to drift off into a sleep from which I'd quite possibly never wake up. There isn't one world anymore, there are *two*—the one where Mom was still here and very much alive, and the other completely broken world from which God had just taken her away. We were confused, but the only person ever able to help get us through something like this was Mom. Everything in my past world that had meaning was now completely meaningless in this new one.

"Crystal, come on. We're going to walk outside as they put Mom in the car," Dad said, tugging on the blanket over my head. "Here; grab my hand and I'll help you up. I'll walk out there with you. We can go together," he said, giving me his trembling hand.

I struggled to stand up, not wanting to witness anything else that might be happening, but I walked away, hand in hand with Dad. We took the same path to the front door, through which that shitty and horrid bed had just rolled.

As I walked outside, I suddenly thought to myself, *Mom would leave in a brand new sparkling black Denali, my girl!* It felt like she had previously planned for that to be her getaway car, just knowing that *I* would be the one who somebody would have to convince to get up and walk outside while they drove her away. She knew at the time it was the car I had been wanting, so I wouldn't be the least bit surprised if she had something to do with conveniently picking that one to take her, I'm sure, with hopes that it might spark a smile on my face. Although a smile was not happening, I did grab a quick huff of breath to acknowledge her fancy ride out.

As the tears drenched my face, I could hardly see them lifting her into the back of the car. I grabbed Dad's waist and hugged him as tightly as I possibly could. He's all I have left. He's the only parent left in my world to lean on and I'm about to need him more now than ever.

Dad unwrapped my hands from his waist and walked to the car just as it began backing out. He tapped twice on the back window and said in a very demanding and severely hurt voice, "You better take extra good care of her! Do you understand me?"

"Yes, sir, I sure will," the coroner answered as he pulled out of our driveway.

In the dark of night, as we were standing at the end of the driveway watching as the taillights faded away, I screamed, "Mom!" as she left us behind.

Rallied together, lonely and beaten, our new family of five stumbled back inside, broken. We walked into a silent living room, because nobody had quite figured out how to pick themselves back up yet and there weren't any words to describe it.

Right away we heard somebody come through the back door. It was Pastor Ed and Nancy. Seeing them again made us feel warm and comforted. Pastor Ed went straight for Dad, wrapping themselves up with each other in such a manly hug. Nancy spread her arms around Meagan, Katie, Rennie, and me as a pillar of strength and a shoulder to cry on. Suddenly at just the mere sight of them, it all made sense!

A few hours earlier when we questioned what Mom could possibly be holding on for, we didn't know. But now, now we knew. Her whole life she lived for her family, and we were now well aware of that. Even though we were all there with her, that wasn't what she was waiting for. She was a woman of strong faith and going back to the moment when everybody in the house had a hand laid on her as we prayed over her—that was what she wanted. We huddled together as one big family, sharing the strongest kind of love and support you could possibly ever give somebody. But it wasn't until the prayer was said that she felt her life was complete and her job was done—*well done*. That's what it was all along—she was waiting on a prayer. She wasn't going out until that happened and, well, cue the music because that truly was *One Hell of an Amen!*

CHAPTER 26

NOW WHAT?

*N*othing can ever prepare you for the loss of a parent. It's simply not possible, nor can anything legitimately make you ready to break the news to your children, especially when it's about their most favored human. For someone like me, who assumes the good ole' internet has all the answers about everything in life, it didn't, not this time.

I take that back. It did bring up approximately 80,300,000 results related to the bad news that I needed to drop on my kids soon. However, not in the way that I thought it should be done.

I wanted to go in feeling supremely confident, like I miraculously still had the necessary strength left in me after what just went down last night. I couldn't go to them as blubbering conglomerate of a mom-less mother—that certainly wouldn't do anybody any good. We knew this, so I kind of just rolled with it, completely unrehearsed. After I dropped that devastating news on them, they went into shock, the resilient type of shock that only comes out in children. Taking the news like little champs only lasted a few seconds before we huddled together on our knees, starting the year-long cries of confusion and heartbreak. It was quite a moment and one that I hope I never have to revisit.

Life moves on, even after your mom dies—like that same day. Little things must be done and more difficult tasks must be conquered. You'd rather just lie in your bed, polishing off a carton of Blue Bell Ice Cream and crying yourself to sleep, full and sad—but you can't—at least, not yet. Don't fret though, those times are coming. Life goes on right away and it leaves you questioning how all this happened in the first place. One minute you're draped under blankets on her couch while your dead mom still lies beside you in her living room and the next, you're searching for the leash to take your dog outside. You know dogs still have to pee, even after your mom dies.

It's hard enough attempting to comprehend what just happened, now consumed in newly fallen grief, but somebody must be the messenger of bad news to the rest of your mom's world. Yes, that somebody is *you*. Just do it, rip the Band-Aid from the gaping hole in your heart and grab her nifty and overly organized address book, because you're going to need it. Put your immense devastation aside for now, because letting her family and friends know about her death has to happen before you can even think about taking care of yourself.

Sadly, despite society's expectation of something being official only when it's been posted on Facebook, the Mom's-a-Goner grenade is still done best by using your actual voice. It feels very unofficial not being stamped to a timeline on social media, but oh, it is very much official. In fact, it's just as official as the *Her Mom Died* label that gets pinned to your forehead the night she dies. The initiation to this sucky sorority is informing others of her death.

I kept repeating the "she passed away peacefully with her family at her side" line, but it wasn't peaceful. It was terrifying. I would have much rather *not* voiced aloud that scenario on an actual phone call, but because my mom was a stickler for proper and personal etiquette, I knew that coming back as a ghost to haunt me would almost certainly happen if I dropped that bomb in one massive text thread with all the crying face and broken heart emoji's. So, I used an actual telephone.

It's awful news to have to deliver, quite possibly the worst, even when expected. So, go ahead and prepare yourself for the most awkward conversation of your life. You'll feel the need to sugarcoat how it really went down, because the human being on the other end of your phone will grapple with devastation and an urge to console you, while you have your own devastation mixed with an urge to help *them*. It's not fun. But someone's got to do it, so stretching the truth by downplaying the details is the surest way of getting right to the point. Short and sweet–until you call the next person on your list.

Because nobody prewarned me that I'd have to tell the other people in Mom's life about her passing, I'm going to prewarn you. *You're welcome*. People who existed on the outer perimeter of her life quickly came out of the woodwork—the ones you never thought of because, well–they were just there. But because they knew her, they needed to know, too. For instance, the UPS guy! Apparently, he and mom were tight. I wasn't exactly aware of this until I encountered him in the driveway a few days later when he joyfully skipped his way up to her back door to leave a package. "Hey! This is for your mom. Is she home?" he asked, handing me the box.

Well, this is awkward. "Oh, umm … I'm so sorry to tell you this," I said, urgently searching for the right words that people use when breaking sad news to the UPS driver. "But she actually passed away a few days ago."

"Oh!" he said, completely distraught. "I am so sad to hear that." It was uncomfortable, clearly for both of us. I could tell, because he went straight into story-telling mode with zero hesitation. "Your mom was amazing," he started. "She helped me get through a tough time in my life after my wife passed away of breast cancer! We had many conversations out here in this driveway when I was supposed to be delivering other packages, but she had such an essence about her that helped me tremendously. I'm really going to miss her." They were even on texting terms, which contained usually the exact same message each time:

> *Hey, Pam! I know you're out of town and can't sign for this case of wine, but I left it anyway! I hid it under the chair on the pool deck around back so don't forget to grab it when you get home! I hope you're enjoying your trip. Talk soon."*

The dog groomer was another one of those "other" people who never really cross your mind when you are newly grieving the world's toughest loss. I offered to take on that task of dropping her two dogs off at the groomer every couple of weeks since nobody was home during the day anymore to do it. "How's your mom doing? I haven't seen her in a while," she asked me while I spun around trying to untangle the dog's leashes from around my waist.

"Oh, my mom?" I questioned, simply using that to give myself a few more seconds so I could figure out how I was going to answer this.

"Yeah," she said, "how is she?"

Now the spotlight was on me. She stared at me as I stood there looking very awkward, almost as awkward looking as that wet Shih

Tzu on the table behind her. "Oh, well, I'm so sorry to inform you that she passed away last month." She was shocked. "She went peacefully, and we were all there with her," I told her. Her eyes widened as she hung her head in disbelief. I continued, "But here's Abby and Carly, oh, and here are their leashes, but I'll just … I'll put them in the bag. I'll be back before 5:00 to get them. Thank you. Bye." It was a futile and desperate attempt to get the hell out of there as fast as I could. It was honestly embarrassing, but not on her part. It was embarrassing for me, because I felt just as shocked and surprised as she did when I heard myself say it.

You end up lying to everybody, like a lot. This is the hard truth about delivering that kind of news. It's for their own good, as you simply do not want them to worry or leave them to imagine, even for a second, the terrifying truth about her fragile mottled skin while she rested there zombie-like in a cancer-induced coma. You drop that charming word, "peacefully," because it allows them to draw up their own version of how her death went down. By doing that, it naturally seems as though she just drifted away, propped up on fluffy cloud-like satin pillows with her hands gently resting on her chest and folded neatly in prayer, with a slight smile on her face when her life just stopped.

You say she went *peacefully* because that's how you wish it had happened. You lie to them, because lying is so much easier than the reality in which you're now left to live. You'll fear their opinions if they hear how you had to coat the inside of her mouth with a sponge just so she could drink something. You become fearful that they won't accept the truth or even worse, you know you won't either. The false manufactured form of reality makes it less complicated when you try to block out those new traumatizing images that are now imprinted onto your own mind.

After a while, lying becomes too exhausting, leaving you to struggle as you continue attempting to smooth out the truth. It eventually becomes even harder to fabricate a more peaceful scenario than it is to just tell them, "It was terrifying painful and scary!" I personally didn't want to tell anyone. I had some weird concept that if I didn't verbalize out loud what happened, then quite possibly my mind wouldn't even know it had happened, therefore—it wasn't real.

I know when people respond with, "If there's anything we can do, please let us know." they're only trying to help. It's a nice and genuine offer given in respect for the grieving family, but after about twenty-six times of hearing it, you just want to say, "Thank you, that's really sweet of you, but unless you can bring my mom back to me, I think we're good for now, but I appreciate it."

Unfortunately, you end up sucker punched in the gut knowing that will never be possible. On the flip side, I do think that talking with other people about death could possibly be a good thing. There were a few others who have been through a loss like mine and for a few minutes, it allowed the focus to shift from my personal feelings of *I'm-hurting-so-bad-I-can't-breathe* to them and their experience and tips on how they got through it. Chatting about death and newly adopted grief, even if it's your own, can allow you to deflect off someone else who knows what you're going through. Everybody has a past, and most have hidden traumas that only come out when someone else is desperate for advice and support. The hard truth and honest struggle with which you quickly become familiar, is what begins to shape and supply you with the strength you'll need for the trying days coming up.

To be honest; I think telling people is the easy part, because the hardest part is breaking the news to yourself.

There's usually someone in each family who's the organized one, the doer, the logistical expert. In our family, it was Mom. Our saving grace was the question, "What would we have done without Mom?" This time it's, "What do we do *now* without Mom?"

Fortunately, Mom always planned ahead. Now that it has been a long three days since she passed away and her actual death wasn't the topic of the town anymore. We had to plan a funeral—her funeral. I'm all about planning some parties or get-togethers, but this one? Yeah, this was not OK. How do you plan someone's funeral when they aren't there to tell you what they want? Or is there even such a thing as "wants" for a funeral?

We sat down on the couch in her living room, racking our brains about where we should even start. We had blank piece of notebook paper, empty and open for all kinds of ideas, but nobody had any. While we lived those last few months in denial of her looming death,

Mom was over there planning ahead, knowing that she wasn't going to be around forever. *Who even does that?* Well, thankfully she did. I did remember her talking about it once before, and chances are that conversation wasn't very long because nobody wanted to even think about that day, but I did recall her mentioning a few things. "Wait! I'll be right back," I exclaimed, sprinting to the kitchen drawer where she stored all her junk that she claimed was "important stuff." I powered on her cell phone, went straight to the *Notes* app, and bam! There it was, labeled "Funeral Notes." I could not believe that even now after she was gone, she still hasn't let us down. She had always been there to save the day and our asses, so people don't start showing up to a church for a funeral that's a complete mess.

What an angel she is, and she hasn't even been up there very long, but she's obviously having no problems fitting in. In her notes, she had listed six songs that she wanted to be played. Songs are hard to come up with, and life is hard when you are trying to comprehend the death of your mother, but she knew that. Thanks to her, choosing the right songs was not hard. She made it easy on us. She wasn't quite mentally all there with us for her last two months, but she was still in there somewhere secretly planning this out on her phone. She probably knew that I would definitely be taking her phone and scouring through it as soon as she had exited the building.

The songs were the only things at this point that were written down on our notebook paper entitled, "Mom's Funeral." We knew the rest of it wouldn't just be given to us that easily. "I can't believe we're doing this," I stated as we walked down the eerie hallway of the funeral home, right down to the casket showroom.

By now, we are all well aware of my love for shopping and Mom totally knew that. But *Mom,* I thought, *this is NOT my kind of shopping!* I looked up at the lighting on the ceiling of the hallway (*pretending I was talking up at heaven*) and told her in my head "Really, Mom? You didn't have to go dying on us just to prove your point about how shopping isn't always a good idea, because this is an awful idea! Not cool, Mom, not cool!"

Dad, Meagan, Katie, and Rennie had already walked into the showroom, while I was still standing out in the hallway carrying on an imaginary conversation with my dead mother, when I felt someone grab me by the shirt and pull me around the corner into the room.

It was so bright in there. So many death beds on display—it was super uncomfortable and extremely odd. In case you've never had this charming type of shopping trip before, let me enlighten you for a second. It's like walking into a Mattress Firm store, the ones on every other corner of your hometown, and knowing you have to eventually settle on the most comfortable bed in which your Mom's petite body has to be stuffed in and put into the ground until the day that Jesus decides to come back.

Doesn't that sound like so much fun?

It was horrible.

"Well, which one *do* you like best?" questioned the funeral director. "We have wood, metal, semi-metal, and now we even have biodegradable options."

What is happening right now? This is hard enough as it is, knowing that we had to all agree on a box that would perfectly suit our mom's dead body, just to be buried. However, having this many options for that task was not helping. I didn't think any of it was going to "perfectly fit" Mom except her king size bed, but apparently *that* wasn't in the list of options.

"Also, you can even choose between mahogany, cherry, oak, bronze, copper, high gloss, or satin finish," he exclaimed.

My facial expression after that said it all, but in case he didn't notice, I looked over at Dad and audibly voiced, "Is he serious right now, Dad?"

Obviously, none of us were thrilled, but after Katie shushed me, the funeral director felt awkward, and Dad forcefully nudged the whole left side of my body. That meant now was probably a good time for us to get out of there. When we left that day, I'm pretty sure we had the most expensive and fashionable casket that place had to offer. Oddly enough, I think Mom would have really liked our choice.

When Katie asked me what I was planning on wearing to the funeral, I told her I didn't know, because if Mom was here, I'd tell her I was going to Nordstrom and she'd proceed to tell me that I have plenty in my closet to wear and not to go out and spend money. But

Mom wasn't here. After glancing in my closet full of things to wear, I couldn't find anything. So, in true me fashion, I went to Nordstrom.

This shopping trip wasn't at all glamorous. I walked in, right past the store clerk who greeted me too cheerfully. "Good morning," she said, but I just glared at her and kept walking.

I got to the dress section, barely stepping off the escalator, and wouldn't you know, another employee appeared. "Hey there! Welcome," rejoiced this lady who had just popped up out of nowhere. I tried this time to be a tad more personable to her. Her name might have been Tanya, but it could have been Karen. Either way, I turned around and walked the opposite way.

Just for the record, every dress I tried on was either too big or not really my style, so I ended up just shoving it all back on some random rack and left. Honestly, I should have just found something in my closet like Mom always advised me to do in the first place. It could have saved a lot of wasted time and way too many tears.

The night before her funeral was the viewing. That wasn't any better. We stood there, a small five-member family, much like an assembly line, just to greet all the sobbing, sad people who knew Mom. They just kept flooding in that entire night like some endless cocktail hour with an open casket on the other side of the room. We greeted what felt like nine hundred people, including those who only knew me in diapers or from a picture printed on the front page of every newspaper back in the day, shouting in huge bold letters, **"NEW TRIPLETS ARE BORN!"**

There were even all those people whom you knew only once in your life, from like a really long time ago, the ones whom you only get Christmas cards from every year. Although they only went to school with Mom or lived on base with Dad in his coast guard days, even the ones who lived next door to us for like a year and then moved out of state—they still *knew* her. I didn't know them outside of their annual bad haircuts or when they got their braces off, but I still had to stand there, hugging them, as they blew snot from their noses. It was weird and sad.

The funeral though—ohhh, the funeral—we had finally planned it and I did indeed, somehow, find something to wear, but now we actually had to go to it.

It was a beautiful ceremony. The church was chock full of grieving people all dressed in black, mourning the loss of my mom. I don't accurately remember much that day, but I do remember the painful cries of my father when he sat down in the front pew of the church just as their song began to play out loud. Meagan sat beside him, grabbing him with all the strength she had as he hung his head, crying with shock and heavy devastation. It was horrifying.

Meagan is much like Mom when it comes to speaking in public or in front of big crowds. Neither one of them ever enjoyed it and usually avoided that type of thing any time they had the chance. Not today though, as Meagan was the one who gave the eulogy, which was perfect. She has a track record of passing out, specifically in church settings, but I do remember that it was such an amazing speech. I think we were mostly more concerned on analyzing her body language in hopes that it would give us a warning sign before she passed out behind the pulpit, but … she didn't!

After the eulogy, Pastor Ed shared a few stories and allowed visitors to come up and speak. They shared their best times with Mom. He ended the service with the things we as a family wanted them to know.

Over those last couple of days between her death and her funeral, I encountered a lot of people. After a loss like ours, you go through the motions in a whirlwind of confusing and defeated feelings. You never really have a minute to yourself, and you haven't even begun to process what happened and where you are going next. I felt stripped of my sanity, questioning everything I did, and wondering if I was being logical and grown up or just plain heartbroken and judgmental. In a way, I'm quite positive that it was all of them. But during those last few days, I heard the same thing said to me, literally on repeat, each time someone else walked up to hug me.

Before the funeral, we sat down with our pastor to go over memories and some of the feelings we wanted to share during her service. I knew I had way too many memories to share and quite honestly, they are so special I'd rather just keep them with *me*.

However, I did share something—not a memory, but a very strong feeling that left me defensive and furious. He was looking for stories to tell that would make people laugh and stories that were worth sharing, but this one – this one needed to be shared even knowing it wouldn't bring laughs, rather a new point of view. He shared it in front of the church and because you weren't there, here I'll fill you in. "I am so sorry that your mom lost her battle with cancer." That–that is not OK, ever! You see, this angered me and let me explain why.

My mom did not lose. She won. Cancer lost!

Now I do believe there are no ill intentions behind that, but honestly what's the good? The word, "sorry"? If that's the case, we can all most likely come up with more ways to say sorry than that. To me, that statement screams horrible reminders of what just took her from our lives. It's giving props and high-fives to cancer, the so-called "winner." It doesn't commend Mom for her courageous fight, nor does it recognize the prize and all that she actually won of where she went and who got her there.

Saying that my mom lost her battle with cancer is like saying she didn't fight hard enough. Like she didn't put enough effort into overcoming it and she didn't have the strength, will, or courage to push through it to the finish line. It sounds as though she was weak and couldn't handle it.

But let me tell you something. Cancer fighters are most definitely among the strongest people ever created. They fight when they don't want to. When you say they "lost," it's a metaphor implying that they were defeated by cancer, undermining them as a person. It's disempowering and isolating. It's an insane framing of something that goes way beyond the definition of a "cancer battle," which I'm not actually even sure truly exists. It puts the burden on those strong human beings and immediately turns them into "the loser" of a fight they didn't sign up for.

Cancer is a disease—not a military campaign! It's an illness that people manage. It's complex, yet a prevailing attitude towards it still exists treating survival as though it was somehow an act of will. The fact is cancer doesn't care how courageous or positive you are. It covertly implies that people in remission must have done more than the others. It puts cancer and its death ending on a pedestal, claiming failure as the reason for why it ended the way it did. If your loved one is in remission, it means the treatment thankfully eliminated all the cancer cells in their body, but not because they fought harder or more endlessly than somebody else. Cancer will never deserve that kind of power over anybody. Only God has that power.

My point is this: words hurt, whether you're grieving or you're the supporter and friend. And actually when cancer takes the life of someone you love, there are no words. Simple words don't do a lifetime of justice. But as a friend, you're compelled to say something of support to let them know you're there and that you care–so choose wisely. Words matter a great deal. They are powerful and, despite our best intentions, they can be so hurtful, even with oncology and sickness, and more importantly … in the most vulnerable of times–*the death of your mother.*

CHAPTER 27

PROFOUND STRUGGLES

*I*t had been a full week now and we had to learn how to get by in our new life. For me, it felt like a dead end. I had no idea where to start, how to do it, and often questioned if I even had a purpose anymore. I couldn't grasp that I'd had my last visit with her—our final conversation and last holiday together. I wanted to say, "I love you," one more time and I wanted to hear her say it back. My memory warehouse was filled with fond and painful remembrances, but I was still holding on tight to the treasured collection of fading photographs.

My faith was dwindling. I had so many questions fueled by so much anger towards God, and He wasn't answering me. It's a lot easier to be angry than it is to be sad. The older you get, the more you forget the difference.

Mom was relentless in her growing relationship with God and quick to remind others to do the same. She found that cancer brought more meaning to her faith, but I felt like faith had let me down. I began questioning everything I had believed in, because nothing panned out like I thought it should have. The path between faith and grief is very crooked, yet faith and death can be deeply intertwined. It's a weird world.

Death appears to be a physical circumstance, but for me, it revealed a spiritual battle. It left me confused with a profound sense of emptiness, when my beliefs weren't helping me acknowledge or accept her loss, much less bring any comfort. Mom always taught me in times of pain that positivity and truth really do still exist, but now she wasn't here to help me through this. The God who she spoke about—the one being so loving and merciful—obviously wasn't my God anymore. Mine let her die. Trusting Him is easy when life is good and our loved ones are within reach, but how do you trust God when you lose someone you love?

I didn't feel that God gave us the tools to prepare for her death. It's so emotional and stunningly final. It makes you question His intentions all along. I've since learned though faith that Mom is in a better place and that I'll see her again. That can bring comfort, but it doesn't remove the pain of her absence. It doesn't undo the trauma that came from watching her suffer and die. I was Mom's shadow and I wanted to be just like her. It baffled me knowing God knew that, yet He still took her away, like the world's biggest Indian giver. If Jesus performed miracles and healed the sick, then where was the mercy and love for my mother?

It's so easy to turn your back on your lifelong beliefs when your sorrow after a loss as big as hers is so deep. Praying felt like a false hope, I no longer wanted to pray for the healing of others for fear they'd die, too. But eventually, we will all have to see the truth behind grief for ourselves, learning to build back the framework of a life that doesn't exactly accommodate our comfort anymore. I didn't believe the heartbreak and pain was fair for our family, especially having to witness the ending. Her struggle wasn't necessary nor was the amount of time she spent in the doctor's office or the flowers and meals people brought by. Although Lisa's Chicken Tetrazzini was the bomb, none of that would have been needed if God had just stepped in. What we needed was our mom, but *He* took her away.

The burden of sadness that I carried, the problems I was facing, and the affliction I couldn't shake began driving a wedge between God and me. I gave anger a foothold, causing a wide variety of negative thoughts and a lot of actions. When someone you love dies, you expect to feel sad and lonely. You expect to cry–like a lot—but you don't really expect to be angry. Anger is a hard feeling to process with grief.

My new motherless world became very complex and confusing to me. At times, even more disorienting was the emptiness I felt now by having fewer responsibilities due to her loss. I had spent the last seven months dealing with her treatments and prescriptions, her appointments, prayers, and Hospice. These things weren't needed anymore, so my life that had been put on hold to be her caregiver now had to be restarted. I needed to figure out how to continue to exist in the roles I had before her death, but I didn't know how. Things were so different now—it all felt meaningless and empty. When people tell you, "God never gives you more than you can handle," well, I was seriously testing that theory.

Here's the thing about losing your mom: you fear that you'll never accept it. This is still a hard one for me, four years later. You'll try to live up to this world's expectations of "moving on" in a timely and reasonable manner, but you won't. Outsiders will often use the phrase "new normal," like adjustment is a cinch, but I can assure you, it goes way beyond that. It's not that simplistic and nothing in your life seems stable right now. Everything in your life now is completely different and there's no part of it that's "normal." We could all stand in a group of motherless daughters and give that unrealistic expectation the middle finger, because honestly, screw the "new normal." Life is never normal.

Society's timeline for grieving is incredibly unfair. Its expectations of how and when you should pack up and move on are an illusion that doesn't make sense. You won't fully live in the way that you were used to doing. You can't because your physical "Life Help and Guidebook" is now dead. No part of this is easy, nor is it fair to have to carry the burden of the world's viewpoint, while you grieve the biggest loss of your life. That dear friends, is simply not how it works.

You know the old saying, "When life gives you lemons, make lemonade," but I'm here to tell you that life gave us a lot of rotten lemons and, well, lemonade is not what I'd call it.

CHAPTER 28

GRACE

*W*e tried picking our lives back up, but life continued throwing punches. Just two months after Mom's death, Grace passed away.

Mom had moved Grace into assisted living back in the beginning of that year. Honestly, she needed her own space, and it was time to learn some independence, even at the age of eighty. Better late than never, right? This wasn't like a normal assisted living facility—it was more like a luxurious apartment complex. We set her up in her own "studio," equipped with everything she could possibly need.

Mom loaded her cabinets up with coffee mugs and decaf herbal tea. She stocked her mini-fridge with Grandma things, like jars of her favorite pickles and too much Diet Coke. She organized all her microwaveable tomato soup cans, boxes of saltine crackers, and packages of iced oatmeal cookies in her food cabinet. She even bought Grace the world's longest extension cord so she could keep her phone charged from anywhere in her apartment.

Now she literally had no excuse anymore for not answering Mom's calls. She attached a schedule of the facility's weekly activities and outings that her roomies were to attend, hoping Grandma would take the initiative to roll herself on out to the dining room to join in—you know, make new friends, socialize a bit, and live life like a little kid again. We just knew she was going to absolutely love it there. It was such a fun little place.

Well, she hated it.

It was like she went on strike in a small ninety-pound ball of sorrow, with daily pity parties and little kid tantrums. Just kidding, that's a bit exaggerated. But she did refuse to keep her phone charged, because she knew by doing that, everybody would freak out when nobody could contact her, so eventually somebody would show up just to hang out. It was all tactics, luring us in so she wasn't bored and alone.

She was a no-show for all the activities about six out seven days of the week, only attending that one day, because when Mom used to visit, she made her do it, physically pushing her down to the dining room gatherings on her walker. Grandma stopped taking her medicine on time and showing up for all the meals. Thankfully, the nurses now have a key to her apartment, so they could use it when they had to force their way in if Grace ignored their knocks at her door. I happened to show up one of the times they had to unlock her door, only to walk in and find her lounging in her recliner, watching her soap opera reruns, with twenty-seven missed calls displayed on her phone that was laying next to her, unplugged with a low battery. God love her.

However, she was a brand-new woman when she had visitors—especially all her great grandbabies! She felt a motherly duty to get onto them when they climbed on her sofa with their shoes, or even when they spilled their crushed-up bags of Goldfish all over the floor. But she did it with a smile and asked for a kiss every single time they were done cleaning it up. It was so much fun for them to push "great-grandma" down the halls on her walker—and they may or may not have left a few holes in the walls when they ran her straight into them, However, their laughter was what kept her going.

Now that Mom was gone, our lives became occupied with so many things we were now learning for the first time. Grandma's days started becoming lonelier and depressing. She was grieving and she was tired. She tried to hold on as long as she could, but her broken heart took her.

Although she went peacefully, the environment surrounding her last moments was very similar to Mom's. The hospital bed, the Hospice nurse, and the same shallow breathing patterns until it just stopped completely. It was awful watching the death of another cherished and very loved family member almost immediately after Mom, but this time around I felt oddly different, kind of selfish in a way.

Now don't get this twisted. I was deeply saddened that I had now lost my grandmother so soon, with whom I was so incredibly close, but I felt weirdly jealous. Jealous because she was now only moments away from seeing Mom again and I couldn't. I was still sitting there very much alive and envying my dying grandmother. But in those moments as I leaned over her face to tell her I loved her, I also felt a strong sense of happiness for her. It was comforting knowing she wasn't in pain lying there, but simply resting until her heart stopped.

When I told her to give Mom a hug for me, I lost it. Grace was eighty and she had a long and full life. Never would I put a timeframe on somebody else's life, but Mom was fifty-eight! I wasn't grown up enough to feel like I didn't need my mom for everything in my life anymore, because I did need her. I wanted her!

Instead of living in the moment and celebrating my grandmother's life, all I thought about was my mom. I compared everything between their two deaths and reverted to anger, because of how differently they each went out. I sat back in my chair in Bubba's living room, while we waited for the coroner to get there. All I could think about was Mom. I wanted so badly to cry for Grandma, but that's not why I was crying at all. The sadness I was living with stemmed from my mom's death and it wasn't fair to Grace. Grandma deserved this moment of shock and grief, but I couldn't convince myself to give it to her. Mom's death was still huge in my life, overshadowing everything I went through after it happened. Sadly, this was just the starting point.

I felt bad enough not feeling sad like I was supposed to that Grandma was now also gone forever, so I assumed at least her funeral would go differently. I tried so hard to allow myself to live in that moment, giving my attention and despair solely to Grandma during her service, because that's what she deserved. However, I just couldn't do it. I kept seeing Mom lying there in the casket at the front of the room. The songs that were played were all about Mom, so I only cried tears for her.

I felt selfish and disappointed in myself, but deep down I knew Grandma would understand. She knew how close I was to Mom, considering she had to call her to come pick me up 99% of the times I attempted to spend the night with her–so she would totally get it, but I felt so much guilt. Even to this very day, I have never been able to accurately grieve the loss of my sweet and sassy Grace. I just still haven't felt it.

I do miss her though. I miss her silly giggle and the way she became so confused when we told her to "brush her shoulders off." She never could grasp the concept that nothing was actually on her shoulder, but it was just funny watching her perform what looked like a dance move to a rap song. She hated rap and she hated when we played it around her. She always considered it garbage and demanded we turn it off, but even then, she would still naively brush her shoulders off. She was the cutest! I miss her soft hands and the way her wedding rings were too big for her dainty little finger. I even miss the cute gray bob on her head that I had to brush down when she woke up, oblivious to her ongoing bad hair days. And, oh–that old beat-up brown leather purse that carried only Chapstick, a dead flip phone, and crumbled-up tissues—well, I even miss that, too.

CHAPTER 29

SHE'S EVERYWHERE

The "firsts" after a traumatic loss are always the hardest. Well, who am I kidding? It's all hard. But it was fall now, which meant the holidays were approaching and up first was Mom and Dad's wedding anniversary.

Nothing screams *comfort-seeking* any louder than it does when your dad mentions taking a family cruise together to get away. Watching him grieve was almost just as hard as loosing Mom. In a sense, we lost both parents for a while. We didn't know how to help him, because our loss was much more different than his. He was trying to navigate this life without his life partner, but we still had our spouses. We knew he wasn't in the right state of mind when he sprang that genius vacation idea on us, so we felt too bad for him not to go, but right now? Really, it was a horrible idea, but off we went.

Our grief overflowed like the all-you-can-eat ice cream machine they conveniently placed on the Lido Deck. That happened, like a lot, and the only way we dealt with it was to either ugly cry until our eyes became raw, or to keep the bartender in business by making endless batches of margaritas and downing draft beer. Most of the time we did both.

Katie boarded the ship sick, which if you are a frequent cruiser, you know that's a big NEGATIVE, but she hid it well while boarding. The vomiting started even before we left the coast of Florida and thankfully before the mandatory muster drill. We scored on that one, because Meagan and I couldn't let her throw up alone, so we skipped the drill, too! Meagan held her hair up as she crouched over the toilet and I stood guard by the door not letting people in until she was done. Ironically, her throw-up session wrapped up as soon as the drill finished, and it seemed like those three loud obnoxious chimes that ring out of the ships intercom system was timed just right, as we could finally get this party started.

We found the nearest pool bar and got right to it. It took a whopping two drinks per person before the crying hit hard. Usually, sharing stories and fond memories about your mother is supposed to bring you joy and laughter, but right now, it was too raw. We screamed and fought with each other out of pure anger and grief, for reasons much beyond the pettiness that started it. Things got pretty wild. Sean launched chicken poppers down Rennie's windpipes from across the bar, our drink limits were maxed out by say, a mere, eh ten AM, and we cried more than we laughed. It was a glorious time! This wasn't our normal family trip, clearly–without Mom, it was just plain weird. Just because we were out in the Caribbean didn't mean our emotions stayed at the dock. They came right along with us, packed in our bags, pre-mixed into our Pina Coladas, and they came out in our tears that fell down our faces as we screamed at each other from across Dad's oceanview suite.

I told you it was glorious.

After a day of swimming with the stingrays and snorkeling the reefs of Cozumel, we plopped ourselves down on the sun deck, sunburnt and sad. The conversations about Mom were constant and our tears overshadowed our smiles. We gathered around in a family circle, some on the lounge chairs and others leaning up against the ship's railing. In between our fake laughs and sniffles, Dad shouted "Look at that!" He was pointing to a lightpost that extended out from the railing over the ocean. A red cardinal came out of nowhere and perched itself directly beside us. Her little black eyes looked our way, winked twice, and flew away. We were dumbfounded! "Since when do birds just fly out in the middle of the ocean and land on a moving ship?" I asked.

"Not only that, but it landed right beside us, nobody else!" Dad chimed in.

"Yeah, and did you see it wink at us before it flew away?" Katie asked. I think we all smiled in unison at that moment, knowing in all of our heads who that had to have been.

"Where did it even come from?" Meagan asked. We looked over and there she was again, landing back on that same lightpost, turned her head our way and flew off only to repeat that sly move of hers for a third time! When Dad tried to reach out and touch her, she flew away for good, right smack in the middle of the ocean with no land in sight.

"What if that was Mom letting us know she's still here with us?" I asked, because in that moment, I believed it.

That was the first time since losing Mom that I became a believer in signs from above. To us, there was no real explanation behind one random bird flying by and landing three times beside us, of all the people on that ship, in the middle of the ocean, during conversations about her.

Here is the thing I've learned: our brains do not carry fear and relaxation at the same time. It's one or the other. As much as we'd like to think that we can find a comfortable place where we partially trust that it was a sign from Mom, sometimes we believe instead that it's just a mere coincidence that can put us in neutral. Being neutral minded is like driving a car with your parking brake on. I had already been trying to drive that car through life without an engine, for crying out loud. But it was in that moment that I decided to just release the parking brake and move forward with comfort, believing my angel had just dropped a sign.

Now that she died, we knew there was no way any of us would be able to recreate the traditions and magic that she brought into the holidays. Thanksgiving and Christmas were her two favorites. She did it all. Dad's only job for Thanksgiving was to pressure wash the patio and cook the turkey. Mom did the rest: preparing the stuffing, the dressing, mashed potatoes, and boats of homemade turkey gravy with a side of disgusting can-shaped cranberry sauce. However, nobody but Grandpa and her were the only ones ever to eat it. Her house was decorated pristinely with the welcoming warmth of fall, transforming the kitchen table perfectly into a gorgeous array of colorful comfort food. Left to our own, we'd surely sit around eating store-prepped cocktail shrimp and microwaving instant mashed potatoes, because we all forgot how to boil water and cook in the oven.

We hadn't yet mastered how to operate in this family without her, but we were trying. She connected us together and grounded us, constantly reminding everyone how many things for which we should be thankful, and not just on Thanksgiving. I could probably count on half of a tiny kid's hand, the things for which I still felt thankful. When I lost her, coming up with blessings that still technically existed was much harder to verbally admit. I still felt like I was dropped off in the middle of the ocean, with my chances of survival being slim to none before the sharks ripped me to shreds. I was lost, angry, and feeling defeated every single day.

"Guys, since this is going to be our first Thanksgiving without Mom … ."

Here he goes again … "I think we should all load up together and go spend it in the mountains." Dad said with his second genius idea of the year. I swore after our lovely cruise, I wasn't going to attend another family vacation without Mom for quite a while. Now that he's come up with another grand plan, I'm wondering what kind of drugs he's on, especially after we had just bombed his last idea of a family vacation. But knowing how hard it would be to sit in our usual seats around the Thanksgiving table in her house, we needed to get the hell out of town.

So, I went.

After eleven hours of binge-watching *Wentworth*, we finally arrived in the Smokies. We spent the next morning glued to the weather channel, hoping the kids would see their first sight of snow. Side note: do weather forecasters really know what they're talking about, because they had no idea what was going on in the mountains of North Carolina that week.

"It's going to snow in the morning!" all the kids shouted gleefully with their naïve little hearts. All they saw on TV was a snowflake icon pinned to the border of Tennessee. The size of it meant our little town of Banner Elk was going to see snow. Spoiler alert: there was absolutely no snow. We drove to the base of Sugar Mountain and found a small mound of dirty, leftover human-blown snow, just so they could touch it and say they saw snow for the first time. Even these moments, Mom shouldn't be missing. She would have been down on her knees basking in their happiness as she helped them build a five-inch-tall snowman just to see them smile. She would have even gone as far as stealing a scarf from one of our necks, if it meant Frosty was complete and warm. God, I miss her.

I woke up on Thanksgiving morning alongside my dog and my husband, wrapped in my Mom's salmon-colored long sleeved shirt, trying to think of every excuse in the book that I hadn't used yet just to avoid this holiday. Anything sounded better than facing this newly pathetic Mom-less holiday that lurked upstairs. It already felt different not waking up to the smell of decaf coffee or the stuffing already baking in the oven. Either that or this house was just too gigantic to smell what was going on two floors up in the kitchen! Dad has always had this weird pet peeve of not allowing anybody to wear jeans on Thanksgiving Day. Like, who even cares anyways? Well, Dad cared and we happened to figure that one out several years back.

We were all still living at home, no spouses or kids, when we walked out of our bedrooms to leave for Grandma's house–in jeans. "You are not wearing jeans today! It's Thanksgiving, you guys," Dad remarked. "Go change right now or Mom and I are leaving all four of you!" he sternly demanded.

"Umm, OK but what's the big deal? We look good," I said in a sarcastic voice, because I sort of thought he was kidding. "Do what I said—go change now or we're leaving you," he threatened. We rolled our eyes in our small half circle as they walked away to the car.

"OK, well, they aren't going to leave us, so let's just take our time" I said.

"I guess, if it's that big of a deal, let's just go change," Katie said because she's a natural-born peacekeeper. To be honest, it still sounds like such a silly thing, but he was dead serious, my friends. We piddled around, rolled our eyes, yelled from our bedrooms to each other about how stupid this completely made-up rule was and huffed and puffed so much that they left us behind!

"He was serious!" Rennie said, just as shocked as the rest of us were. It was then that Meagan came up with the best idea to date: "Well, if they want us to dress up and not wear jeans then I say we dress up!" She had such a conniving look on her face and I liked it.

We picked out our fanciest prom dresses, with Rennie in a suit, and drove to Grandma's house. It was a fabulous idea and this way, if we ALL did it, then we ALL went down together. We walked in her front door, sparkling gowns shining, Rennie looking spiffy and very well put together. The look on their faces was priceless!

I do have to say we were a tad bit nervous about what their reaction would be considering they were already so pissed at us, but then again it wasn't the first time the four of us had gotten in trouble together–so we just went with it. I knew they were stunned when Mom spit her wine back into her glass when we walked through the doorway, and I'm positive we could have heard a pin drop in the silence of the kitchen at that moment. It was awkward until Mom busted out laughing! She was always there to save the day somehow, making light of situations that really didn't matter at the end of the day.

Needless to say, after the initial grand entrance, we didn't last long in those stiff gowns, so off we went to change into our god-awful khaki pants that you never wore until they're all of a sudden the only appropriate thing you have in your closet for Thanksgiving at Grandma's.

When I woke up that morning in the mountains, I realized I had only packed jeans. I randomly opened the closet doors and *voila*! Wouldn't you know, a stunning bridesmaid dress was the only thing in that entire closet, hanging right in the middle of the rack, as if Mom had put it there knowing how I would be the one to only pack jeans. "OK, Mom, I see what you did there," I mumbled to myself with a smile as I put it on. I walked upstairs to everybody else crowded around the bartop in the kitchen. Dad was sipping his black coffee, Rennie was looking up the times of the Thanksgiving Day football games, and Katie and Meagan were already slaving away at Mom's famous recipes. I felt Mom all around me that morning, as it was totally her idea. I'm still convinced to this day that somehow she angelically put that dress there, because she knew it'd be the best way to start my first Thanksgiving Day without her!

Thanks, Mom.

CHAPTER 30

THE HOLIDAYS

I knew, despite our *Griswold Family* movie addictions and irrelevant bickering, Christmas would be the best it could be without Mom this year. For me, it wasn't starting off so great, as just the thought of it caused a blubbering meltdown in the middle of Nordstrom.

"This sucks!" I mumbled to myself, absentmindedly browsing the stocking-stuffer table. Nordstrom during Christmas is what I imagine heaven being like–happy and colorful, full of all my favorite things. But times were different now. Every shopper that passed me seemed so jolly and thrilled for this holiday. There I was, feeling very alone.

I wrote in a text to my siblings.

I don't think I can do this.

They all wrote in their own variances,

Yeah, I know but you'll be okay.

When Mom died, our family was collectively left behind and not by choice. She had kids with four very different relationships that existed in four very different ways, each one of us dealing with grief in our own way. The two things that we did agree on was the fact that it was so fiercely unfair. The other was knowing without a doubt that Christmas would never remain the same. I am very proud of them though, to this day, for the constant positive vibes they often shot my way.

I, being the natural-born procrastinator that I am, had too much shopping left to do. One minute in the shoe section I'd be all, "*Ohhh, Jaxon would love these!*" and the next, I was pouting. I recall becoming tearful and annoyed, staring at a mother and daughter duo. They were bickering as they compared prices of yoga pants that her dear sister would love as a gift. I suddenly despised them merely for the fact that she had a mother that she could negotiate prices with, and I didn't. Shopping had become such a depressing and emotional affair for me. I have always wondered if I didn't storm out of Nordstrom that day what I could have found for Christmas gifts that year. Oh well …

Do you know those families who have an obnoxiously tall Christmas tree with gifts stacked up to the ceiling? That was us—our family, every year thanks to Mom (*and Dad's wallet*). When it came to Christmas morning as a child, it was pure perfection. My internal alarm clock was on point every twenty-fifth of December. It'd wake me up bright and early—and by early, I mean six a.m. early!

Katie and I shared a bedroom across the hall from Meagan, which happened to be completely across the entire house from Rennie. Both Meagan and Katie were like grandmas on Christmas, never budging when I tried to wake them. In my head, I knew if I woke everybody up before Mom and Dad, then they'd have no choice but to get up. Four excited kids jumping on their bed would have been too annoying not to walk straight out of that bedroom when we came barreling in clothed in our pajamas.

"Leave me alone," Katie told me every year without fail. When I couldn't get her up, I didn't even try to wake up Meagan.

"OK, you're boring," I'd say as I scurried my way across the house to Rennie's room. I knew he would wake up with me. Most years, I'd already find him sitting on his bed waiting for me to barge in. Rennie and I have always been a dynamic duo, to say the least. We'd sit there, Indian-style atop his bed, talking about what presents we thought we'd be getting and discussing whether that noise in the middle of the night was in fact Santa himself. Everybody else was incredibly lame that early in the morning.

Usually, it took about thirty minutes of patiently waiting for the most unenthused family members ever to wake up, before we decided we were going to make them wake up. In my Tinkerbelle nightgown and Rennie shirtless, dressed only in his checkered Umbro shorts, we'd scurry back across the house to the girls' bedroom. We had this weird habit of making ourselves cover our eyes when we ran past the living room, thinking that was the only way we'd have the self-control to avoid spoiling the big gifts that Santa left us. You know, the ones that are unwrapped, because they were "too big to fit in his sack of toys on his sleigh."

We'd count down from three, flip the lights on, and jump on their beds like obnoxious two-year-olds throwing a temper tantrum because their mom didn't buy them *tic tacs* at Publix. Now that Katie was just as excited, we'd tag-team Meagan with planned antics. One would go straight to her window, opening and closing her blinds, another flipping on and off the lights while the third jumped directly on top of her. We were really annoying.

Here we were, running back across the house in a straight line, eyes covered, all the way to Mom and Dad's room. We at least had enough respect to try and tiptoe in quietly—that was, until the door creaked as we snuck in, so now it was on! We bombarded them. "Wake up!" we yelled, jumping up and down on their bed. "Let's go open presents!"

"Get up!" we chanted in unison. Dad, being a morning person, always hopped right up. "Not yet, I have to take a shower first," he'd tell us.

"Ugh!" we loudly sighed. Mom still laid there pretending to be asleep, like she really believed we thought she was serious. She'd throw in a few moans and groans here and there and rolled over about sixty-seven times before she finally decided to open her eyes.

"You guys have to wait. Your dad is in the shower," she'd so sweetly say, putting the blame on him.

Finally, Dad came out of the bathroom already dressed and smothered in Jovan Musk aftershave (*which by the way, he still wore up until about a year ago. Believe that!*). It was then that Mom decided to pull this charmer: "Let's sleep another hour." She cannot be serious right now!

"Ummm, no way!" we all yelled, so serious at this point we could have smothered her with her own pillows. That was the worst idea ever, yet it happened to be her genius plan every single year, like we'd never heard that before! Sprawled out at the end of their bed watching *Coyote and Road Runner,* patiently (or impatiently) waiting, we realized we'd lost Dad a long time ago.

"He must be out there already! Let's go out now!" demanding Mom just let us go already.

"You guys just wait a few minutes—I still have to brush my teeth," she said as she stuffed the toothbrush to the side of her cheek, standing halfway out of the bathroom just to make sure we weren't escaping on her. Do you want to talk about the biggest and longest sighs you've ever heard come out of four people's mouths at the same time? You should have been in the Heath household every Christmas morning!

Mom and her pearly whites with her dress-like night gown, freshly brushed hair, and body perfectly spritzed with Elizabeth Arden Red Door perfume was finally ready! We jumped up out of her bed and ran for the door. Just as we grasped the gold round door handle, her hand went up against the back of the door. "No, you have to wait! I have to go out and start the oven for the Egg Dish (the best breakfast casserole that you're so unfortunate to have missed out on).

"Then I need to turn on the video camera and let the dogs outside before you can come out," she said in that sweet angelic voice she had.

"Oh my gosh, Mom!" Katie butted in. Since the time Rennie and I woke up to this point of the morning, it felt like hours had gone by. Our excitement was now building to the point where it was just about to burst at the seams.

"I can't wait any longer!" Rennie exclaimed.

"Then let's go!!" I yelled with my fist towards the sky. We snuck out of their room into the hallway; one by one, on tiptoes with a hand on the person's back in front of us. Just as soon as we made it to the corner of the kitchen leading into the living room, we got caught!

"Dang it!" Rennie yelled. We hit the backs of each other as the line abruptly came to a halt.

Mama Bear came in hot, rounding the corner with hands glued to her night-gowned hips. "Now line up one by one in birth order before you come around the corner," she ordered, shaking her finger back and forth in front of our curious little faces. "I mean really!"

That puts me dead last of this line and what's the point of that anyways!? Once we get around the corner, it's a full-blown brawl fest! With the video camera rolling, the smell of breakfast baking in the oven, and the Christmas tree lights still twinkling from the night before, every Christmas morning in our household was one for the books!

How crazy is it that these childhood memories go by so slowly as a kid, but looking back as an adult, you realize they actually flew by. Those times of eye rolling, accompanied by laughter and smiles, are so sacred and special. It made our childhood perfect and brings so much comfort into our futures when it's needed the most. I tried very hard to keep up with as many of her Christmas traditions as I could, but in no way, shape, or form did I have the motivation to shop the amount of stocking stuffers to fill a stocking as big as a sumo wrestler's leg like she did. Plus, I don't even own a video camera. It's amazing how one person can make something so magical.

With nightmarish expectations of memories remembering our past life when Mom was there, it was truly painful this year. Who was going to make the deviled eggs that Bubba and I would stuff in our mouths two hours before dinner? We couldn't just show up anymore with raw yeast rolls that still needed to be baked (*cough-cough, Rennie*) and nibble on all her hard work. She wasn't there anymore to depend on having a full stick of butter available in the refrigerator door, so I could complete the pineapple casserole I brought half-prepared, because I am pretty sure Dad hasn't restocked the butter since she died. I couldn't possibly grasp why she died in the first place, but could she have at least been allowed to last through this Christmas and maybe even the next forty-five after that?

Those questions always ended rudely unanswered. The only thing that came to me in the form of a response was reality's big fat "Nope" as it slapped me in the face. It all felt so heavy. The thought of having to face it without her brought so many tears and dread. It's an odd feeling to imagine Christmas without Mom. She did much of the holiday's obvious work, plus a hundred other little things behind the scenes that we'd likely forget in all the holiday rush.

The truth is that there is no right or wrong way to do a holiday without your mom. You just kind of figure it out. It was painful the first time when one of the kids said aloud, "I wish Memaw was here," because so did we.

Christmas Day came and went just as quickly as the tears that flowed down my cheek as we stared at the sight of a living room that looked like a bomb of wrapping paper had exploded five times over. This year the soft background music wasn't "Jingle Bells," but the sound of dishes being washed in the kitchen, because Mom wasn't there anymore to do it. (I tell you though, she'd hate to hear me say that, because she was "not our maid!" But I'm pretty sure we're all aware how those things really go). She wasn't there to help us stuff leftovers into her Tupperware containers she made us swear that we'd bring back. What are moms really for if they don't loan us their Tupperware containers on days like Christmas and Thanksgiving and actually believe that we're going to bring them back?

She was always there to perfectly pack away the gifts Santa brought into giant holiday bags and help carry sleeping kids out to the car. Who was going to be there to send that one last "Merry Christmas, I love you," text before I crawled into bed in my new unwashed pajamas? Here, I'll give you a hint: it wasn't Mom.

"Well, babe, we made it through our first Christmas without her," I said to my husband as we flopped down in bed, exhausted and broke.

"Yup, we did, but she was there the whole time. We got this, baby," he replied. As we cuddled up next to each other, I closed my eyes and a shower of those same cherished childhood memories started playing in my head again. Tears streamed from my tired eyes, right down my cheek onto the pillow.

Christmas is quite an emotional holiday to begin with, and now it's just heartbreaking. I tried so hard to fall asleep, but my mind was still wide awake with emotions. Suddenly I heard Mom, as if she was narrating all those memories bombarding my head. "Crystal, I am still here. You must move on and make Christmas just as enjoyable for your children as I did for mine."

I could hear that statement plain as day. I finally fell asleep wondering if I even had that capability somewhere deep inside me. There was so much to live up to, such big shoes to try and fill, and so many traditions I didn't know how to carry out. I was genuinely thrilled that Christmas was gone now for another whole year.

I was all about it "being the first Christmas without Mom." The numbness was still wearing off, coupled with the pressure of trying to make it a good Christmas, despite the empty chair at our dinner table.

I tried to feel the magic and get excited thinking about candy canes and snowflakes and stockings hung up. But, well, there were no candy canes, snowflakes, or stockings this year. My mom was the Spirit of Christmas. She was the one to decorate the house so magically, to dress up the presents with perfect ribbons and bows, and to get the family all excited about spending the holiday together. As much as I've tried to keep them going, I've seen the traditions fade away this year. I've felt the pain with every mention of "Christmas." It's a shame, but it's the truth and that's why I'm writing about it here today.

Because I know that there are other people out there, some whom I know personally and some who are strangers, who are feeling this same pain that I am describing. They know deep down, aside from all the fluff and positive talk, that nothing will replace the void that is felt, while looking at the empty chair and seeing the bare spot under the tree where her presents were once placed.

The holidays are meant to be spent with family and loved ones. That has been etched into our psyche since the day we are old enough to comprehend what a holiday actually is. But what happens to the joy and warmth of the holidays after you lose a loved one? Living every day without your mom is already one of the biggest hurdles you'll be forced to jump one day. It's a huge void that can never be filled. Unfortunately, with that comes all the constant year-round reminders of her and everything she did to make your life magical.

But what is it about the holidays that magnify our grief? Holidays are such joyous times that come with so many memories attached—good and bad—that even the smallest things can send you spiraling down immensely. These memories that are implanted into our brains as children, most of the time only resurface in the winter. As hard as Christmas is for me without her, some of those memories do bring comfort. Those are the ones that get packed away in the back of your mind until they're needed again. Those are the times that we cry for and long for that make us ache to the core.

If you've lost your mom and you've suffered through the holidays, my advice to you is this: store away those good times and bad in a very sacred and safe place in your head until you find yourself blubbering into half a box of tissues on the bathroom floor Christmas morning. Trust me, you'll need those memories to help you stand up, pull yourself together, and go play Santa Claus, as you pass out all the gifts to your children who are getting extremely impatient, just waiting for you to come out of the bathroom.

You got this!

CHAPTER 31

LEAVING IT BEHIND

"Three, two, one, Happy New Year!" There it was, a bittersweet midnight, leaving our shittiest year and heading right into the next. I was confused, happy, and sad all at the same time. The way my brain works isn't something I can explain to you, because I'm still not exactly sure of it myself. I wanted to hold my middle finger high up to the sky as I watched the ball drop leaving 2017 behind, but instead I scoured the live tourist-infested Times Square webcam feed, trying desperately to find Dad, feeling like I was competing in some Where's Waldo World Championship.

Dad must have felt like a brand new man or something because, oddly enough, he decided to take off and go to New York City alone just to celebrate the ending to the worst year of our lives. Now keep in mind my dear friends, Dad is someone who despises being alone. So why he decided to fly to New York by himself is something way beyond my brain's comprehension. He said he enjoyed the time away, but I can assure you he really didn't, because we have about fifty selfies of him with a different New York landmark that we received in a two-day time span to prove it. That pretty much made us feel as if we were right there with him. I have always wanted to visit New York City during New Year's Eve but, thanks to Dad finally learning the concept of a text message, now I don't have to. I went everywhere with him on that trip. Thanks, Dad, I'll be sure to check that one off my bucket list.

When you lose someone special, your whole world lacks celebratory motivation. You feel lost and sad and then, the loneliness deepens to the point where it feels extremely isolating. Pretending you aren't hurting anymore is not your truth, but a lie to your soul. Believing that your holidays can stay the same as they were in the past isn't the truth either. Your life is different now and so are the holidays.

Those traditions carry on for a reason and we have to do our best to make them our own traditions for the children we are blessed with. I can tell you from painfully experiencing it, that you will get through it somehow. You are not alone, nor will you ever be. Thanksgiving, Christmas, and New Year's will come and go whether you spend it with family or sulking in your own tears while you down Ferro-Roche chocolates in your bed. It will happen regardless, and it will pass, just like the rest of your life. The holidays can be a magical and memorable time, but they can also be a time of incredibly trying faith. I have struggled with losing faith and finding it again, so I feel you.

During these holiday times, I seemed to lose the string of faith that I tried so hard to hold onto all year long. I'd be lying to you if I said I didn't question whether God really is there. I was convinced that if he was, I wouldn't feel all this pain and sadness and my mom would be sitting right in front of me with her glass of Pinot and glasses on the tip of her nose while she read *The Night Before Christmas* to my sleepy children. Jaxon said to me in his little sad voice, "Christmas won't be that much fun this year!"

I asked him "what do you mean by that?" Pointing to the sky he replied, "Because Memaw isn't here anymore."

Little Tanner chimed in and said in such a hopeful way, "I'm not sure what God got Memaw for Christmas this year, but I bet he got her pretty flowers!"

If those statements don't rip the pieces of your broken heart right out of your chest or drain every ounce of tears from your throbbing head, then I don't know what will.

Losing a loved one feels very much like you're being robbed of all the holiday joy you've always ever known and looked forward to enjoying. Although he's completely right, hearing my child confirm the feelings I have of fear and wondering if I can make life as good as she did makes the pain hit that much harder. I feel like I am struggling and failing horribly at making these holidays as special as they once were.

Does God really care for me? Did I do something so terribly wrong that he had to take my mom away from me just to prove a point? Those questions I'm still trying to figure out, but if Mom were here, she'd tell me to stop it and instead, just believe and pray. Pray for those who are entering their first holidays motherless, fatherless, or childless. You don't have to accept those Christmas or New Year's party invitations. You don't have to bend over backwards worrying about the Christmas cards you forgot to send out this year. Give yourself a break because it really is okay to do so.

I'm here to tell you that I know you're doing your best to move on, and I promise you're not the only one. You may not always be able to hold onto life with both hands, but never completely let it go. Hold strong on your grip! The grip of yourself and the grip of your life is your own story of loss, but it's just *one* chapter in your book. Maybe it's a huge chapter or several chapters put together, but it will never be the whole book.

CHAPTER 32

FULL-TIME GRIEF

I struggled relentlessly, battling major depression to a degree that didn't even seem real. Just when you think you've mastered the fine art of living and "moving on" without your mom, a new twist emerges and suddenly your work is just beginning. Sleeping at night flew out the window the night her soul flew to Heaven. I didn't even know what sleeping meant those days, much less the feeling of being fully rested and refreshed. I had already cut down my work schedule to strictly an "as needed" basis. I tried numerous things to keep my mind occupied, so I wouldn't fall further down into this well of sorrow and become completely limp and feel worthless. Unfortunately, that didn't work out so well.

For the first month or two I enjoyed being that "stay-at-home-mom" I had always wanted to be. My days consisted of whatever I wanted to do and that's how I liked it. I always had this perfectly planned day in my head that I swore to myself I was going to do now that I had no schedule to follow and nobody to boss me around. It was a new level of freedom that I hadn't known, and life seemed good again.

Don't get too excited, because that ship sailed quickly.

One night before her last surgery, Mom and I sat in her hospital bed and she started talking to me about what my future might hold without her. I didn't think too much of what she was saying, because I didn't believe anything bad would *ever* happen to her. She laughed when I told her, "Mom, one day when you're not here, you're going to have to give me a sign!" She dropped her head and shook it side to side, knowing how silly that sounded, but just how serious she knew I was.

"No! I mean it! You know I won't be able to live without you, so if you aren't physically here, then you better leave me signs, all day every day, like you're right there beside me," I demanded.

"OK, the next time you're in Target and you feel somebody tap you on the shoulder, you need to turn around and leave," she said, "because I know you, and most likely, it'll be on a day you're supposed to be at work."

I laughed, partly because she was totally right and it would definitely be a workday, but partly because she must not realize how serious I was. "Well, that won't be good enough, Mom. What happens if I don't feel your tap or if I turn around and someone else is behind me?"

She thought quickly and tried to convince me, "Crystal, you'll know it's me."

However, knowing myself, I probably wouldn't, so I continued to debate with her, "No I won't! That won't be good enough, Mom!"

She laughed again, finally concluding, "Fine. Then when you're on an aisle by yourself and something falls off the shelf, then turn your ass around and get the hell out of Target!"

Oh! She cussed, she's definitely serious! We laughed hard, because we both knew I would be back to Target at some point soon and she would be seeing how scared I'll get when something does fall off the shelf. It will be quite comical for Mom from above.

Since Mom is now gone and I'm miserably motherless, I'm completely on my own during school hours. My repetitive schedule went like this:

1. Drop kids off at school
2. Book writing at my favorite coffee shop (which by the way has the absolute best avocado toast in the world)
3. Target ($200 later)
4. Three-mile run around the lake
5. Ask my husband to pick the kids up because I'm still "so busy and won't make it back in time"
6. Home to quickly throw together something for dinner because I spent all of my day out and about
7. Wine, Netflix, and more wine

It sounds like such a "stay-at-home-mom" type of day, right? Well, not so much. Eventually, I became broke and the laundry at home piled up to the ceiling. One of my biggest issues is having so many clothes that I'll just let my dirty ones pile up and keep wearing the endless stock in my closet for weeks. (I highly don't recommend this unless you want to spend five full days confined to your laundry room washing an endless amount of clothes. Just sayin' ...)

I used to complain to Mom about how much I hate laundry and she'd tell me in her you'll-learn-one-day voice, "Crystal, I don't feel sorry for you. If you just wash a small load every day, you won't have to spend so much time washing mounds of it. It's not that hard."

I mean that woman was always right! I may or may not have just hoped she'd say, "Just bring them to my house, honey, I'll wash and fold them for you," like she did when I was a kid. Nope! Mom wasn't going to lend a helping hand where it wasn't needed. She always had a way of putting lessons in every type of scenario.

I'm a mother now and that's part of a mom's job description. I didn't even consider the fact that I wasn't working regularly anymore. Now I had more than enough time to get the laundry done. I still hate it and it's entirely too boring. If you know anybody that just wants to do laundry every day, send them my way. Help a sister out!

After she passed away, it took me months, and I mean months, to muster up enough courage to actually go back to Target. I just couldn't do it and, to be honest with you, I was legitimately afraid something was going to fall off the shelf in the home decor aisle and I'd have to leave my cart sitting there abandoned, while I ran full speed out the front doors.

The day I felt ambitious enough to just suck it up—mainly because I needed more shampoo and conditioner, or a new purse (same thing) —I proudly stuck it out and did it! I think I was ridiculously nervous that day because, when I pulled into the parking lot, I felt the eeriest and weirdest feeling ever. I didn't have to drive around in circles that morning looking for a parking spot like I usually did because, what do you know, there was one space wide open at the front of the store. I mean, this couldn't have been any more perfect, I thought, as I turned down the radio to pull in. (Like somehow turning the radio down was going to make me park safer. Weird)

I felt like a straight up VIP pulling into the front, having never before parked there. That feeling lasted all of three seconds until I looked up and a big, black cloud hoovered over the entire building!

"Hmm, that's weird. It's not even supposed to rain today and nowhere else is it cloudy and dark around here."

I tried ridding myself of my bad habits. OK, let's take a step back to where we start believing in obvious signs from above. This was the epitome of a "Pam-type" challenge. It was so obvious! Here she is reeling me in with the most perfect parking spot as close as you can get to the front doors, shouting out, "Look how close you got! Now you have to go inside, Crystal!" just tempting me to grab my purse and start my shopping spree right then and there with no questions asked. But, in true "mom fashion," there's always some sort of test in it somewhere.

Knowing I was about to go spend money on things completely unnecessary, she never easily gave in to that irresponsible action of mine. That's why she threw a big "No-No" sign above the store in her dark and gloomy rain cloud, trying to tell me not to do it. I sat there pondering on it for a good two minutes, heart pounding and wondering what I should do.

"I know I shouldn't be here spending money I'm not making at work today, but I'm sure there's something in there that I can buy." I tried telling her as if she could hear me from above.

Nothing shouts "Don't do it,!" louder than the voice I heard in my head saying, "Here, Crystal, go right ahead and shop," or ... "You can see I'm very much here in this rain cloud trying to tell you it's a horrible idea. If you walk in, I'll give you a tornado."

I laughed a little as I opened my car door and looked up to tell her, "Well, Mom, I know that's you and I *reaalllyyy* appreciate your efforts, I do, but you know me better than anyone, so I'm going shopping!" Off I went. Although nothing fell off the shelf that day, I knew Mom was there, watching me browse the things I definitely didn't need to be buying.

After finally realizing I couldn't keep spending my husband's money at Target every day, and seeing that the house chores were not getting done in a timely manner, I found myself curled up in a ball one afternoon outside on the front porch chair, hysterically sobbing. "Hey, babe! How was your ... what's wrong?" Sean asked me as he walked through the door.

"I don't know, I just don't feel like myself. It's like I'm not useful to anybody or anything anymore. Why am I even still here?" I cried, gathering my shirttail to wipe my face off. I realized in that moment that the depression and grief had completely overtaken my entire life. The important things in life took the trunk (even farther than the backseat!) and I was searching for materialistic things to fill the void of where true happiness once had been. I became obsessed with things that at the end of the day shouldn't have mattered.

I clung to my normal comforting things like running, hot baths, binge watching Netflix, gaining more gold stars on my subscription of endless weekly wine deliveries, and excessive sleeping. I missed (still do) my old life. I missed my friends and the memories we made when nothing huge burdened them. I miss having a mom here— our talks, our laughs, her advice, and all her inspiration. I miss the push she had behind me to live as the best person I can possibly be, because right now is when I needed it the most. She had always taught me just to surrender my pain and put it all in God's hands. I was doing an awful job of that. I felt like my faith had failed. It wouldn't protect the best of us.

When the worst happened, I thought if I had faith, then we could all just fly away with her and land in a world where this hadn't become a reality. When it didn't go that way, I could not understand why. She had always shepherded people in the worst moments of their lives, but now she's gone, and I am totally not grown up enough to do that for others, especially because I can't do it for myself. I couldn't love my family, if I didn't love myself. She was like my lifeline of living, so now I'm left here drowning with no liferaft to grab.

Before Mom passed away, my passion was exercising, becoming healthier, and losing the baby fat that I still tried to use as the excuse for my flabby stomach and not so perky boobs. Although that blame train had passed by a long time ago, considering my children are not babies anymore, I still used it to motivate me after she died, because it was something that wasn't necessarily "my fault." Blaming others, whether it is your dear sweet children or something totally irrelevant, makes it a whole lot easier to focus on getting better.

I became so obsessed with losing weight and looking good that I didn't realize I hadn't been spending nearly enough time with my own little family who desperately needed me now more than ever. Each time a pound of fat melted from my stomach, it'd just feed my ego and brainwash me into thinking I was "so much happier." I became consumed in not only the sweat pouring from my skinny bone-protruding body, but the unfair and unrealistic image that I had in my head of becoming America's Next Top Model.

I used to run about three times a week when Mom was still alive. Even when she told me, "Crystal, you shouldn't be running out there by yourself on such a busy road—it's dangerous"—I did it anyway. (Shocking, right?) Bless her bones, she was so caring and protective. I'd tell her in my know-it-all way, "I know, Mom, but I'll be fine! I am on a busy road, so if anybody tries to kidnap or murder me, there's bound to be somebody who will stop and call for help. Plus, I have my phone, so if I'm not home in thirty minutes, come look for me, because I've probably been left for dead in the woods down by the lake." She hated that response.

When I run, I have such a strong sense of peace. If you haven't tried it, even if you dress the part and just walk, you should. The "runner's high" is a real thing and it's much safer to be high in *that* way. I believe it does good for my soul and it helps to clear my head, which often seems like it's working on acid. (No, I've never done acid or any drug like that, but I can imagine it's similar to the way my brain feels every day.)

When she passed away, I lost my partner, my person. Who am I going to talk to while I'm stretching before my run? It sucks without her. I miss the sight of her reading glasses way too far down on her nose that there was no way she could be reading her iPad. I miss her laughs when Ellen pulls a prank on someone during episode thirty-six of the reruns that Mom's seen a million times. The sound of that rocking chair she perched herself in for too many hours of the day, won't ever exist anymore, because nobody has balls enough to sit there again. The glass of wine she'd have poured for me after my run … God I miss her.

I started running about five times a week after losing her because, somehow, I needed to survive. She never joined me on my runs because as she said, "I'm getting too old, Crystal. I'll never even make it a quarter of a mile." So now was the perfect time to run, because she'd be with me every time. I felt her in the sunshine that burned the tip of my nose and in the wind whispering through my ponytail. It was relaxing and calming, and I just knew she was right there with me.

I was disconnected from the entire rest of the world. I was lost in a world of strictly myself and the spiritual being of Mom. She was that imaginary friend to whom you tell everything and then laugh out loud, while the rest of the world stares at you, wondering if you're either demonic or completely insane.

I realized that I'd rather be alone than ever feel so much heartache again. I didn't understand why everybody just walked on by without blinking an eye. Other people seemed to be going along with life in their perfect ways, but I was just not there anymore.

I thought it'd be better to stay on guard than feel shattered again, since I hadn't even picked up those pieces in the first place. Pulling away from your family is a terrible side effect of tragedy and loss. You, too, will feel like your family has been blasted apart, totally different from whatever it was before. You'll shut everybody out. You'll feel guilty for doing so, but you're terrified of losing them, too. (Oh, and by the way, your extended family will go nuts!)

For me, it was too painful to be around them without her. I often still feel that way. I've started coming around more, because learning how to relate to them in a different way was the only option I had to hanging onto the family I do still have. But being around Moms' closest friends, who were like second families to me, is hard to do. It hurts terribly to hang out with them in her absence. Although that's the wrong way to look at it, it's normal and it's okay (at least, for a while anyway). Working at it may never stop—I'm still etching away at it, too, babe.

I became equally as obsessed with shopping as I did with my body image. I thought that if I spent every day doing things my way, all those fun new goodies I bought would bring back some of the happiness I had lost. Actually, the complete opposite happened. Now, not only was I totally broke, but I was extremely unhealthy and even more unstable. The things I bought that I thought made me feel satisfied found themselves stuffed away in old purses in the hall closet or completely unopened in the back of my bathroom drawer that I haven't even opened until just recently. The clothes I splurged on still hang in my closet with tags on them and the growing stack of workout clothes started getting entirely too tall to manage. I was so confused, sad, and lost. Nothing was making me happy anymore or mending the heartache that I tried so hard to heal. I didn't understand why.

You see, I learned once during a church sermon that sin has its way with everything you do and everything in which you partake. When your mind is not in the right place, it has voids that need to be filled. Human psychology works that way, unfortunately. Sinners like you and me fill those voids with false gods—it's part of our makeup. We indulge in things such as materialistic happiness, excessive alcohol consumption, or a morbid overdose of drugs. It's too easy to fall deeper into the darkness when that void in your heart is filled with all the wrong things.

During those days in my life, I was filling my emptiness with things that only made me temporarily contented or deathly hungover the next day. I certainly drank my fair share of alcohol, hoping it would numb the pain of losing her, like liquid Xanax. Although I've never done drugs, I didn't stop my doctor from overdosing me on depression medication. I felt the more medication I took, the more my mom's death would go away. I accepted the daily anger, felt brutally incomplete, and lost sight of how it felt to be truly happy.

Great news! You aren't crazy for feeling incomplete at all. Let yourself find peace somewhere. Remember that she loved you with a pure, unwavering, endless love. Take that love she showed you and share it with others. Make her love your legacy.

Grief ultimately takes away your ability to be human. It only has room for the bare minimum of intellectual processing, and even then it won't seem to be enough. Grief is uninvited and no matter how good you are at wishing or praying it away, it seems as though it's there to stay. Linear isn't the word I'd use to describe grief. It's winding and erratic, messy at all costs, and most definitely not logical. The only way to work through it is to *walk* through it. *Feel* it. Be kind to yourself and remember that grief is necessary. You must be very careful with yourself and the people you're around. They need to be tender to you, too, because even the most kind-hearted people will do and say the wrong things and it'll set you off. They don't mean it and you don't mean it, but that's grief for ya! I still do it myself. Most of their missteps are forgivable, but you'll decide which ones aren't and that's important, too.

My mom's death isn't something I've survived, like at all. It's something with which I'll always have to live and have to work hard at getting through it. I didn't do anything after her death except learn to stay alive, partially wanting and not wanting to do so. I miss her terribly, but if your mom is anything like mine, she deserves to be missed.

Our identities are a funny thing. How we define ourselves, the way we think of ourselves, and the stories we tell ourselves about who we think we are—all comes together to create our own personal makeup. And yet, we aren't always conscious about our identity or even the loss of it. It's naturally stored away in the background, similar to the soundtrack of a movie. We don't often become conscious of it until something changes.

As human beings, we tend to only focus on the tangible "things," such as when we lose a person, a job, or a relationship. Although that alone is a huge part of your grief, there's another side of grief of which we aren't often aware. The loss of your mother is the whole shebang of losses, but what you may not realize until it's almost too late, is that you are also suffering the loss of your "being," a secondary loss of great magnitude. It will only create far more grief with which you'll have to cope than that of just your primary loss. Sadly, I learned the hard way that when my "self-clarity" correlated with my depression, it resulted in intensifying the post-traumatic stress experience.

Remember that our own personal identities shift to relational roles when we transform from daughters to caregivers, when loved ones become ill. One day I was a daughter, but the next I became a caregiver for my dying mother right before my eyes. My focus shifted as did my role in life. This happens as life changes, because nothing ever stays the same.

For most of us, when that loved one passes away, your caregiver role stops immediately and you're left with a sense of unimportance, while your purpose in life becomes less clear. Trust me, it's taken me years to realize that my identity is not only connected to the present, but it's also bound immensely to my past.

If you take the person you used to be and let it help mold you into the person you want to be, it can be a very healthy way of healing. Everything you go through is fundamental and necessary to keep you alive from day to day. Your negative setbacks will eventually encourage the positive moments in your future. Take your time and embrace it. Remember who you are, who you make proud, and just roll with it, sister.

CHAPTER 33

SIGNS

"Don't worry! She'll send you a sign when you're least expecting it." That's always one of the very first statements you'll hear as a new motherless child. I know it's chalked up to being comforting in your hopeless new days of grieving but, to me, it wasn't comforting at all. Most people who extended that unprofessional and non-proven "fact" hadn't even lost their mom yet.

If there was ever a mother-daughter combo that would certainly keep in touch after the veil fell between them, it was Mom and me. I tried holding on to that truth, but the truth of that loss exceeded it all. I juggled back and forth, wondering if she really would send me a sign or if that generic statement was totally made up, because nobody really knows—right? I had a small amount of hope that still gripped my heart. I just knew we'd talk endlessly in some odd spiritual kind of way. Probably just as much as we did before the shell of her body just up and called it quits. I hadn't experienced a ping of weird telepathic communications when her soul left, but I tried reasoning with this one, too. Maybe our spiritual connections are just delayed? Maybe she's still getting all settled into her cloud castle or maybe she's just busy attending Heavenly Happy Hour with her previous dead loved ones? Mom did love Happy Hour.

I tried desperately to believe that was exactly what was going down way up in the sky, but that logical reasoning lasted all of five whopping minutes. I was broken, so terribly sad that she was gone now and knowing there was no physical way of talking to her anymore. I spent days upon days searching for a sign with every step that I took. Up to this point, I never found her and I never felt or heard her.

"You know, Crystal, sometimes our loved ones come back to visit us in the form of animals, or maybe some sort of relevant form that they know is bound to get our attention," I was told. But the truth is, imagining my mom reincarnated as some wild animal didn't quite do the trick. It was hard to believe that one, but I tried—trust me. However, the very minimal of logical thinking I felt I had left didn't grasp that concept at all. I don't want a sign—I want her!

Let's think about this one. How can my mom possibly transform her cute little soul into some 2017-dated shiny penny I just forced down the coin machine in the Bank of America lobby? Or what about that one penny that fell out of the bag while I walked into the bank that's now lying on the sidewalk in front of me? That can't be her! It's too hot outside for her to sunbathe, and she hated that anyway.

I know the squirrel that ran up to my blanket last week just to steal my last cashew wasn't her either. She hated cashews and most definitely wouldn't ever have left me hungry.

She was always the most beautiful person in the world. We know this, but the butterfly that zipped past my face wasn't going to be Mom either! *But … she did love the color yellow, so maybe just the yellow butterflies are her? No! This is so idiotic!* I said to myself, as onlookers seemed to be tilting their heads, thinking that I for sure had escaped the crazy ward from the hospital down the street.

Your mind thrives on grief. It's an expert at turning its thinking process into something absurdly strange, like convincing you that your mom is now every strange animal on the planet. But in those lost and lonely days, it feels like you have nothing else to lose. Embrace it. If you question it or ever wonder if your dear sweet mom is really the neighbor's noisy parakeet, well, read on.

You can either choose not to believe it or you can choose to go with it because, either way, it'll happen whether it's her or not. So just go with it—it makes things easier. Trust me. Think of it this way— are you having a serious motherless meltdown? Like are you having a shitty day, because you're missing her the most? In that case, any animal that scurries through your line of sight is most definitely your dead mom.

Or how about if the animal is like really super cute? If so, that's definitely her, duh!

If it's a beautiful red cardinal flying above you, yell out, "Hey, Mom," because it's her! Every red cardinal that soars the skies above you is almost always filled with somebody's dead body and if she found her way to you while you're downward-dogging it during your yoga session in the backyard, consider yourself lucky, because she's there, too. *Gosh, she's so sweet!*

Lastly, are you desperately trying to scrub the animal poop off your brand-new car while you think there is absolutely no way your mom pooped on it? If you answered, "Yes!" Think again. Believe it. That's definitely a dead-mom-animal. I didn't believe it because my mom was always too proper to poop anywhere except a toilet, much less outside on my brand new Audi.

I hate to break it to you, but since you haven't given any attention to all the other sweet and genuine signs she's dropped you, pooping on your new car was her last option. Open your eyes! Do you know how many times you ejected poop onto her as a baby? Even as proper as proper gets, being in Heaven now means it's all fair game! It's the perfect time for her revenge, because God can't get mad at her for it.

She's there. You have no choice but to believe it, because not believing will only make it worse. She's there in everything around you, so lean on that and keep moving.

I know, you're probably thinking–"Crystal, well that's easy for you to say, you didn't know my mom." Well, indeed you are correct. Maybe I didn't, but I did know mine. Once a mom, always a mom! I knew mine had promised me that night in the hospital that she would leave me a very obvious, over-the-top sign that nobody but me would ever think twice about. Because let's face it, throwing things off the shelf in Target could quite possibly happen if a toddler were standing in the same aisle as me. I needed something very apparent and something very much her. I'd miss it if she injected herself into a dragonfly and landed on my hand, because there's no way that I'd be able to contact her back through that tiny little body of a bug.

I struggled daily, looking for something—anything— that could be her. Nothing that cued that *ah-ha* signal in my brain ever came up. Pennies, butterflies, cloud messages from planes in the sky, or even songs on the radio didn't help me in the way I had always heard it would. I wanted to know she was still there, around me, watching me and even making sure I'm trying to keep up with one load of laundry every day like she told me to. I was needy in that sense.

After eight months of this "no-mom" life and no obvious or weird telepathic communication from the other side, I felt unbelievably hopeless. "I don't understand it," I said to my husband at the start of another selfish pity party, confused. "She knew I'd need a sign, but she hasn't come back, not once! Why?" Even *he* didn't have an answer. That was a hard one.

"She told all her friends that if and when something happens to her, for them to watch over me, because I'd be the one to struggle the most. Where is she?" I asked Meagan, kind of rhetorical, but kind of wanting an answer.

"You're right—she did say that. In one of our last conversations, she made me promise her that I'd always make sure you were OK. And I agreed, but only under one condition," she told me.

"Well, what's that?" I asked.

"I told her that I would always make sure you were okay, as long as she promised to me that she'd fly over *you* every single day," Tears fell down my face. "She promised me that she would, Crystal!"

It was comforting, but at the same time it was upsetting. I wasn't okay. In fact, I was the furthest from that. "Well, I don't see any flying going on around here!" I told Meagan as she laughed. "Actually, I take that back. There was a bird this morning. A bird that I thought could maybe possibly be her."

"Oh, do tell," Meagan said inquisitively.

"Well, it pooped on my car and then flew away!" I responded, making her laugh. I was serious but it did sound a bit crazy. "But it wasn't her. She would have never done ... *that*! You know her!" I was confused and I didn't understand. Even after hearing what she made Meagan promise her, why hadn't she come back to at least say hello yet? So many members of my family had received a significant hello from her by now and here I am, left immensely grieving without a simple visit.

Those unanswerable questions only intensified my dilemma. It didn't help—it only made matters worse. Why did God have to take her in the first place? Why does everybody get visits from Mom but me? What did I do? If God loves me, then why did he do this to me? I don't believe I'll ever get those answers.

Yes, I'll admit, I did believe that the bird on our cruise was or could have been her, but that belief sizzled out the longer I went without any obvious signs from her. She knew I was drowning and needed her, but here I am still lost without her.

I briefly thought about visiting a psychic. I'm surprised I didn't just drive to the nearest neon sign flashing, "Psychic Mediums," the night my mom died. I had found a few "world-renowned" psychics on the good ole' Instagram, but never really caved to that idea. They're all fake as shit anyway. I mean, if my mom is going to talk to anybody now, it's definitely not going to be some crazy witch-looking psychopath with clairvoyance and a deck of tarot cards.

Maybe this was another way for God to teach me a lesson (because trust me, there's been plenty). Maybe he was trying to teach me not to depend on someone to make me happy inside. The smiles, laughter, and joy in my life were still very much there, but I blew those off as irrelevant mishaps quicker than you could imagine. I didn't allow them to take residence in my heart very long, because I didn't want to believe them. I believed that all those blessings were solely because Mom had been here and now that she wasn't, those weren't real to me anymore.

There wasn't much, if anything, that provided me comfort at this stage. I had built a wall around myself and my heart that was bigger than the Great Wall of China. "That could be why you haven't mentally received anything from your mom yet because you aren't letting her in," I was told by a dear sweet friend, who was both truthful and worried. I sat on that statement for a while, picking and prodding at every word she said, as if I was dissecting some pig brain like I did back in my middle school science class. It didn't ease the confusion. It only maximized the "Why?" question to which I could never seem to get an answer.

One morning in March I woke up on the complete wrong side of the bed (trust me, my mood proved it long before any words from my mouth did the job). I was in the biggest slump, totally oblivious to everything going on around me. With no recollection of any conversations that I had that day, not even the tiniest smile had flashed from my face for those next ten hours. I experienced every non-happy state a human being could experience all in the same day. "Why did my mom have to die?" I kept asking myself, desperately searching for some form of an explanation legitimate enough for my comfort. "Dear God, why *my* mom? Why?" but He didn't respond.

That was the same question I asked my mom every day for the last four years, the same damn question that nobody could answer! Lying in bed beside her and crying during her fight against cancer, I reminded myself that the very person I was trying to keep alive had CANCER. I'd ask it over and over until I fell asleep under her covers. Mom never had an answer either, but she did a good job reasoning with me—enough to form my thoughts into positivity and hope, realizing she really is an angel on earth.

Even up to the day she could no longer verbally shoot me the same response aloud, "Don't ask why, Crystal. You'll never know that answer. It is what it is, so don't ask why," she'd say too often. If I got an extra day with her for each time that I asked that question, she'd still be here, for crying out loud!

One of those bad days after she died, I pulled into my driveway that night, shut the car off, and laid my head down on the steering wheel. "I don't know how to go on with my life without her," I cried. I'm not sure how long I sat in that slumped over position, wondering what the hell I was supposed to do. All I know is that I heard a snore coming from the backseat and suddenly remembered my two babies were still back there, sound asleep! *I'll have to get them into their beds,* I thought, ashamed of myself for forgetting they were still back there.

I lugged two sleeping boy bodies to their beds before I plopped myself down helplessly on the couch. I sat there in pure silence, dark and alone, asking the same "Why?" question over and over in my head. Wedged between the cushions, I became an expert at wallowing in my own sorrows. I replayed my life those last several months, wondering how I'd even made it this far without her. "God should have taken somebody else instead," I mumbled to myself, obviously angry. Now, I know that was quite selfish of me, but don't be too quick to judge. Yes, that was horrendously selfish, childish, and insensitive, but at the time, I had third-degree raging burns all over my insides. Trust me, it was mortifying and pathetic.

Shaking my head back and forth, ashamed of God, I asked Him, "Then why did you give her to me to love with everything I have and then rip her right out of my life? Why?" but he still didn't answer. Now I'm alone, totally losing my shit in an I-feel-so-sorry-for-myself meltdown.

Grieving is not fun at all, but doing it all alone is even worse. I grabbed my phone and thumbed through my text messages, desperately searching for the one labeled, "My Husband ♥" and began to text:

Babe, why did my mom have to die?

I waited there in that draft text for a minute, just hoping the logical part of my brain would kick in any time now before I clicked SEND. I knew I hadn't gotten anywhere with that question this whole day (hell, even these last eight months!), so I deleted it and threw my phone on the floor instead. I knew he wouldn't have that answer, so whatever it may have been wouldn't have satisfied me. What was the point anyway?

A few more useless minutes passed, and I took one for the team! I decided to get myself up and find something productive to tackle (mainly because that couch is so uncomfortable for anybody but my dog), and I needed something, *anything* to do, besides asking the same question over and over, because nobody was listening to me.

The black medical scrubs, in which I live ninety percent of my life, weren't cutting it anymore. I walked into my closet, and climbed the step stool as my only hope of reaching the t-shirts on the top shelf. I looked to the floor before feeling my way back down.

There it was, smack middle of the floor. I climbed down to the last step and sat for a second. "What in the world is that?" I asked, squinting to see it better. It was a small light-brown colored tag laying there by itself. Mind you, it was not there when I walked in! No, I'm not crazy, it really wasn't! I picked it up and flipped it over. Suddenly, I saw my sign for the first time, almost losing consciousness when I read the only three words printed boldly on that tag: **Don't Ask Why.**

My jaw dropped as I fell back against my shoe rack utterly blown away! That very obvious sign that she promised she'd give me, yeah … there it was. In fact, she *would* place her sign in my closet, because she knows that's my happy place. I have never seen that tag before. Even in all the ungodly amount of shopping trips I've made, I had *never* seen it. I wouldn't have ever bought a shirt or anything else from a store without first looking at the tag, much less one that only contained *those* three words—it never happened.

I swear that was some sort of initiation, because I am now a proud member of the Believer of Signs Club, thank you!

I knew that was her without a sliver of a doubt! Whether she's here or there, she's still the only one who responds to my annoying and repetitive question that I've never stopped asking and in exactly the same way she physically voiced it to me all these years. She might as well have been standing there right in front of me (I wish!) with her finger pointed towards my face during her response. Nobody else would have understood the amount of meaning and significance behind those three simple words.

That little cardstock tag, placed perfectly in the middle of my closet floor where she knew I'd see it, brought me so much overwhelming joy. It brought me the comfort I direly needed, mainly to continue moving forward–for my sanity and for those around me. And it brought along with it so many tears. After all, my mom always knew how to make me feel better when I was sad or having a bad day. She always spoke the truth and she always and I mean *always* kept her promises.

CHAPTER 34

NEWLY SINGLE DAD

I can only speak as the daughter of a mom who was ambushed by cancer and forcefully removed from this earth. But in my selfish, totally-not-professional-at-all-never-been-in-this-position opinion, I can tell you that being a spouse left widowed would completely suck! I watched it and it's terrible. I'll spare you the sugarcoated advice that counselors will load you with during your therapy session and I'll just tell you how it really is. It's not fun at all. After thirty-eight years of marriage and then suddenly becoming newly single is something in life I never want to experience. It was brutal and I was so judgmental. It's like I was still in Denial Land, because I'd never even fathomed the thought of Dad dating after Mom died.

When it started happening, it was sickening. Finding out that he was dating again came as a shock to me. I battled a different kind of gut-wrenching sadness, as I saw him cheerfully walk around with another woman who wasn't my mom. Not only was I hurt, but I was upset by the way I found out! I received some good ole' pictures in a text from a friend. She spotted them at the same restaurant where she was having dinner. It wasn't the way he wanted us to find out, but that's how it happened, and shoving that into his face only intensified *his* grief. (I'm so sorry, Dad!)

"She's really nice, you guys, and she has her own job and her own house," he exclaimed, trying to uplift her really boring description, so we'd give him our dating acceptance.

I figured that there was no way I'd ever replace Mom, so why should he? She wasn't going to give me "Mom advice" or love my kids like their Memaw did, so what's the point in dating someone new anyway? As far as I was concerned, his romantic life was now over. He had a good run, and it was wonderful while it lasted, but it's time to close shop and call it a day. *Pat on the back, Dad, you did great!*

Although that sounds like the most logical reason ever to deal with things as a scared, possessive, and selfish adult-baby like me, it wasn't. I was OK with the new father/daughter relationship we had, now chatting it up on the daily with each other, trying to fill the gaping black hole lodged between us. Unfortunately, that only lasted until his "love life" started shifting into a world as foreign to me as it was him. His world was thrown into a different dimension now, and as life-ruining as it can be, it was totally unfair.

"Well, she's ugly!" I'd tell my friends. "She's so strange" I kept openly sharing. I judged entirely too much. People would often ask me, "How's your dad doing?" and I'd painfully drop this beautiful reply, "He seems to be doing just fine. He's dating someone and she's a real bitch," I'd tell them.

I told myself I wouldn't even mention her in this book because she's so not worthy of that, but I'll throw in a quick mental picture of her for your ever-so-wondering mind. She was like a scrawny and wrinkled wanna-be Barbie who ended up as a very deformed and fake drag-queen puppet, whose bobble head was totally wired wrong. The only talent she had was to pathologically lie every time she opened her overly red lipstick-coated lips. *Enjoy that one!*

I withdrew from my relationship with him and convinced myself that I had lost both parents. I didn't know this newly single man and I didn't like what he was doing. I felt that I'd never be okay with it and any woman who walked into his life will now be in mine, so I would never approve. That lasted several months before I grew up and realized Dad was severely hurting and trying to find his way.

"I will always love your mom for the rest of my life, but I am very lonely," he told me. It made me sad but, putting it that way and hearing just how lonely he was in his voice, I decided to accept it for what it is. Inside me, I was screaming with feelings of betrayal, but if agreeing with him meant that he'd find some sort of happiness to move on then, *fiiiiiiine.* He hadn't asked my permission or approval, but he did lovingly ask for my agreement.

"Of course, Dad, you deserve all the happiness in the world," I reassured him of my true feelings deep down. I realized how unfair it was to defer happiness to him, but to beg for it for me. In hindsight, the tears my father shed weren't just for my mom. They were for his children who were trying their hardest to stop any further happiness that didn't include our mother. It was incredibly selfish, and Mom would have never wanted it that way.

Listen, if you lose a spouse, are you going to want to die lonely? Would you want to spend your nights chugging bottles of wine and running out of tissues to wipe away the tears over which you have no control? What about your kids? Do you want to lose them along with your spouse who just died? That's what I did. I allowed the space between myself and my dad to widen by the day. I was choosing to walk away from him, because I didn't like what I was witnessing.

I had to really search my soul because he was going through something completely different than we were and he was now completely alone. What about walking around town with a huge target on your back, while people judge your actions after a loss *they* haven't experienced. Do you want to be that person? Would you want to go home to an empty house, staring at your spouse's clothes or the stale coffee they left in the coffee pot? That happened to him, too.

Is it appetizing and comforting to you to let the leftovers they cooked mold in your fridge, because you can't bring yourself to throw them away? Would you be willing to end all adult conversations with your best friend the day she dies just to go to bed at night having only spoken ten words all day *to yourself*? I didn't think so. I definitely didn't want to carry that on *my* shoulders any longer. It was exhausting trying to keep up with the bombardment of feelings that weren't completely necessary.

He experienced the world of rumors and sabotage. He experienced unwanted judgment by people who called themselves "friends." I watched from the outside and realized how much I really do love him and he's still here. It wasn't fair to him. He was ambushed by cancer just as much as we were, and I wasn't there to defend him. And because I wasn't legally able to walk around punching every grown ass adult "friend" of his in the face after something I'd heard they had said, I needed to do something to help him. This was my dad and acceptance was the only thing I knew that was right.

It's tough to go through it and watch your newly widowed parent search for another companion. But trust me, if you're in this position, you've already conquered a harder battle. I couldn't possibly yell at him on the phone anymore or cry any harder than I already had. It was exhausting trying to stalk the bitch who walked into his life after Mom died.

When I found out she lived in my neighborhood, my dog no longer wanted to poop in her yard anymore, because I had already let him dump his feces in it for the last month! It was full and there was no more room, just like my emotions. They were full of sadness and I had no more room to give all this madness any more attention.

I threw in the towel and had a serious "coming to Jesus" moment, when I remembered it's my Dad we're talking about. The only parent I have left, the one who's always been strong, and now *I'm* causing him to break even more. I love him, but if I push him away for selfish reasons, what would I have left?

Of course, Mom was still the one who helped me turn this around. I realized what I was doing and the sadness I was throwing at him were only causing bigger problems. The same night in the hospital that she had told me to stop investing my dwindling income into Target, Mom also gave me permission that I had forgotten all about until now.

"Dad is going to need to find another companion when the time comes. Crystal, *you* need to know that I am okay with that," she told me as I gasped, completely not okay with that statement. She knew me and she knew if and when that really happened, I'd be the one ready to murderously kill somebody. OK, not really, but it sounds a lot more dramatic for the sake of this story. She loved him with every ounce of her frail body and that type of statement meant she loved him enough to want him to be happy again.

If she had never given me her permission for him to go off and find happiness in another living woman, then I would have spent the rest of my life terrorizing any relationship before it even started. She gave it to me, knowing I needed to hear it to be able to move on in that way. I pulled a "her" and finally accepted that Dad, out of everybody, needed happiness right now. I lost my mother, and he lost his wife. Those are two totally different losses, and it's only logical and downright fair to realize and remember that. With that being said, it wasn't a piece of cake (which is fine, because I'm not a fan of cake anyway), but it had to be accepted by more people than just him.

Do you remember how important it was to you that your parents accept your new boyfriend or girlfriend back in the day? It's equally significant and important to our widowed parent when we are confronted with the bomb of their new relationship. They went through drastic changes just like we did, so they, too, are trying to rediscover who they are without their life partner.

Just imagine how terrifying it must be to find yourself alone, after thirty-eight happy years of marriage, while mourning an immense loss. Your previously over-protective Dad who ran background checks on your high school boyfriend may decide one day it's a great idea to invite a woman he met downtown to fly across the country with him or stay at his house for two weeks. While you're thinking "gold-digging-Craig's List-killer," understand that your Dad is an adult, too, and has been around a lot longer than you have. He's perfectly capable of making his own decisions and is willing to risk the mistakes that may follow. Give him a break! No matter how you feel about the uncomfortable and oddly unfamiliar "new normal," you won't change it. And to be blatantly honest, you'll just lose him, too.

At this time in my present life, he has now found another woman and married her. No, not the bobble head drag queen, as that was an exception to the rule, because we would never have let that happen. I'd have to take back everything I said in this chapter, if that were the case.

His new wife, Rhonda, is a wonderful person, who is beautiful, smart, independent, and extremely caring. It was hard at first, watching her take on that role in his life. It was new and scary, but growing in my journey of loss and learning to accept it was what made it a suitable future. I do believe, and I have since told her this, if my mom could handpick one person in this world to love and cherish my father in a similar way that she did, it would be her. She won't love him like my mom did and she won't have the memories he shared with my mom, nor will she ever be "my mom," but she deserves happiness just as much as the rest of us, and Dad's happiness is at the top of my list. Mom would be proud of me for finally acting like a grownup and interacting with his new wife. Rhonda has made that transition easier.

It was tough in the beginning and it wasn't easy for all parties involved, but Mom (and God) were at work up there. Rhonda knew her boundaries coming into this hot-headed family and has grown to love each one of us in different ways. I struggled with my children and all the grandchildren on how they'd react to a new person in our lives, but they've done great and so has she. It's a given that there will only be one Memaw and nobody has ever questioned that. Their lives started with "Memaw and Papa" and I've seen the growth and resilience in them, too, so "Papa and Rhonda" is how it remains.

Not only does she make good dinners and have a keen eye for pristine interior design (which by the way is my favorite part), but she deals with my dad's weirdness (his break apart reading glasses and endless frozen meat deliveries), and she *likes* it. And best of all, she's given my mom the one thing she had requested that none of us could give—dad's happiness.

In his defense, what a miserable experience it must have been to lose the love of his life and learn to date again at the age of sixty. So, my advice to you is this: love him endlessly, support him in everything he does, and stay in his corner because, at the end of the day, that sweet man you call "Dad," is all you have left.

CHAPTER 35

COUNSELING

*Y*ou know how they say: don't reject, just accept (just kidding, nobody says that. I made it up, sorry). I did try to accept the fact that my mom died of cancer, but I still couldn't deal with how it went down. It was holding me back from healing. Bad news my friend, it doesn't go away that easily–in fact, it doesn't go away at all! My life spiraled out of control. I went days without eating or sleeping and days I didn't smile or laugh at all. I'd find myself wandering around without any productive tasks being completed.

When I went to bed each night to try and fall asleep, I often wondered what I did that day. "I don't even remember what I did this morning," I'd incoherently admit to Sean. "I must have done something because my kids got to and from school safely, but I don't even remember driving."

My thoughts were mush at this point. Most days I found myself sitting in the carline at school staring through my tears. I listened to what you aren't supposed to listen to when you're sad and cried all day, every day. I had a typical routine of parking, crying, turning up the radio, crying, texting my family, and crying even more. I felt so incredibly lost.

When I started to realize that I wasn't giving any effort to anything or anyone around me, I knew I needed to do something. After all, I am a mother! Katie had been telling me for months that she thought I needed to see a grief counselor or someone who could offer some sort of help to save me.

I had refused those ideas numerous times, because I didn't feel like I could be helped. I was too far gone. I couldn't remember anymore what happiness felt like. I didn't see the positive in any situation and negativity was my life now. I never smiled and honestly, I hadn't heard my laugh in nearly six months.

After every family member at this point begged and pleaded with me to just give in and go talk to somebody, I couldn't even think. I was this hollow human being who wasn't present anymore. I felt like the Crystal I always knew had left the minute Mom died, but I had no clue how or the desire to bring her back. I didn't want to face the fact that I'd come back without my mom here and I honestly hadn't figured out how to live motherless yet, nor was that what I wanted.

A small piece of me deep down in the depths of my broken soul seemed to still be somewhat logical, as it kept trying to push the issue to pray and seek the help that I so badly needed. Why would I pray, after God ignored all my prayers? He didn't listen to me in the first place and He definitely won't now. What a bad state of mind to be in, I'll tell ya! I don't know if it was the power of prayer and secretly hoping it'd work or just coincidence of yet another really depressing day, but I finally decided to break down and make an appointment with a grief counselor.

The days leading up to that appointment just confused me. I didn't know what to expect and I didn't know how it was going to go or what I was letting myself experience. My family kept reminding me that when I go, I need to be completely honest with the counselor and completely open up my heart and mind so she could help me.

I kept trying to think of every excuse why I needed to back out and cancel my upcoming appointment, but something kept telling me not to do that. Mom tried to get me to see somebody after Grandpa died a few years back, but I didn't go, because I still had her to help get me through it. I think it was her voice playing in my head telling me that it was the right thing to do and if it will help even a little bit, why wouldn't I give it a try?

I arrived about twenty minutes early that day, which is such a big deal, because I'm not usually early to anything, like ever! When I pulled in, I turned my car off and just sat there. "It's not too late to back out now and just leave!" I kept tempting myself. I felt so anxious, nervous, and already upset. Here I am, about to walk into an office I've never been to, open up about the most painful time in my life to a complete stranger and she's supposed to just magically make it all better? Now the "being early card" was thrown out the window because with all the tempting you-can-still-go-before-it's-too-late thoughts, you've now made yourself late, Crystal.

It was a very plain office, and quite boring, to be honest. It was cold in there (or maybe that was just my nerves) and it was a very awkwardly quiet place. "Thank you, Crystal, you may have a seat now" the receptionist told me as she pointed to the corner near the plain white end table full of expired magazines.

I sat there for a few minutes, flipped through a few pages of *TIME* Magazine's mental health issue and wondered when it was going to be my turn. I set the magazine down and asked where the restroom was. I went into the small bathroom around the corner, locked the door, and sat down with my head in my hands. "What am I doing here!?" I whispered to myself.

It was sad and terrifying in an unknown place. I was uncomfortable and motherless. I almost made myself sick. I could still faintly hear Mom telling me, "Crystal, you aren't going to get anywhere sitting in the bathroom. Now get up, go out there, and deal with your grief the way I've taught you!"

I went back out to the waiting room and the minute I sat back down, the doctor walked out. "Hi, are you, Crystal? I'm your grief counselor. Are you ready to follow me into my office?" she asked me, staring into my eyes like she was looking through my soul already.

"Uh, *suuure*," I said as I slowly stood up to follow her. She took me into this small office with a couch, a desk, and a coffee maker. It wasn't very homey, and it definitely wasn't what I expected.

She obviously had no problem with starting right away: "So what brings you in today?" she asked me, as I had just barely tried to sink myself into her couch, hoping I'd just disappear.

"My mom died, and I need a miracle," I abruptly got to it just like she had. I've always had this weird thing when I get defensive and guarded, I start to judge people by the way they look, talk, smell, or in her case, the décor in her office and the awful green leather couch on which I was sitting definitely didn't give her any brownie points. Her taste in style was nowhere close to mine, so I wasn't going to bond with her—I could already feel it.

"Well, I am very sorry to hear that, Crystal. I'm sure you have had a very tough time trying to cope with your mother's death."

I wanted to shout, "Well, no shit!! Isn't that why I'm here?" But I let her have her welcoming speech that sounded very much rehearsed like she says it to every new client that comes in after such a big loss like mine. She asked me to give her a summary of what happened, so she could better understand the severity of my loss. I told her pretty much this whole book in a nutshell, added a lot of tears, and ended it with a big sigh of relief, because I had just explained out loud to her the absolute worse experience of my life.

"I am so very sorry your mom lost her battle to cancer," she tried to say before I immediately shut her down.

"OK, I know you don't know me at all yet, but one thing you should know right off the bat is that to me, my mom did NOT lose her battle to cancer! She won and that's not a comment I ever want to hear again," I told her in a very hurt and defensive manner.

She proceeded with an apology and told me just from our conversation, she could tell just how hurt I felt and how close to my mom I was. She repeated numerous times how much she is in awe of the kind of person Mom was and the giant impression and impact she clearly had on people. She now understood why I made this comment about her and thanked me for giving her a different outlook on a person passing away from cancer.

After our discussion she gave me some advice on giving myself a break, because getting hit with cancer, and three deaths within four years is more than most people my age go through in a much longer time span. Trying to be a wife and raise a family, while grieving those losses is incredibly devastating. We talked about my faith and I explained to her how I grew up only knowing good faith. However, I struggled tremendously between believing in that and giving in to my anger since the death of my grandfather.

Now that my anger and grief is off the charts, I didn't know where to go except backwards, because backwards contained my mom. I kept bringing up the question, "Why did He take my mom?" and she calmly stopped me by placing her hand on my knee and told me she can tell that's a question holding me back from healing.

She left me with a very interesting point that has stuck in my head to this day. She said to me, "Imagine sitting face to face with God right now, just you and Him. If he told you to ask Him anything you wanted and he would give you the answer, would you ask Him that specific question?"

I smirked and huffed through my nose, "Umm, duh." "If you asked Him that, you know that no matter the answer He gave you, it wouldn't be the right answer to you unless He took back her death and brought her back, which you probably would not go for, am I correct?" she asked.

She did this weird thing to me as if she reached right through my chest, clinched my heart, and made me answer her with, "As much as I want to have her back, I would never make her leave a perfect world like heaven to come back down to this horrid place."

How did she do that? She made me realize my feelings deep down inside my heart and admit a feeling I hadn't known I felt. It was as if the greedy side of me walked right out that door.

The response I gave her brought me a little comfort that day because I hadn't known those feelings were in there. The only ones of which I was aware I had were the dark grief and sadness in which I had been living. I felt selfish most days because regardless of what my mom went through, the daily struggle I was enduring is what took the front seat above all of it.

Counseling ended up being something I hadn't continued to attend. Maybe it was the selfish emotions I went through, or maybe it was the counselor herself, with whom I just didn't click, but I quit, thinking I could figure it all out on my own.

The days continued to pass, and the struggle was real. Some days went better than others, while some days seemed like a complete waste of anybody's time. I was coping and learning, even if learning meant that counseling wasn't right for me.

CHAPTER 36

MOTHER'S DAY

*T*here's only two days until Mother's Day and this entire world won't let me forget it. My email inbox is flooded with, "Send Mom the perfect flower bouquet today!" and "50% off handbags for Mom!" Reminders kept coming through every ten-minutes of this dreaded day, causing me to question why I should have ever subscribed to any of these heartless retailers.

"Excuse me, overpriced clothing brand," I wanted to reply. "Don't you know my mom died in July and this will be my first Mother's Day without her? I posted about it on Facebook, so it's been official now for a while. There is absolutely no reason that your data-tracking software shouldn't have been informed by now! Thanks a bunch!"

As if every other day you've gone through since her death hasn't been hard enough, Mother's Day is an inevitable blow to the face from the universe that you never viewed from this aspect before! Forget the sense of humor this world is supposed to have. It's just an asshole, quite honestly!

It seems like every type of store now, as they put up their joyful Mother's Day ads, is definitely just out to get you!

For the last ten months, I had become a pro at making myself get up out of bed every morning and I learned how to cry in secret very well. Whether it be in my own car at a stoplight, staring through my tears in the back row at the yoga studio, or letting my sadness roll down my cheek joining with the water droplets in the shower, I just hadn't seemed to be able to move very many steps forward. I had taught myself my own pep talks to be able to act as humanly as possible with each passing day. Sometimes the pep talk I gave myself helped for a mere thirty minutes, while others helped for the entire day. However, what I quickly realized was there is no pep talk that could ever prepare me enough for this Mother's Day!

Most people only put dates down on the calendar or in their planners to be able to count down with excitement that next approaching jolly day. However, for me, my mind wouldn't let me forget that this holiday was approaching quite abruptly, which only heightened my struggle through her loss.

It's unfortunate that when you become motherless, you look at the world and its holidays as just another sequel to the movie *Revelation; The End of Days*. You feel guarded, shut off, hopeless and just full of pure sadness, because you can't buy the Mother's Day cards with chocolate anymore. I try to steer clear of any such store during the month of May, because I'm no longer in that club and it's extremely unwelcoming.

I begged God all night to let me sleep through the whole next day. I thanked him for giving me such an incredible mom like mine. I felt guilty knowing I was going to celebrate Mother's Day tomorrow without my mother, whom this day has always been about. After all, is it even Mother's Day without that strong primary attachment you have to your living Mom anyway?

The tad bit of thankfulness I thought I had, quickly diminished before the daily question and answer session began. "I loved her," I said to God, "so why did you take her?" I fell asleep that night in the middle of my prayer and still woke up the next morning completely against my will. I stayed in bed sulking in my own "lost-mom meltdown" before I remembered that getting up as the mom I am, is only fair to my children. I had already ruined my own Mother's Day by anticipating how depressing it was going to be since it was the first mom-holiday I had to go through after her death.

However, God always has a way of bringing you back to where you belong. I had prayed and begged him to keep me asleep that entire next day, but instead, he woke me up to the sweetest little voices whispering, "Wake up, Mommy, it's your day! Happy Mother's Day!"

I rolled over to the smallest little arms wrapped around my neck, asking me if I had presents for him, too! For just a few minutes I had forgotten about everything in this world, except the two sweetest little blonde boys at my bedside, who had made me an actual mother!

I heard Mom's voice in my head saying, "Crystal, you must keep moving forward. You are a mother, too and your children deserve a day to celebrate you, just like you did for me."

That made me realize what my brain had been refusing to accept. Mother's Day is going to come and go every year for the rest of my life and it's something I needed to learn to cherish. My children have just as much right to celebrate that day, as I always have. What kind of mother would I be if I gypped them of that right? It's just one day a year and that day is something I'll have to learn to live through.

Unfortunately, I learned the hard way that grief and sadness can take over your every thought, if you sit and wallow in it. It seems to escalate on holidays and most of the time doesn't ever truly dissipate. It had taken me all day to stop crying and wipe my tears before I could go to bed that night and reminisce over the countless memories that we shared together. I felt unlucky having to celebrate my mom on Mother's Day without her. I felt angry and jealous of all the people in line at Target who stocked up during all the Mother's Day sales. After all, they can go home and sip wine with their moms around the dinner table and not have to worry about anything else.

I decided to send every "Mother's Day sale" email from Anthropologie to my spam folder starting every March! I began binge watching crime shows on Netflix come early spring just to avoid the Hallmark tissue-grasping-heart-shredding Mother's Day commercials on TV.

I will admit though, as time goes on, it's exhausting to keep up with your feelings of depression and sadness before each approaching holiday. It wasn't fair to my children that their mother wasted the day away sleeping and crying, because she's now without a mom. It has become more evident each passing year that letting my guard down and crumbling that wall of grief is much more appealing than trying to fight against those feelings, because you feel guilty for moving on.

I'm finally learning not to feel guilty because not only had Mom allowed us to celebrate her on this day, but she celebrated her daughters as the mothers we are. It would be selfish to put a halt to this annual holiday because my mom has gained her wings. My children don't deserve that and lucky for them, I am still here, and I am always ready to be celebrated! *Plus, I'm a boy mom and if you saw the amount of pee I have to scrub clean every day, I'm pretty sure you'd be down to celebrate me, too!*

This is the way the world works. Its looming arrival will always cause an emotional internal explosion, much like a ticking time bomb, so get used to it. But you don't have to skip over this calendar celebration altogether. I found comfort in this day as my boys showered me with the love they knew how to give. I mean, there isn't a whole lot that can beat those school-made Mother's Day handprint cards that you have add to the growing artwork collection in your attic every year anyway!

Realistically, it's a very special day set aside each year to celebrate and honor those women who have been blessed enough to endure the painful, body-contracting, bloody mess of childbirth! That alone puts you in a category definitely worth celebrating and more than just one day a year, if it were up to me! Maybe more like one day a month, sounds fair—right?

Having a mother is a gift, but being a mother is an even bigger gift. I could have chosen to continue and carry on year to year the sadness and tears every holiday easily brings along being without a mom. However, if your mom is anything like mine, you know she wouldn't want that. I don't know your mother like I do mine, but somewhere hidden in your closet (or hers!) is a box full of old cards you've saved and somewhere in there is a Mother's Day card from your very own mother, stating how proud of you she is. Take that card or old letter out and use it as your ammo and perseverance to move forward.

One day (hopefully many countless years from now) your time will come, too, and your children deserve to celebrate the mother they had, also. Now I know for myself, I wouldn't ever want my children to sulk and mope around, crying nothing but tears of extreme sadness when I'm taken home and I highly doubt you do as well. I want them to celebrate, laugh, and smile every time my blonde head pops into their memories.

If you are motherless like me, let's make a pact with each other! As Mother's Day comes rolling around, promise yourself that you will spend the day just like you would as if your mom were physically still here. If you have to drive to your Dad's house just to judge his award-winning ribs, because that's what he cooked on Mother's Day every year, then by God do it and always pick him as the winner! Do it with grace and thankfulness!

If you have to sit solo at the bar of you and your mom's favorite brunch spot and down peach bellinis or watermelon martinis, then once again chug away, sister! Even if it means having to hit up Nordstrom's Mother's Day sale utterly alone and spend entirely too much money on Dry Bar hair products, then I believe that is productive therapy and is one hundred percent necessary. If you want to talk or cry about her all day, or even post old and embarrassing photos of you and her on your social media accounts, then girlfriend, you post away.

You will always have a mother whether she is physically here or not. Mother's Day isn't just about honoring the living! Go ahead and shower yourself with flowers and graciously accept (and maybe share) the edible arrangement your sister sent you (because let's be honest, nobody in their right minds can eat that much fruit by themselves in one sitting anyway.) Make a big deal about the handmade "All About My Mom" construction paper booklet that your son brings home from kindergarten or the Popsicle stick picture frame your grade schooler made of you and him! Your dear sweet babies are excited to celebrate you, so allow that.

I made a pact to myself to try and conquer each upcoming holiday from here on out with a mind full of positivity. Now don't fall out of your chair; I said I'd try. It was a little easier to move into the next several weeks thinking that way until her dreaded birthday popped up on the calendar, and the feelings of hopelessness and sadness came barreling back.

"Today would have been Mom's fifty-ninth birthday," Katie said. This is when those movie scenes where the body melts down into nothing but a puddle of jeans, a tank top and shoes happen! The constant reminders of what I don't have anymore, is enough to make me want to melt into non-existence. Unfortunately, that was my way of trying to deal with it. I thought that if I could just disappear, then the holiday that I was going through would somehow disappear, too. Apparently, that's not how life works. Shocking, I know.

This was the very first year of my entire life that May 30th was just another day. It felt wrong, it felt awkward and just pure shitty. Can I still buy that Boston Crème Pie from Publix anyway? What if I still buy a bottle of Red Door perfume just to keep up with tradition? Is that weird?

Truthfully, I felt like I was allowing myself to spiral instead of heal. In my head, it was OK to continue all that, but in my heart; it wasn't OK at all. As bad as I wanted to be telling my mom how old she was getting, just so I could hear her voice say, "You don't have to remind me, jeez, Crystal," it would have made the day just as perfect as she was. That conversation might be simplistic to most, but to me it meant everything. Well, almost everything. The back end of that statement came just nine short days later on my birthday that always started out with a phone call blasting her Celine Dion vibrato voice singing ,"Happy Birthday," at promptly 8:46 a.m., just a mere one minute after my brother's phone call, and two minutes after my sister's.

Having triplets was forever exhausting, but she handled it, knowing that was her job in life. She never complained of having to make three phone calls every morning on June 8th. She never complained of the tripled friends' list for birthday parties and she never thought twice about buying triple the birthday gifts, because to her, raising triplets was her gift! To this day, my birthday has never been the same. How do you celebrate the day you were born when the person that gave birth to you is no longer here? It's a difficult concept to understand and let's be real, it's just plain wrong.

I am only celebrating this day, because she endured the pain of bringing me here. After her death, I decided I didn't want to celebrate my birthday any more. It didn't seem right and the meaning of it was gone. It's difficult, but it's another day that comes and goes with which I have to deal. I tried the whole, "Dad, will you call me on my birthday at 8:46 am just like Mom always did?" but that doesn't ever turn out like it did with Mom. In Dad's defense, phone calls that early in the morning just aren't his thing. Mom was well prepared and organized like that, but it unfortunately doesn't seem to be a Dad thing to this day. I miss that phone call and I miss her voice on the other end of the phone. Bless her bones, she swore she could sing better than even the best Grand Ole' Opry performers out there. I loved it as I let her fifteen-seconds of fame echo right through the speaker of my phone every year.

I sat on the floor against my bed the night before my first birthday without her, freakishly going through everything on her cell phone like a stalker. I had done this before, but each time I somehow felt as if I'd find something else that I didn't see previously, as if it'd be some sort of surprising comfort to me if I did.

This time I came across her voice recording app that I don't remember seeing. I scrolled through several dates saved on her phone and it kind of confused me. How did I not see this before and why does she have so many voice memos on her phone? Does anybody really use this voice recording app besides her?

I scrolled down and came across one she recorded in the beginning of May, saved on a date nowhere close to anybody in the family's birthday. Low and behold, there it was! She was singing in the most angelic voice, "Happy Birthday," without addressing anybody's name in the song. I was so stunned and taken back that I immediately broke down into tears. I wasn't sure how I felt. *Did she record this for anybody specific?* She couldn't have, because it has no name in it and it was recorded and saved on a random date without any meaning.

Was this a sign from her? I couldn't believe that something so simple like her singing to me on my birthday would be such a dud from this year forward. Yet here it was, as if she planned that out knowing I'd find it. She amazes me. It was the best gift I could have been given that year.

I sat there for a few minutes on the floor next to my bed just looking up and smiling through the tears that welled up in my eyes. *Should I send it to Katie and Rennie, also?* I wondered. *I know they are missing the birthday song from her and since I was given that gift, I need to share it with them, too,* I reasoned, so I texted:

> *I am not sure if you both want this or not, but in case you do,*
> *I found this voice recording of Mom on her phone, if you want*
> *to play it to yourself at the exact time you were born tomorrow*
> *morning.*

I sent in a group text labeled, "Heath Triplets." They were as thrilled as I was.

What an honest and sincere gift she gave us from that year on. To this day, at 8:46 a.m. every June 8th I sob like a little girl listening to her sing "Happy Birthday" to me. I close my eyes and imagine her right in front of me, as I blush, embarrassed listening to my mom sing to me. Even as an adult, those moments bring me back to being a little child embracing traditions my mom always upheld. No matter what it was, she could always bring a smile to my face.

Whether you're a mother, have a mother, or know another mother; you deserve to celebrate this day. Start weird new traditions that your kids one day can carry on as their kids laugh about how silly they are. Go skydiving or set up a Mother's Day brunch with your other motherless girlfriends and split a bottle of wine (or six—no judgment here). It's a bummer of a day, but let it grow, sparking the joy that really does still exist. Celebrate how far you've come and what you've come through.

Don't just sleep your way through the day sister, because you'll regret it. Avoid having the mentality of just suffering through it—own it, for God's sake! Some of the most cherished blessings in life are the one's you've already received, even during the time of your mother's passing. The friendships you gained and the trust you instilled in individuals not previously present in your life, are the human beings who respect it the most and they're the ones who have been sucked into this madness right along with you.

You'll never be alone, because if you think about it; every day is Mother's Day.

CHAPTER 37

ONE WHOLE YEAR!

*P*erhaps you feel like you've conquered every "first" there is to conquer after her death, but unfortunately, you haven't. (My apologies!) There's one more date on the calendar to deal with being half-parented now. Quickly approaching in what seemed unrealistically fast was the one-year mark of her death. This was in no way, shape, or form considered a holiday, nor would it ever gain any type of privilege like that in anybody's planner. But it was coming, whether I was ready or not.

I tried very hard to forget that day and the fierce significance behind July 16th, but I couldn't shake it, no matter how hard I worked at it. I tried to pass it off like life was just supposed to miraculously skip over that date altogether. I wanted the universe to do me a favor, for once, and go ahead and take that day off all calendars forever. Knowing for the last year that nothing seemed to have gone my way no matter how hard I tried, I knew I still had to face it boldly.

I decided to go into work that day, highly anticipating that my mind would scatter elsewhere. Plus, still seeking Mom's advice, I could hear her forcing me, "Crystal, go to work. There is no reason you can't go to work today." So, I did. And I'll tell you, I am certainly proud of the decision I made. I woke up that morning feeling sad, but also unexpectedly feeling some sort of calm and positive emotions that flooded the outer surface. I'm not sure if it's because I was so determined to tackle that day and get through it any way I could or if I genuinely felt calm, but I was going with it.

I felt confident in making it a great day and remembering Mom while doing so. I poured a Styrofoam cup of black coffee from the break room after I clocked in and went right into work mode. It went pretty smoothly, considering it was the busiest day of the week. I stayed on task, talked to many different patients of mine, and just kept chugging along.

It wasn't until I slowed down and my patient load dwindled at the end of our daily schedule, that I had some time on my hands to allow my thoughts to wander back to the happenings of this day exactly one year ago. It was too late to talk myself out of it, as the cloud of darkness and pure mourning invaded me. My personality suddenly shifted into a big useless ball of emotions. I had tried so hard to avoid it all day long, but I didn't have the strength any longer to keep holding up that wall.

Before I lashed out at everybody for no reason legitimate enough to back up my actions, I hopped in my car to speed home. I could still envision the family huddled together around her Hospice bed in the living room. I couldn't rid my brain of the sight of Mom's body lying in the middle of everyone, helpless and motionless. Instead of trying so hard to steer my thoughts away from the biggest traumatic event I'd ever endured, I just let it all out. I let the tears fall and my heart pound as I flipped to my "life sucks" playlist on Spotify. I wanted so desperately to avoid those feelings and tried hard not to ruin the somewhat good day I had, but reliving this day in memories wasn't going to allow me to do so.

I do believe that sometimes certain emotions are far from invisible and must be let out to be able to get through them. I paid a visit to that cement headstone her body lay under at the cemetery where she was buried, because I felt like it was necessary. I hadn't ever "felt her" there when I'd visited, but I felt somewhat guilty if I didn't at least stop by. My dad and sisters met me out there to join in the grieving party together. Life works hard at distancing people after a death (or even *not* after a death, if we're being honest). It was nice to be able to huddle around, hand in hand, and reminisce about Mom's life as a whole.

Meagan had this genius idea to light paper lanterns in her memory and watch as they drifted off into the sky. It was a pretty amazing sight to see and, truthfully, I'd much rather paper lanterns be the thing drifting off into the sky than my Mom's soul, but let's be real. I was heartbroken and just couldn't wrap my brain around the fact it had already been one whole excruciating year without her. Her voice in my head was still so prominent and profound, and the sight of her face never left the forefront of my mind.

If only I could have attached a note to those lanterns and let them drift into Heaven. That may have been the only way I was going to be okay with standing there without her. Unfortunately, reality checks come and go while mourning and those lanterns didn't make it into Heaven. In fact, they floated up quite a ways and then started falling into the woods down below.

"Oh my gosh, they're falling!" Katie said. "Great, here we are trying to do something in Mom's honor and now we are about to set the whole north side of town on fire," I told them as we laughed, truly hoping they'd burn out before they hit the ground. Needless to say, we ended our little honorary grief ceremony without any wildfires. (Still thanking God for that one.)

Everybody started to wrap up our bean burritos from Taco Bell (also in her honor) and head home, but I just wasn't ready yet. So I stayed a little longer, alone and broken, to give myself the opportunity to finish crying it out. I talked to her, cried to her, and prayed to her, hoping she could hear me.

After a few pity parties of my own, it was too dark to even see her headstone anymore. Pulling myself together somewhat, I wiped the dirt from the base of her headstone, straightened the flowers in the vase atop it, and kissed the ground where I pictured her head would be. I walked off into the darkness back to my car and headed home to my little family that had been waiting for me this whole time.

Before bed that night, I shared with the world the most beautiful picture of her face. She looks like an angel sitting in the back seat of a car. Window down, arm propped up under her chin, and the most stunning, genuine, sincere smile on her face. I gave into the silly thought of, "It's not official unless you post to Facebook" bullshit and submitted a post to my timeline. It read (as if Mom could read it or something),

> To the most beautiful person I've ever known: One year ago today was the most traumatic, gut wrenching, heart shattering worst day of my life. I can't believe it, just as much as I can't believe you aren't here anymore. This last year has been tougher than I could have ever imagined, and it hasn't seemed to get any easier. There isn't a moment that goes by

without my thinking of you. It's completely consumed me and changed my life forever. I try to remember your advice of how life would be without you and I try really hard to make you proud. Nobody will ever know how much you mean to me. There isn't a single soul in heaven or on earth that I have loved more than you. I miss you so much and can't wait until I see your beautiful face again. One year without you is one year closer. I love you so much my angel and miss you terribly!" (insert all the crying emojis)

Now, let's be real. As I sit here and re-write my post from the one-year anniversary of her death, I can proudly say I've come a long way. To me, that post screams pure obsessive heartbreak and full-blown grief to the extreme. Like that friend you keep begging to leave her abusive relationship, only to find out she stayed and got battered again by the drunken asshole she just can't seem to leave. I couldn't leave the heartbreak and I couldn't seem to get away from the depression. If you asked me any day of that whole year how I was doing, I would have never responded with, "I'm good" or "I'll be OK," because I wasn't and I didn't believe that. I had convinced myself that I would be broken at that same severity for the rest of my life. Time doesn't heal, but it does help push you to a level of acceptance so you can continue to live the life you've been given.

Granted, there are still days when I feel just as broken and helpless without her as I always have, but as time passes, I get busier with my growing children and I'm thankful for that. Often on days that I am stressed out and running around like a crazy mom who's completely unorganized, I remember one of the most important reasons God placed two children under my care in life as a mom. It most definitely has its reasons and it's times like these I am thankful I have those two little blondies to lean on when Momma just can't hang on any longer.

CHAPTER 38

TRYING FAITH

*S*ince Mom's death, I've had to learn how to realistically cope with life's grief triggers. Life's realities are extremely different from my own reality, and that's very hard to try to tackle. When my life was at its hardest, deepest, darkest point; I didn't think I could live anymore. This wasn't ever a feeling I shared with my husband or family, because it made me ashamed and embarrassed and I thought it would freak them out. I knew it'd make my mom very upset with me and I had children that needed me to care for them.

Sadly, I plummeted to the lowest point on the human mentality scale, for sure. At the time, I felt like giving up completely. That was until I met a friend who took me under her wing and cared and loved me even before she met me.

> **Real talk:** *She was one of the most amazing and helpful women I've ever met in my life. The second you meet her, she puts the "church girl" stereotype to bed. She even looks like the kind of mom you spot at a PTA meeting and immediately identify her as the cool mom whom you want to be friends with. I use this overly dramatic cliché, because in her case; it's true.*

One night sitting at *Panera Bread* downing black coffee and bear claws, she admitted to me that she'd heard of me in the past and knew who I was when she saw me, but never had the courage to introduce herself. She had previously heard through the church body about what I was going through and told me she started to pray for me daily about a year before she finally met me in person.

I couldn't believe that there were people out there who hadn't even met me yet and were praying for me like she was. Not only that, but the amount of love and positivity that she showed me on the hardest of my days will speak volumes to me for the rest of my life.

She took me in like a sheltered and battered homeless girl, when she didn't have to at all. She led me back to God alongside her. I shared with her my pain and heartbreaking story. She physically took me by the hand and allowed me to join with her in her growing journey of faith. She even forced me to pray out loud with her right there in the middle of *Panera Bread*. Talk about uncomfortable. But I did it and thankfully, nobody else was there except the closing crew who was mopping floors and rinsing out coffee pots.

Her husband was a pastor and one of the nicest, most genuine people I've ever met, but *she* by far took the trophy, as the rarest gem you could ever find as a friend.

When she told me she had come into our church and started up a women's Bible study, I felt oddly intimidated.

I can't tell her all my true thoughts, because she's not going to think very highly of me," I thought. *Boy, I was wrong!* She convinced me to come and try a night at her women's Bible study, just to see what I thought. It took a couple of weeks to truly convince me, but I finally decided to give it a try, because at this point, I had nowhere else to go—except home, in my comfy oversized grief-infused California king. As much as I hate to admit that I believed living in my tears and deep sorrow was going to inevitably be there for the rest of my life. I am in fact happy to admit that that's not where my life stayed. I decided to take a "leap of faith" and see what all the hype was about. I thought to myself, "It's not going to help me, but I guess it can't hurt me anymore and especially if it's about the Bible, right?" *Well, sort of.*

The whole day leading up to my first Bible study was nerve wracking. I felt sick to my stomach and I swear I must have come up with over a hundred excuses as to why, "I just can't make it tonight. I'll reschedule." Thankfully, the little voice in my head (thanks, Mom!) convinced me to branch out of my comfort zone and just do it. So that's what I did.

I walked in there with one spiral notebook and a mechanical pencil almost out of lead. This outgoing-sometimes-overly-chatty-girl that I am, felt extremely shy and awkward. The Bible study was like a huge Mom's-night-out. She got up and spoke into the microphone on the stage in front of all the women there, and she instantly grabbed my heart. As if her country accent and pregnant belly didn't make me love her enough already, she spoke about God in ways I had never heard. Her sweet soul is one that's been blessed with many gifts. Her most cherished one in my book is the way she makes you feel. She genuinely speaks to you on a level that most people may not even know how to reach.

At that first study, we focused on the books of Corinthians and Colossians. She dug deep into the meaning behind the words written in those books and, in my opinion, it was intriguing. A little back shadowing: I grew up attending a Lutheran Christian school from third grade to eighth. I graduated from confirmation and attended church as well as Sunday School every single week. We weren't allowed to miss it. I vacationed with my youth group at Christian camps and served as an acolyte during "adult church." *I mean something had to have been etched into my brain besides "Truth or Dare" and flashlight tag at midnight or how to sneak in walkie-talkies connecting the girls' and guys' cabin, right?* I thought I had known all there was to know about the Bible, front to back.

I sat in Bible study that night, sipping late-night coffee and munching on little tea cookies at a table full of very friendly and welcoming strangers. I suddenly realized that I knew nothing about the Bible. I didn't know the meaning behind any of the books written, and I certainly didn't know the timeline in which it was written. I realized that there was so much more to learn about it and the reason behind why God even wrote it in the first place.

I felt extremely confused and embarrassed because it was so much more complex than the outside world realizes. I took down two pages of pencil written notes about things I had never even heard of (mainly because everybody else at my table was taking notes and I didn't want to be the weirdo not writing this stuff down).

When I left, I cried. I felt so overwhelmed. The thought of how proud my Mom would be, knowing that I even walked through those doors in the first place, instantly brought me to tears. *Oh, how I miss her!* "If only she was here to see what I did tonight!" I told a friend in the parking lot. "She knows, Crystal, she sees you, and she's extremely proud of you for it!" She tried desperately to cheer me up.

After giving in to my first Bible study, I started to attend church every Sunday. She had gifted me with a notebook that I ended up filling to the brim from the very first page to the very last. Each page was dated and labeled with titles of Sunday church sermons. I found myself in Books-A-Million often, looking for the best Bible I could have for my own. Over time, my faith kept changing and strengthening. My grief started to diminish a little more and I found myself talking to God numerous times a day. I sat in the same seat in the second row at church every Sunday, and even became friends with the people around me. I just couldn't resist little old Ms. Anne's hugs every week! Suddenly I felt like I had a home away from home. I felt wanted, cared for, and loved. Not that I hadn't felt loved up to this point, because I most definitely did, but this was a different type of love. This was an inspiring, faith-growing, Godly welcoming type of love.

My faith became a huge part of my life. My mom had always taught me to continue upholding my faith no matter the day or situation. She taught me to trust in God and I thought I had done a great job of that, until now. I realized after a while that I only had faith in Him when it was convenient for me and when I was in desperate need of a miracle. My faith dropped to the bottom of the list most days and my prayers became totally selfish. I bargained with Him way too many times and I promised I'd "Do this, if He'd do that." But I came to realize when he didn't grant me those wishes, that that's not exactly how it works.

Up to this current day, I have three notebooks full of sermon notes and Bible studies. I have three Bibles with highlighted material and cliff notes of my own. I poured my heart into them and spent most of my time learning about the Bible, its background, the authors, and its true meanings. Without that, I don't know that I would have survived the amount of grief and depression with which I was living. Mom knew what she was talking about and tried her hardest to bring me back to God. Now that I was doing that, comfort came around more often.

I'll admit I haven't abided by that thought process every single day. I'm human and I've earned a couple of scars. There are days I still drive down the road and glance over at her favorite store, only to break out in ugly hysterical crying. A small whiff of someone in Saks Fifth Avenue wearing her perfume, Red Door by Elizabeth

Arden, and I'm a total mess! One stanza of *Oh Holy Night,* and I'm launching back into my childhood memories as an angel at the altar of our church in an itchy oversized robe with a halo that wouldn't stay on top of my head while I looked out at the congregation to see her beaming with joy watching her babies in the church play. There are songs on the radio that will play as if she's singing them to me. There are days my anger gets the best of me and I take it out on any soul who walks into the room at that time. (Usually it's my husband, bless his bones.) Those downfalls are naturally a part of this life and they're here to stay for a while.

Complicated grief is something that should never be taken for granted. It's not a laughing matter nor is it something that should ever be taken lightly. It's as real as real can get. Moving on after a loved one's death simply takes up everything inside you.

I had to learn the hard way that significant grieving can cause mental, physical, spiritual, and substance abuse all at the same time, and I have juggled with all four of those. Struggling with faith is a very real but normal part of one's life.

Being a mom, I now realize that even your own struggling faith can change your husband and your own children. My boys attended "kid church" every Sunday while Sean and I went to "adult church." They came home with more and more knowledge of God and all His stories to tell. They started sharing with friends and family where their Memaw is and what they are going to do to get there. As a parent, hearing your child talk about God and all the knowledge they've acquired at such a young age is a blessing and such a big gift, all in one. That faith and eagerness they have has stemmed from someone very special who knew all along what she was doing in raising her own kids and grandkids. That's what angels do, you know.

Grief and depression are harder to endure when it comes in waves. Over the last three-and-a-half years of being motherless, I've experienced an excessive amount of uncontrolled emotional waves. At least for me, it seems to have been more detrimental than even that of a tidal wave.

Marriages can suffer, and parenting can suffer, as well as friendships. I know, because I've been through all of them, more times than you can count. Having a strong hold on your feelings after a tremendous loss isn't easy. It is something I believe can improve as time passes. It can alter every aspect of your everyday life in ways you didn't know ever existed.

"No! I don't want chicken—I want steak!" I yelled to the Outback to-go employee over the phone when she so kindly told me they were out of steak. Anger came out and it came out quick. It creeps in inconveniently at times, unexpected and totally unnecessary.

We all know what it's like that morning you're late for work, because you hit snooze twelve times, decide to get up at the very last second, skip your morning shower, and throw your hair up in a messy bun. You just honk and cuss at every driver on the road actually abiding by the law and driving the speed limit, as if *they* are the reason you're late to work.

I get it, sister! It's frustrating because nothing seems to be going your way. No matter what you do or what road you take, there's always construction and roadblocks complicating your life even more and you just don't need that right now!

Your mind is a tricky son of a bitch. It's the reason we do what we do and the reason we think the petty way that we think.

I'm pretty sure that grief and our minds are like best friends forever. It's only going to feed into the needy emotions and hurt you if you don't take control of it. I like to think half of one's mind is the devil, and the other bigger half is God. It's up to you to determine which part of your mind you want to listen to and which little buddy on your shoulder you're going to follow. I'd rather pick the angel over the little devil, but some people have a hard time deciding.

Amid my depression, I've surprisingly found myself lifting others up and actually listening to my advice. It seems to help friends who keep coming back for more, but for myself, it's slightly tougher. That's when Mom steps in and throws a clothing tag down on my closet floor, telling me so blatantly not to ask why. I mean, she is right though. I can ask, "Why" until I am ever so blue in the face, but the answer for which I'm looking will never come.

Same with grief—if you let it take over you, it'll turn your life into one spiraling, devastating, and hot messy tornado. Even then, your answer won't come and, truthfully, I think that's what's best for all of us.

CHAPTER 39

A MOTHER'S SPIRIT

"Someday you should share our story, Crystal," Mom said in the passenger seat of her own car as I pulled through Wendy's to load her up with her favorite Frosty on the way home from chemo. At this point in her life, it was an honor to lug her around wherever she needed to go, because that meant I was spending time with just her, and occasionally Kane Brown joined in on the radio. Our times in the car were such fun. Nothing was held back, and no conversation topic was off limits. It got awkward at times, but Mom had an ear for listening and a heart for caring. That type of person is someone everybody needs in their life forever. "Mom, you could write a book and maybe you should. It'd be an amazing story to tell!" I tried to shift the task onto her. *God I miss her.*

I had engulfed everything into my mom and her memory. But look, I'm a natural born, materialistic, too-expensive-for-my-own-good person who still sends Christmas lists to my dad (and my husband). I like things and I still lust for any present to reward a struggle or bought just because. Without Mom here to do it for me, I started giving those things to myself. The picture frames in my house were switched to Mom and me. The wedding rings—*oh the wedding rings ...*

I had somehow convinced my dad to open his safe before he sold his house, so I could get something of Mom's to take home. I hadn't expected her wedding rings to be in there, considering he had her one huge diamond turned into four 14-karat gold necklaces that were crafted together outside the United States for his kids. (*Dad, you're the sweetest!*)

But when he opened it up and said, "Take anything you want!" I grabbed her wedding bands. The day I replaced my own wedding bands with my mom's, I actually thought it was OK to summon Sean for his opinion on how pretty they look on my dainty fingers;

he responded with, "Umm, yeah they look ... great." He inspected them with a confused tone of a mid-thirties man, who doesn't need bifocals yet, but I could tell something was wrong. "Hmm, he must not like them," I thought as I walked away.

It turned out that watching me mope around the house in my lost and depressed state, and now seeing me happy over materialistic things that honored my mother, was extremely hard for him. We still had a family and I was still the wife and mother. "Oh no, maybe I should replace *some* of the pictures of Mom and me around the house with Sean and me and our family of four," I said to myself, realizing obsession was becoming a problem.

Why am I telling you this silly irrelevant-seeming story? You see, when you're fogged with devastating emotions, an obsessive disorder based on who you lost may help heal that wound, but it's opening another one that's going to need healing, too, eventually. I was drifting further from my family as I started my own shrine of Mom.

Grief will tear up parts of your life, whether it's one part or fifty. It's not balancing your life by any means and you must put a stop to that right away. Go ahead and replace a few pictures here or there with you and her, but remember that you're still here, living and breathing.

It's hard, I get it. It feels like you're an orphan after you lose your mom, because your typical family foundation is now gone in an instant. Being a mother yourself, you still want to be mothered. Nobody's been through motherhood like our moms. Without them, how are we supposed to learn the stuff they knew? "My mom didn't leave a tutorial or instruction book," I said, completely flustered and annoyed.

Moms take care of everyone and keep the family together. If there's a conflict, Mom is the mediator. *Now, since Mom isn't here, the family will fall apart,* I thought. Assuming my mother's role would be the only way to regain our family stability.

Loving your husband and mothering your children can't just stop when your Mom dies. That has to keep going and mastering the nurturing aspect in the way your mom did, is what you're set out to reenact. It's an honor because nobody else in the world has the role model you do. Use it, pursue it, and live it up like she did!

This world tends to overlook and underestimate young adults who lose their moms, because they unfairly feel like the mother-daughter bond at that age doesn't need as much maternal guidance as you did when you were younger. They are so wrong! Over these last four years I've learned so many lessons that can't be taught verbally and others unless you physically endure them yourself. I've learned that appreciating your mother is by far one of the biggest blessings God gave you to appreciate.

A mother is the hardest job on the planet. A mother is the first person to love you. She's the glue in your entire life. When you lose her, it's one of the most devastating and traumatic events you could ever possibly live through. But that's just it—you will live through it. She created you. She nurtured you. She loved you from the time you were physically formed. You were the one to hear her heartbeat from the inside, and she was the one to give you your heartbeat. She's so special. Don't dismiss that and ruin it with your ever-growing state of sadness.

You mother's mortality is inevitable. Although it's universal, everybody will grieve differently. It's an event that no matter what the circumstances are, it will be one of the absolute hardest things you go through. To me, she was my home. She was my safe place. Being around her brought me joy that I had no idea ever existed until I was old enough to feel it for myself. The tone of her voice was comforting. The sound of her laugh was hysterical. The sight of her smile was undeniably amazing. Being a mom in my opinion is the toughest job on the face of the planet. I mean, who else can spit a human out of their va-jay-jay and live to talk about it? Much less raise those human beings with endless grace and love.

True change must come from loving yourself enough to care for your own needs and be the best version you can be for your family.

We all get lost in the darkness sometimes, but the failures and screw ups are lessons and often gifts that wake you up to what's most important in life. That is, if you choose to see it that way.

Motherless daughters may have issues with other relationships in life. You'll tend to feel especially distant from your peers, because of both jealousy and lack of commonality. Even intimate relationships struggle because we are far needier after losing our moms because nobody seems to ever fill that void. You'll try to search in others, especially our husbands, for the nurturing trait you are used to getting from your mom. It's hard to give as much back to our partners at this time and it's only going to cause resentment. Fortunately for you and me, it can be recovered and conquered.

Unlike the physical symptoms that can manifest while grieving the death of your mother, the psychological impact of it is less predictable. There's no "correct" emotion in the wake of such an enormous loss. Even the most adult-like people, who can put on a brave face and go back to work immediately following the death of a loved one, may still be suffering a clinical condition, if they remain preoccupied with the death. It may become more complex and much harder to handle—take it from me, a self-proclaimed complicated griever.

Simply allow yourself to explore different life prospects without the approval of your mom. It's normal for your mom's image to stay static, but over time, people will naturally change.

You won't take these life changes and real struggles for granted if you have to earn it back. Don't go back to who you used to be. Instead, make a newer and wiser version of who your dear sweet mama loved so much.

Your emotions are nobody's responsibility but your own. You will drown trying to change the emotions of fellow grievers. The best way to apologize to yourself is by changed behavior on your part. You might not have your mom here anymore, but you still have faith somewhere in there. Without blind faith, what do we have left anyway? You must wake up and refuse to live that way. It's hard, but it's that simple. It's a decision, a mental commitment that will become the most important decision you'll have to make in your life right now.

The world pushes us to "get over it" too soon after a significant loss. We must be able to grieve and do so on our own terms. But we also need to adjust our expectations of ourselves. Be intentional with your healing. Strive to live and learn, because the decisions you make now become impactful in more lives than your own.

Be strong yet gentle, unrelenting yet yielding, because at the end of the day, that's what a mother is. After all, you've learned from the best and her spirit lives on in you forever.

CHAPTER 40

THE NEW YOU!

*T*here will always be unspoken truths about what it's like once your mom kicks the bucket. Because nobody warns you about them ahead of time, I'm going to. Buckle up and prepare yourself, because it's real. Maybe not in the exact way it was for me, but in some sort of similarity, it may walk into your world as well, *Just sayin* …

You'll have days when you feel you've only been left with her recipes and a Polaroid infestation on old Whirlpool in the kitchen. Those are blessing, because the longing memories from another time will shine through as you open the fridge searching for the half-eaten container of Hershey's chocolate icing you put in there last night after your cry fest during that Hallmark movie you should have never watched. But that's your life.

You'll feel like you're falling backwards, like your slime-left being is seeping through the cracks. You'll feel so lost that those cracks you're slipping through are embedded on the back alley roadway you wandered down in an eerie, dark, off-the-grid town and its only occupant is you. You can scream if you want. In all honesty that's exactly what you'll do, but eventually you'll be down to your last breath. You will envision where you want to be, but the voice inside your head is saying you'll never get there. That's a lie. That's grief's best friend called doom. You don't know this yet, but these are the moments that you will remember. These are the moments of struggle that will shape you into the person waiting on the other side.

No matter how badly it hurts or how much water weight you lose in tears streaming down your face, you'll live, sister, you will. *I did!* Don't be that sulking emo introvert forever. (Nobody likes them anyway.) You aren't honoring your mom that way. You're only disappointing her by staying there. Be the one that's got to do what you've got to do. She knows your strength—she instilled it in you. Don't let her down. Show her you still have it and then some!

"Crystal, you don't need me to survive. You are a lot stronger than you give yourself credit for," Mom told me as I lay doubled over on the bathroom floor while she tied her cute purple scarf around her bald head. I didn't believe her, but she told me that because she did.

Your inner strength is stronger than you can imagine. It overpowers any physical strength your body is capable of holding. Our minds are the most powerful things on the planet. Surprise! Now use it, but in a positive way. Our moms are the fear and fire in every life fight. Now *you* are left to uphold that CEO position of your life company's crumbling breakdown.

I have learned that the essence of our mom's will lives on and seeps into every part of our lives, great or small. She comes out in my voice when I'm yelling at my kids, "because I'm your mother, that's why!" I still try to duplicate her recipes for every holiday, even though I never really perfect it like she did. It's frustrating to not be able to pick up the phone and ask her what aisle the green chilis are on at Publix or what temperature to set the oven on for her famous meatloaf I just bombed. Small things that seemed so irrelevant when she was alive turn into such a big deal to me now that I'm motherless.

I've taught my kids to grab the milk carton at the back of the shelf at the grocery store, because it will have a longer expiration date on it. I've realized now, it's important to thaw your meat in cold water in the kitchen sink the morning when you're going to cook it, instead of spending twenty minutes pounding on a raw meat block trying to break it apart ten minutes before you're supposed to be serving it for dinner. She encouraged me to always clean the kitchen as you go, so there's less you have to do when you're done. We all know the rule that makes every kid gasp with disappointment when Mom exclaims, "I cooked it, so now you can clean the kitchen!" Now, I've adopted that rule in my household and I'll tell you, it's a marvelous thing.

"Crystal you won't have mounds of laundry to do, if you'll just do a small load every single day." she'd purposely say, interrupting my complaints about how many piles of dirty clothes I still haven't gotten to the washing machine yet. *(It's with great sadness, Mom, that I admit I'm still the world's worst at this one. But hey, there's always tomorrow!)*

It's like you just hopped onto a speeding rollercoaster and the tracks feel like they're coming off the rails. You'll wallow in the icky, uncomfortable, overwhelming, and confusing emotions of jealousy, resentment, and good ole' hatred! The severity of shock, numbness, sadness, denial, and despair comes faster than you can even think about it. The pain will become overpowering as you try navigating life motherless—*who else is supposed to tell me that I'm being absolutely ridiculous and I just need to grow up?* But the emotional strife is the added extra credit you'll earn for tumbling down life's messy landslide that this world likes to call, "grief." Losing your mother takes a stronger hold on your psyche than anybody ever expects, because the thought of loving someone so much is captivating and having them ripped away from you leaves you incredibly lost.

Humans have a hard time expressing their true feelings in ways our brains can comprehend. I'll admit, I wished I was dead sometimes. Not because I hated life, but because I just wanted to see my mom again. I knew she'd be the first one to welcome me home and I thought I was at peace with that. I can see her now, "There's my girl! Come on, baby, let's fly away in goodness together!" After time passes, you'll realize that's not OK. She was at peace with knowing where she was headed when her body gasped for its last earthly breath.

"It's OK, honey, I'm not scared. I may not always be here, but I'll always be right there," she told me as she pointed to the breaking heart in my chest.

I mean, if she knew I was thinking of dying following her death, she'd most likely break out of her grave and join the Anderson sisters on Hocus Pocus just to come haunt me forever. And believe me, I've seen her mad. That is not a place I want to revisit!

It stings more than the wine you down every night watching reruns of *Friends*, but when you set out to conquer your struggles, you'll win. It'll always feel like you're pouring sea salt into your gaping open wound, but I can assure you, that clock on the wall will not cure it all. Don't wait for a sensible time to pass you by—you aren't made to come in last. You, my little angel, are the only one who can finish your journey. You are the only person capable of defeating grief and the time frame that comes with it is of your choosing.

"I have children to raise and a husband to love and support for the rest of my life. God chose me for that job, nobody else," I had to remind myself repeatedly. That's an honor! Remember that your children look at you like you looked at your mom. Take that and use it to motivate your future. Bad news, my readers—there are no second chances in life, so don't waste your time waiting for it.

The struggles after a loss like yours come at varying degrees. Some days just seem easier, while others seem entirely too tough to have to manage. It's impossible to explain to outsiders what exactly you are feeling and why you just did what you did. You'll do things you don't believe in, and you'll act like a person you've never liked because in reality, you're just as confused about who you are now, as you are trying to understand the reason behind why she died. It's too hard to pinpoint the reasoning behind most things you've done wrong, but you know deep down it's because you're hurting.

The timing of somebody's grief is such a foolish expectation that this world carries. I personally don't agree with it and, if you are the one walking down this path, you won't agree with it either. Chugging along to your own timeline is very much okay. Some grievers seem to be able to move on a little quicker than others. Nobody can judge that but God. If you find yourself judging somebody's grief timing, then by God, I pray you never have to go through it. The people around you will quickly become impatient with your healing process. It's not that they're impatient with you specifically, but they're impatient because they want you to feel better so much faster than you do. It's not about how fast you get there. It's about the real-life struggles, the climb to conquer it all, and the will to come out on the other side a stronger person.

I have specifically chosen to take all the time I need while writing this book because, just like life, there are many emotional triggers, and this has been the hardest one. You don't realize exactly what you go through until you write it down on paper. I'm here to tell you the sustained grief felt years later can have cognitive, social, cultural, and spiritual effects. It's easy to question God, but it's not easy to get an answer. I've suffered from depression since the day my mother was diagnosed with cancer.

The truth is, when you're ready to get your mind right, your tracks will become straight again, but for someone with complicated depression, those tracks seem permanently crooked. Healing is a wild journey—it'll never be a straight line. People have their own ways of coping. I have mine and you have yours. Triggers will come and go, but you must learn not to torture yourself with them. Instead of causing more unnecessary pain, wouldn't you rather ask yourself how you can honor your mother instead?

"One day when I'm gone, I don't want you to cry. I want you to smile when you think of me," she said to me, like she expected it to be that easy.

I didn't realize then, that if I physically smiled at every thought of her, that my smile would never go away. It'd be glued to my face just like her love is to my heart. Time has a way of generously giving back your love and peace, so eventually you will find the "you" that you were always meant to be. Uphill battles are inevitable and there are times you'll have to lose. But if you just stop there, you'll get no further. Keep your head held high because, even though this loss seems so detrimental right now, the truth is that there's always another mountain you're going to have to move.

Every family has traditions growing up, and when you have your own family, new traditions emerge. That concept is fine with me, but what isn't fine are the new traditions that losing your mother forces you to create. There were only a select few traditions that were able to stay somewhat the same after Mom's death, but the majority had to change. They didn't change because we wanted them to, but because she headed all those traditions. Nobody else knows how to do it quite like she did.

Every Christmas Eve she read the book, *Twas' The Night Before Christmas*. That tradition started when I was a baby and lasted all the way up to the year she passed away. I couldn't bear the fact that I had to be the one to start reading that book aloud to my kids now. Frankly, I didn't want to, because I still wanted her to read it to my needy self. It wouldn't mean the same if I did it. I can't accentuate my voice into five different characters in one story like she could. I'm not that cool.

The first year, my dad kept that tradition alive and read it to the grandkids, but even for him it wasn't anywhere near the same. I can't tell you the last time my dad even read a storybook to any child, much less his family grands! Thankfully though, a smidge of her self-preparedness seeped into my veins when I recorded her reading it to them that last Christmas Eve we had with her. *Papa, you had a great one-year run with it, but Mom will take over from here, thanks. Love you, mean it.*

You now have to recreate the Christmas magic for your babies because even though your mom died, Santa didn't and he's still coming in hot, folks.

It's then that you'll find some happiness still buried deep inside your morbidly depressed soul. Recreate it in your very own way, even if it means sitting on your couch every year after that, listening and watching the video of her reading it to them. It's the next best thing to her physically being here and, hey, it's a different type of tradition, right?

Oh, but it is. So, you do you, my friend. No judgment here.

Tradition is a hard one to tackle on the seven-mile lengthy list of things you must overcome when you're initiated into the Dead Mama's Club. It's about learning to let go of the things that you aren't ready to release. That's where you'll find the peace to keep pushing on.

Let me go ahead and throw this one out there for you to latch onto: smiling is okay! Did you hear me? I said smiling is OK. You aren't alone anymore. (Thanks to Kevin for staying *Home Alone* and giving me that one liner truth to use.). It might be hard to do most of the time, but remember how your smile was one of your Mom's favorite traits she liked about you. I get it, though. For a few years, my smile was fake. It hid a lot of pain and sorrow behind it, and it created a barrier between my physical appearance and my heart's appearance on the inside.

However, it did a fabulous job of hiding my true feelings and tricking everybody else into thinking I was okay, when I wasn't. I was far from OK. When I dove into the Bible to learn more about

God (someone whom I strongly disliked in the worst times I could have disliked somebody), that smile slowly became more genuine and real.

God thankfully has brought comfort back to my darkest days, and I had convinced myself that I could never say that again. God provides. Happiness, faith, and love are all eternally irrevocable. It doesn't matter what you go through. It stays stored away inside until you decide that living with it is, in fact, remarkably better than living without it. When you accept that those are all pertinent factors in the days ahead, you'll come to realize that to whom much is given, much is expected. Your healing process and overcoming tragedy is a test that is given by God, so don't waste it. Your mother didn't waste it, so why would you?

Run on faith if faith alone is all you have. But guess what, if you have faith, then you have it all.

You may see yourself as broken, thinking there's no way you can ever be fixed again. But that's not how God sees you. It's like standing in a garden full of flowers and weeds with God–it's a mess but it's wild, wonderful, and perfect. That mess is you.

As difficult as it is to understand, God is in the middle of everything we perceive as a mess–working for our own good. That's what He does. Even when we see our world as a mess, to God it's beautiful.

The real underlying flaw in my life was that I didn't see Him as "good" after Mom's death. Immense mourning blinded me from that perception. I didn't realize how much He loves us, because I didn't know Him that well. I didn't allow myself for quite some time to even give Him the chance, knowing I wouldn't understand it anyway. There's a big picture, a plan, and a purpose behind every tragedy. He's always at work.

To plant a new "you," you must prepare the ground. Dig up the old roots or they'll return to harm the new growth. The sap from a single toxic twig can kill you on its own. But combine it with the nectar from a flower, and together it has incredible healing properties. Us + God = Healing.

The fallout of losing your mom is not something you can outrun. Especially in the months following her death, you won't outrun your grief no matter how hard you try. Instead of fleeing, just feel it, live it, learn from it, and show up every day doing the best damn job you can.

Studies have shown that losing a parent will have a lifelong, permanent, psychological effect on humans of all ages. The lengthy denial and anger phases of grief are very serious, but it's how we handle them that matters most. In the early days (or if your denial is particularly needy like mine, it'll last way too long—not recommended), you'll hate people with a homicidal rage, because they still have their moms, and you don't. You'll hate the strangers you see sitting across from you at The Cheesecake Factory yelling into their iPhones at their moms on the other end.

You'll end up hating your friends who do nothing but complain about all the petty and annoying things their moms do. I became the wrong friend for someone to complain to me about their mom. I shut it down quickly, because I would have done anything to be the one on the phone who just hung up on my mom while she tried to tell me I needed to be more responsible and to just listen to her. You'll give anything to still experience that mother-daughter pissed-off-but-loving bond. You'll resent the moms you see walking hand in hand with their adult children through Central Park, galloping their happy asses right through the sunshine or the grandmother sitting in the front row of the bleachers obnoxiously yelling for her "doodlebug" grandson to hit her a homerun. You'll scowl her way in hatred, too! Trust me, I do it all the time. You'll even hate the people who have terrible living moms because, even though that's incomprehensible to you, trashy humans can still be good moms, too.

You'll hate a million times over before you realize this weird and unfair surge inside you is actually quite terrifying. It will embarrass you at times and you'll start to feel deeply ashamed of it. I found it difficult to admit, even to my pretty-faced best friend with her blonde highlighted silky bob and understanding teary eyes. My anger wasn't the kind you're "supposed" to feel. It wasn't serious raging fury at simply the fact they still had their moms, but the fact mine was dead now. We are all living boring and unpredictable lives, but the only difference now is that some still have sensible, living, mom-jeans wearing, breathing mothers who they can still go home and vent to over endless bottles of Pinot Noir. *Damn, this sucks!*

That type of anger for me was conceived and birthed the day I found out my mom had cancer. It was fed and nurtured excessively the day she died, and I was still mothering it (no pun intended) years later. Sure, I had other it's-the-end-of-the-world-because-my-mom-died emotions, but the anger was there from the beginning and it bubbled over my life-pot constantly. I hated everyone who got in my way. From the sweet nurse who complimented our mother-daughter twinning looks, to the nutritionist who gave my Mom life-surviving superfood shake recipes. After she died, my rage strangled everything around me like a demonic octopus tentacle with more than a death grip. I'm telling you this so you can avoid it when your toxic best friend named Grief tries to take you by the hand and lead the way in *your* life!

You aren't going to wish away your mom's death no matter how hard you try. Unfortunately, you won't bring her back no matter what you do or don't do. Trust me I've tried it all. The moments you go through all have meaning and it's building you into a person you never thought you'd be.

I've questioned God so much. "Why did He let her die? Why didn't He stop it?" I've realized that I'm sitting back trying to make sense of a very incomplete picture, looking through the knothole of my pain. God doesn't try to justify what happened. He's trying to heal it only if we allow it.

Be ready when your kids tell you, "Mommy, as much as I miss Memaw so bad, I wouldn't bring her back to this bad world even if I had the chance." That will prove to you right there, that lessons have been learned through her loss despite transforming you into a blubbering cry baby because you're hurting, but also somewhat proud that your kids are acting more grown up than you are.

When they ask you, "Mommy, if you could have three wishes, what would they be?" and you know you cannot respond with "To bring Memaw back, bring Memaw back, and bring Memaw back," you'll realize they're onto something good, so play along. Two of Jaxon's wishes were something realistic like "a million dollars and a Ferrari," but his third was, "to create a perfect world that I could bring

Memaw back to until we are all ready to go to Heaven together!" *I'm telling you—what a little gentleman he is.* That doesn't only show me how much he misses her, but it shows me the extensive degree of his love he still has for her, who once was his world. It also shows me the blind faith in God that beams from his heart and loving thoughts. Those comments of his true feelings completely solidify the lessons Memaw taught him and the traits she instilled in him.

There are so many Memaw traits that have been etched into the human-formed beings of her grandchildren. It's comforting for us sad adults to see every day.

It could be as simple as the password on their new iPhones that the two oldest grandkids selected. (Mine may or may not be the same, but that's not the point.) It's meaningful things like Memaw's pillow that Jaxon can't sleep without, or the teal blanket that warmed Mom's cold body that Maddie cuddles with in her bed nightly. It's the simple hand-drawn pictures of Memaw with her blonde hair topped with an oversized and crooked halo, holding a teal flower that Tanner submitted as a class project. Even the flowers he thinks God gave to her on her birthday up in Heaven is such a simple example of blind faith in the Man who took her. It's the facial features on Chloe's face that mimic Memaw to a tee. *Talk about twinning!* Kinslee's golden heart is just as sweet and caring as Memaw's was and Barrett's love that he unknowingly gives is all Mom that seeps out of his little body every single day, even though he's never met her. Little Hannah who just came into this world was born with Mom's name attached to her like a giant "Memaw stamp" that'll be carried with her throughout the rest of her life.

It's in the tears that they cry because they miss her so much, while we try to instantly gain composure and grow up like adults so we can wipe those tears away. We remember that the sun shines so brightly because "Memaw is up there making it such a beautiful day," as Tanner says is all her. When that red cardinal flies by and lands on the neighbor's tree next door, they know it's Memaw watching them play. Though, let's be honest, she's probably making sure they aren't brawling and drawing blood in my front yard. But either way, it's cool. Hey Mom!

As a mother, my heart melts when my boys step up to the plate in a championship game, draw a cross in the clay, and look up to say, "This is for you, Memaw," before aiming for the fences. These things can't be taught. These are things with which their little bodies have been instilled because of the love and impact she made on everybody, including them. Those things will never be taken for granted and she will live on in their lives and their hearts for as long as they live. What has been taught though, is the way *I've* had to carry on from watching *them*. I can't give up now! They bring just as much joy to the world as she did, just in small multiple ways. She's here and still very much alive in every part of our lives.

You will try to get by, just simply by living inch by inch. Random shit will pop up and draw you right back to the swirling hot sadness that once felt like it burned your inside organs to a crisp.

You'll try to watch the movie "Stepmom" and NOPE!

It will suck when your phone updates and deletes all the old voicemails she left you.

You'll keep waiting to feel better and eventually, after putting in the work, the good days will become plentiful.

When E! News announces that another celebrity died of a drug overdose, you'll stop subconsciously jumping on that public mourning train, because our loss is collective, so you subconsciously hope this will make your grief socially acceptable and everybody else's tears will camouflage yours.

Eventually you can start seeing her as a real person, instead of the idolized version of her that's stuck in your head.

The first time you hear yourself voice ,"If she was here, she'd say... ", it's really hard.

You will come across pictures of yourself and think "Damn, I look like my mom!" – embrace it. It's a good look on you.

It's normal to wonder how different life would be if she was still here.

You'll sometimes imagine her watching over you.

Catching yourself telling your friends, "Oh, my mom loved those," will seem obsessive, but who the hell cares.

You'll appreciate the times when she pushed you harder and you'll thank God for the times she didn't—like your old deadbeat high school boyfriend. Thank God she talked you into dumping his ass.

You will one day realize you can talk about her without falling apart.

You'll adopt a "self-care" routine–(AKA just trying to pick yourself up and feel better), but none of them will seem to work out very well.

Every morning and night you'll start kissing her face on the picture frame you set beside your bathroom sink because, in your head, you imagine it's real and you can still feel it as if it was.

One day you will feel sad because you'll realize what an idiotic grieving mess you were and you'll cringe at the thought of how your family felt watching it, because you didn't listen to them or anybody else for that matter.

You already know what she would say in certain situations, but you do it anyways, because that's who you are and she loved you regardless.

If you're like me, you'll stand outside at 3 a.m. gazing up and talking to the brightest twinkling star in the night sky, telling her how much you miss her, all while your mini goldendoodle sniffs out your whole front yard just to pee for five seconds and then run back in.

You will memorize the last things she said to you, because those are the most impactful pieces of information that a human can't physically forget. Be thankful—you'll need them soon.

After some time, you can laugh and remember her fondly. You can even make jokes about her, especially if it's the way she ate a chicken wing. And Mom, don't leave your grave—it was all Rennie's idea!

You'll describe her to people that didn't know her, and you'll make them wish they had.

Most importantly, you will remember when she told you repeatedly, "I am so proud of you!" and you'll use that to keep moving on. Because the truth of the matter is this, she was always proud of you and she always will be! Mom knows best. The intuition and love they have are ones that can't be defeated by anybody or anything, ever. Our moms will always live on forever.

I'll go ahead and burst your bubble for you, because the rest of the world won't be this blunt and honest with you.

The truth is this—it never gets easier. It never hurts any less. In fact, it hurts worse with time. You won't ever stop missing her. It will get to the point that your heart feels like it's shattering into even more pieces right inside your chest, the one that's still bumping up and down as your heart continues to beat. The tears you shed will not diminish, pretty much ever. But they will lessen as your life moves on and your busy schedule continues to grow. You'll learn to cry in public less, instead you'll cry in private more. You won't ever stop mentioning her name or thinking of her every time you drive in the car alone, sobbing to all those sad songs written by artists who still have their moms.

The pain of her loss will shape and mold you into a person you've never met. There will be days when you won't like the person staring back at you in the mirror, and other days when you'll wonder where the strength that you've displayed really came from in the first place. You won't know you have it in you, but trust me, it's there and you'll need it.

When you see a friend post a sappy, heartfelt message with an image of her and her mom attached to it on Instagram, you'll want to break your computer screen. You will have moments that you hate her, that is, until you realize that you really don't—you're just jealous. It's a jealousy you've never had until now. It's a want that can never be fulfilled again.

As you read this and think to yourself, "I'm not going to be like that. I'll be happy for her now that she's not in any pain." In some cases, you're probably right about that one, but just wait. Wait until you walk into Nordstrom right past the perfume bar and you smell that Red Door perfume the clerk just spritzed on Susan, as she inquired about a purchase for her mother-in-law this coming Christmas. You'll break. You'll walk around aimlessly, feeling sorry for yourself, because you can't buy that bottle of perfume as a gift for *your* mom anymore. You'll search for the nearest restroom just to be able to sit and hide behind a closed door, while you wipe the tears from your face with toilet paper just so you don't look like a blubbering hot mess as you ride up the escalator to the handbag department.

When you start seeing signs about Mother's Day and hearing your girlfriends' plans about a surprise brunch they're planning for their moms, you'll get angry. You will try to figure out a way not to have to wake up on that empty, hollow May morning. But you won't figure that out, because you're instantly reminded that you're a mother yourself and your kids don't deserve a pitiful vegetable of a mommy on that morning that sun will still shine. Trust me, it's totally glamorous.

You will end up being awkward in conversations that contain the word, "mom," and you'll skip over the movie *Stepmom* on Netflix, almost as fast as you feel like downing the bottle of wine sitting next to your bed, just to mask your problems for yet another night. *I've been there. I feel you!*

But because I have been there, I can tell you this: that wine won't make you feel better. It won't mask anything. It may make you laugh and feel carefree, but that's only until you realize you indeed *do* care and you're having a full-blown meltdown Indian-style, drunk in your own driveway at two in the morning. Buying that eighty-dollar perfume bottle that you smelled in passing will only make you broke, because you'll still be sad. When you decide to flip the radio station to rap music, just hoping to find a song about something besides sappy heartbreak, you still won't smile. You'll just look like a depressed Snoop Dog trying to ridiculously nod your way into thinking you actually feel better, but you won't.

I had someone come up to me at a pop-up shop asking, "Are you the one who lost your mom?" and even though that's not how you want to be labeled, because it's an ugly and hurtful truth, I still admitted that I was. It is true, "That's me," I say.

I saw a painful but excited look on her face. Painful because that look only comes from someone who gets it, but excited because she found somebody who truly understands. It's a fact you don't want to admit and it's a pain that you don't want anything to do with, but regardless, it's real. It surfaces when strangers approach you, because they know your story from afar. They want to hear it and share it with you, so it validates that they aren't alone in this motherless world.

They want to know that you're OK, because it shows them that they can be, too. They're hopeful that their broken world indeed has a chance of somewhat mending back together like it once was. You're a friend to them, but on another level.

When you lose your mom, you're thrown into a world that lacks validation and the raw truth about what you struggle with daily. You seek comfort in only those who know that kind of pain. You have a bond with those who live the truth of loss that most people dread.

But that's a blessing. It's one you can only pray about. You pray for it, because being solo in a motherless and unfair world becomes relentless. Take it all in and enjoy the fact that people recognize you, even though it's because of death. You're already an inspiration to them or they would have never approached you to begin with. *Help a sister out!*

You're showing them it is still very much possible to live past the day of her death. Most days, you'll probably wonder how you made it this far, but that's not up for question—it just happens. You'll realize that your plan doesn't compare to God's plan and His is the only one that matters. His plan is the only way of life—yours is paved by lust and want. Yours is filled with loss and grief and, quite frankly, even though the validity of those feelings is there, they won't ever diminish until you accept His plan and His plan only.

You'll withdraw from family and friends simply, because nothing seems to matter to you anymore. Isolation becomes your comfort zone. You fear that getting close to others will only end in devastation, too. But that's not true. You can't stay there.

The first time you hear yourself laugh again, you'll remember that you still have a soul and a purpose. As hard as it is to feel pain, trust me—it's much harder to feel nothing.

There will be much sadness on a lot of happy days, but eventually that happiness will overcome your feelings of sadness and it'll mask it enough to get you by.

No matter what you're going through, the sun will still rise. It gives you a brighter outlook, knowing that the world is giving you another chance at turning yourself around and digging your way out of that useless state in which you've now become too comfortable. You can devour all the self-help books imaginable, and it may help a little. But what will truly help is the strength and fight in your heart and mind. I know that cliché, "What doesn't kill you only makes you stronger," will sound like a lie to you, because it does me. It's not though—it's the truth.

Eventually as time passes, you'll stop comparing every celebrity's death to your mom's age of death. "She was my mom's age, I know what they're going through!" or "Well, she was much older, it's only fair, right?" No, wrong—comparison didn't change your odds of survival and it won't change your odds of healing either. Emptiness will grab your soul and loneliness will find you. You *must* conquer those two. You have to learn to let go of things that are hard to release—this is the hardest one for me. I'm still learning, but that's the thing—I'm learning! I chose to brush up on my survival skills, because I didn't have many choices left. Choosing to stay empty, distant, and lonely is nothing shy of heart hollowing and that alone will tear your world apart even further.

It'll be hard to grasp the truth of knowing that one minute she was there and the next she was gone, slipped away. There will be many moments in life with her name written all over it and you'll say to her in the clouds, "I wish you didn't have to miss this." That's OK and I agree—I wish mine didn't have to miss this either. It's OK to feel jealous of heaven and the angels flying there. I felt it, too. How do you keep from getting jealous at the success of other people's moms when they conquer cancer and all their chemo treatments? It doesn't seem fair. But jealousy never ends well, and life has never been fair. But the good news is you *will* see her again real soon. This isn't where it ends.

You'll run down the path with "warning" signs flooding the entrance, and you'll walk in a way you never should. But that's growth. Those are more lessons you'll have to learn to continue to survive.

When you realize the only way to see her face is to shut your eyes, it hurts. Your memories are the only thing you have left of her. Cherish them and hold them tight. They are permanent creases in your mind that are etched there for a reason. Don't be overly willing to remake your entire life. Modify it according to the changes you're still living through, and grow it into something you can tolerate and enjoy. Dreams are important, as they can be a way of opening a window and letting all the bad air out.

For a few years, I had dreams of Mom and me quite often, but we were always fighting in those dreams. I never understood why because, in real life, we rarely argued. As the storm passed and I continued moving forward, I understand now the reason behind them—I was angry. I'm still angry. I had to learn how to take control of that anger, because it had taken up all the time I spent with my mom in my dreams. I had let the anger consume me when I didn't have to allow that. Take a deep breath and listen to God's voice. Don't look at the past and all the bad things you've been through, because none of that can hurt you anymore. Look at God—He's not going anywhere.

You'll never be equipped to take care of your family, if you can't take care of yourself. Grab hold of that severe depression and fight. Practice what you preach on the good and positive days that will still come. Then look back to see how far up you've actually made it from way down at rock bottom. You are still you, the you whom your mom loved without end. Whether you see it now or not, you are still capable of steering the reins in your life. Grab hold and move along because remember this, nobody changes until the pain level gets high enough.

When it comes to the death of a parent, there is no such thing as "getting over it," no matter the type of relationship. Regardless of what you think or believe (because believe me, I've felt it all), you will learn to live your life without her in ways she would have. It profoundly and permanently alters your every being, mentally, physically, and very much emotionally for the rest of your life.

Grief is not always expressed through tears. It may come out in forms of anger, sorrow, guilt, fear, selfishness, negativity and, at times, even peace. Sometimes it hits you on a regular day, yanking you right out of your happy and pleasant thoughts. I want you to remember that overwhelming grief. The stronger your grief is, it isn't necessarily a bad thing. It stems from having loved our moms so very deeply. Mom and I had an unbreakable bond, because she knew me from that first second of existence to her last. That's a blessing. I believe God gives everybody parents to help guide and teach them lessons in life that you will need to know, so you're able to actually survive after they go.

They teach us hard lessons and easy ones. They teach us what true love means and how to become a better person starting from the inside and working its way out. They teach us feelings, emotions, and how to handle unexpected experiences. They are put here to instill in us true and genuine faith and to remember that, no matter what you do, it should be done bringing glory to God, who one day will welcome *you* into His gates of Heaven, too. I can attest to the fact that it's truth to believe that God sent His son to die for us and save our sins so that we may live in Heaven eternally with Him and our loved ones. That alone is the most comforting promise He's given.

Give yourself credit and make a promise. Instead of wishing you can bring her home, promise yourself to do whatever you have to do to guarantee yourself a place in God's home, which is where she's waiting.

Love them while you can, because one day it'll be too late to wish you could get the time back. It doesn't work like that.

My love for my mother may sound obsessive and I can assure you, to some degree it is. It wasn't until quite a while after she passed away that I realized my heart, in fact, is still very much capable enough to hold more love in it for others. I've had days where I think to myself, am I really a good wife and mother? Love is meant to exist in a relationship. That's all Jesus wants for us. We are the center of His love and purpose, even if we can't see it, but Jesus was human. He's the best way any human can relate to God. To see *Him* is to see God.

I questioned the fact that if being a so-called child of God comes with having a good heart, why am I feeling like my whole world isn't worth anything now, and I have feelings of being extremely unimportant and completely useless? I'm not supposed to feel like I don't have enough love left to give to my husband and my kids. I am supposed to use every ounce of my being to do what I can to be here mentally and physically for them.

I'm Sean's wife just like Mom was Dad's wife. I'm my kids' mother just like Mom was mine. She died, and fortunately for me, I don't have to yet. There are times when I feel grateful for that, and other times not so grateful, but I've learned that's all a natural part of it and I'm OK with that. That's very painful to write down and admit, but then again so was the rest of this book. It's like being on a sinking boat, when God gives you His hand and the conversation goes like this: "Grab my hand, let's get you out of this boat. You can do this," God tells you.

"No I can't!" you reply, scared.

"Not on your own, you can't!" He says.

"I'll sink!" you yell back, stubborn like always.

"No, you are imagining a future without Me, and that future does not exist. I promised to always go with you and I'm right here."

When you finally grab His hand, you'll ask, "now what?"

He'll say, "Just start walking."

One day my husband, my kids, my father, and my siblings will read this, and I hope they get out of it exactly what I have gotten out of it—comfort and peace in faith and in healing. Though I've struggled through excruciating pain and I've lost what, to me, was the world, I have come through the struggle so much stronger and I am still very much here.

I've lived through that pain and I now have the opportunity to tell about it. Some things are very difficult to read, but behind every difficult confession is a very real and extremely weak heart. But I still found enough courage to share my story with high hopes of helping other weak hearts find their way, too. You will be okay. Maybe not for a while, but I can promise you, eventually you will. Since we don't have our mother's physical being, we are left with the love, strength, and knowledge that she gave to our souls. Use that to give to others. Love them and love yourself like she did. We've experienced so much in our lives and through all of that, she can live through us. If you talk to God daily, know you're talking to her as well. She hears you. She sees you and she will love you forever.

For as long as you live, make a promise to carry on with her spirit in everything that you say and everything that you do. Spread that wealth to others, including your children and grandchildren. Together, if we continue to live this way, the essence of our mothers will live on forever and because of that honor, the truth is, she will always be there!

ACKNOWLEDGMENTS

To Mom

If you could read this, I think you'd sigh with relief knowing this helped get me through the days that nobody else, including myself, thought I'd ever get through. Thank you for being you and for being the world's sweetest, most loving and caring, genuine, funniest, smartest, and prettiest mom that God ever created! Your amazing grace will forever be admirable and never forgotten. If you could read this, I want you to know that I'll always use the fact you threw out there so many times that I am the one that holds the other half of your heart, just to one up everybody else. In all seriousness, Mom, you're missed tremendously. I will indeed always love you more! Yes, I saw that Denali you rode out in and I'm still yelling, "That's my girl!" with pure pride. Take care of the mainland, Mom—we will all be there soon!

Oh, also, I floss daily now and I go to the gynecologist twice a year just like you told me to do. You'd be proud.

I love you the most! This one's for YOU.

Thank You's

To Dad: Thank you for being you. You're so strong and you're so loved. The truth is, I couldn't think of a better (or scarier) man to be able to put up with the shit we did as kids. Thank you for loving Mom and in doing so, showing us that true love and respect really does exist. Thank you for being open to me sharing this story, even though the amount of negative feedback may expand once the nosey extended world (or family) gets hold of it. You don't care, so neither do I. Most importantly, thank you for planking on top of the golf cart like you did—it's made the best payback picture anybody could ever have.

I love you.

To Sean: Thank you for supporting and loving me through this traumatic time in our lives. Thank you for sharing your love with me when I had nothing else to hold onto. There are really no words to express how grateful I am that you are my life partner. Thank you for loving me endlessly, even when I lose my cool and lash out at you like wife-zilla when you try to wake me up in the mornings. I am the luckiest and I love you a lot, a lot.

To Meagan: Mom always told me I'd be OK if I just listened to you. Although, I don't necessarily agree with that word for word, I am thankful for you. You've assumed a role in this family that nobody else could handle but you. Thanks for always having an open ear, even if we're fighting. I'm also thrilled that you like wine just as much as I do, so I don't have to spend tearful wine nights by my lonesome. Thanks for being there, I don't know what I'd do without you.

Love you.

To Katie: Thank you for being the sweetest person on the planet. I know I'll never be alone in life as long as I have you by my side. You're so much like Mom and it helps me heal knowing I still have her overprotective, sometimes absurd advice over the actions of this family. You're like a breath of fresh air and a whirlwind all at once. We are so lucky! Also, I'm so sorry Rennie and I tormented you into making us PB&J sandwiches at midnight or blaming the dog's poop in the bathroom on you. I'm also sorry that we voted you as the one to sit at the kids table every holiday—you looked cute though.

I'll love you forever.

To Rennie: Thank you for giving me all the insane and hilarious moments in our life that I was able to share in this book. Having you as my only brother is a blessing that I'll never take for granted. You made Mom so proud and because of that, I'll always be proud, too. Your bear hugs after she passed away are something I'll never forget, and I'll never be able to thank you enough. I'm sorry if I got snot on your shoulder, but I'm glad Maddie is good at laundry! I also wanted to tell you, we were the bomb.com together growing up. We may have not made it easy on Mom to have such a trouble-making dynamic duo, but it was definitely worth the stories to tell in our later years. Oh and PS, I'm still mad at you for not filling me in on the secret of hiding Katie under your bed on Jonathan Lane while Mom freaked out and called the cops because she had a missing child. You know I would have kept that secret, too. It was good though, five stars for that one.

I love you so much.

To Jaxon, Tanner, Maddie, Chloe, Kinslee, Barrett, and Hannah: You were the light in Memaw's world. The love she had in her heart for her grandchildren was something incredibly sacred and that can never be taken away. She loved you all before you were even born and I'm pretty sure she loved you all even more than her own kids. She never wanted you to forget her and I think we can all guarantee that will never happen! Your love for her shines through your sweet little smiles and I know how happy she is up there watching every one of you. I hope one day when you're old enough to read this book, you can share a newfound love for the amazing person she was and always will be. She will always watch over you and she will always comfort you in times of need. Memaw will always love you to the moon and back, back to the moon, around the stars forever and always. Never forget that! And, by the way: you know Memaw, and I think we can all agree that she has an endless amount of whipped cream cans up in her Heavenly fridge just waiting to overflow your little mouths with white foamy goodness once you all get there! Just make sure it's a really *looonnnnggg* time from now! She'll wait!

I love you all to the bottom of my heart.

CPSIA information can be obtained
at www.ICGtesting.com
Printed in the USA
JSHW022000281222
35470JS00003B/20